Reviews of *The Tenth Planet: Revelations from the Astrological Eris*

It's not often that a professional is on the cutting edge of his field but Henry Seltzer is no stranger to breaking new ground in astrology. In this latest contribution, he graces us with pioneering insights on Eris – a dwarf planet that he proves deserves consideration. The pages are filled with well researched chart examples and analysis supporting his archetypal views on how Eris functions in a horoscope. This book deserves space in your mind and on your shelf; Seltzer's contributions on Eris is a definite enhancement to astrological theory.

Maria DeSimone - www.InsightfulAstrology.com

In this cogent study of Eris, Henry Seltzer is doing bold, groundbreaking work on the astrological frontier. I've marveled at the slowness of the astrological community to embrace this new planet despite its being slightly bigger than Pluto. Perhaps that is because these new worlds always represent new, emerging possibilities in consciousness, and thus tend to frighten people. Thank you, Henry, for not being afraid.

Steven Forrest, author of *The Inner Sky*

Mr. Seltzer's book on Eris offers groundbreaking research into the field of astrology. His description of Eris in each of the houses is eye-opening and offers fresh insights into an area of life in which we need to develop the feminine warrior aspect of ourselves as part of our life purpose.

Jan Spiller, author of *Cosmic Love*

What we have here in Henry Seltzer's new book is more than a well researched treatise on Eris, it is a fantastic look into the workings of the mind of a true astrologer. Henry displays all the intellectual resources, the philosophical depth, and the respect for our ancient craft that go into the making of a definite addition to our astrological home libraries. Plus, we get to learn all about the properties of this newly discovered planet. Bravo!

Alan Oken, author of *Soul-Centered Astrology*
(with a natal Eris/Sun conjunction)

Henry Seltzer's passion for Eris, his fine writing and ample research will sweep you into a relationship with a new planet. This pioneering work brings us face to face with an emergent archetype, the feminine spiritual warrior. Behind Henry's enthusiasm lie years of astrological learning and a keen astrological mind. Let him take you along on his quest to understand an important new planet.

Lynn Bell, author, consultant, teacher and speaker in astrology, based in Paris, author of *Planetary Threads*

Henry Seltzer has given us a wonderful introduction to an archetype whose time has come: that of the avenging warrioress. A new symbol can empower us to address ancient blind spots; and, as is often the case with pioneering studies, it seems fated that The Tenth Planet should appear just now. Its subject is urgently relevant, to both visionary activism and personal psycho-spiritual work. Seltzer uses references from legend, art and contemporary culture to put the reader in touch with an impulse that is quickening within consciousness seekers everywhere: the urge to rebalance a world made toxic by the imbalanced masculine principle. Welcome, Eris!

Jessica Murray, San Francisco, MotherSky.com

Henry's interpretation of dwarf planet Eris provides a fascinating entry point for exploring the feminine warrior archetype. After 5,000+ years of patriarchal conditioning and its distortions of our connection to all species on planet Earth, Eris provides the opportunity to shift the male dominated world. Evolution is demanding that human consciousness balances its gender wounds as well as our relationship with all living, breathing beings. Eris is ready to take us to new levels of understanding the journey ahead. Bravo, Henry!

Kim Marie, Evolutionary Astrology Network

The Tenth Planet

Revelations from the Astrological Eris

Henry Seltzer

The Wessex Astrologer

Published in 2015 by
The Wessex Astrologer Ltd,
4A Woodside Road
Bournemouth
BH5 2AZ
www.wessexastrologer.com

Cover Design by Leslie Benson

A catalogue record for this book is available at The British Library

ISBN 9781910531013

To Shari with appreciation and love;
her unending patience and support
have made this project possible

Contents

Acknowledgments

Many people have helped to make this book possible, including close friends and family and of course the many mentors over the years of my astrological apprenticeship, both in their written works and in person. I would like in particular to express tremendous gratitude to my son, Asia Seltzer, who has helped me greatly in my astrological work, and in marketing the very well-received astrology software program that I created and that he has helped to design, the *TimePassages* program and app. He has also been a partner with me in our joint design of what is now rapidly becoming one standard Eris glyph, with the arrow going straight down, a combination of the glyphs for Pluto, Mars and Venus.

I have also been incredibly blessed in my staff at AstroGraph Software Inc., located on the web at Astrograph.com, that is Stephanie Shaffer, Leslie Benson (who did such a wonderful job graphically on the cover also), Lisa Stutey and Phoenix Toews, as well as a terrific assist from Bella Shing. I am continually in awe of their combination of amazing commitment, intelligence and energy for this work in which we are engaged – of spreading the revolutionary information that astrology indeed does "work" no matter how; and of course that "how" is a very great mystery that deserves attention in this time of failing traditional values. Magic is afoot in the world, in spite of every indication to the contrary, and we have the evidence clearly at hand, or as astrologer Richard Tarnas puts it, in his seminal *Cosmos and Psyche*, when we open-heartedly address the universe with an understanding of the language of astrology, the universe is capable of speaking back, directly to us.

I want to give a special shout-out as well to my extremely capable editor and captain of the publishing ship, Margaret Cahill at The Wessex Astrologer (well, who *is* The Wessex Astrologer). Her encouragement and tireless dedication to this project have made it a far better representation of the information and the evidence regarding the proposed existence of a brand-new astrological archetype than would have been the case otherwise. I thank her from the bottom of my heart and applaud her courage in taking an unusual stand by espousing the thesis of this somewhat controversial and revolutionary book, even amongst fellow astrologers.

Acknowledgment is also due to the following copyright holders
The University of Pennsylvania Press for permission to quote an excerpt from "The White Negro" by Norman Mailer, published in the fall 1957 issue of *Dissent* magazine.

Random House, LLC for permission to use passages out of *Memories, Dreams, Reflections* by C.G. Jung, translation copyright 1961, 1962, 1963 and renewed 1989, 1990, 1991 by Random House LLC. Used by permission of Pantheon Books, an imprint of the Knopf Doubleday Publishing Group. All right reserved.

W. W. Norton & Company, Inc. for permission to use passages from *The Red Book* by C.G. Jung, edited by Sonu Shamdasani, translated by Mark Kyburz, John Peck, and Sonu Shamdasani.

The Penguin Group (USA), LLC for permission to use passages from 'The Captain's Doll' from *Four Short Novels* written by D.H. Lawrence, copyright 1923 by Thomas Seltzer, Inc., renewed 1951 by Frieda Lawrence. Pollinger Limited for these same rights, electronic.

HarperCollins Publishers for permission to use the first few lines of "Howl" from *Collected Poems 1947-1980* by Allen Ginsberg. The Wylie Agency (UK) Ltd for the UK permissions to use the first few lines of "Howl" from *Collected Poems 1947-1980* by Allen Ginsberg.

Rotten Kiddies Music, LLC for permission to use an excerpt from *Burden of the Angel Beast* written by Bruce Cockburn.

Part I

Intimations of a New Archetype

A new planet has been discovered and named in this dawning 21st Century, although concealed under the appellation of "dwarf," yet, still a planet.

1

The Challenge of a New Planet

In September 2006 a new planet was announced by the International Astronomical Union (IAU). It was named Eris – for the Greek goddess of Chaos and Discord – and true to its name, this planet's birth did not come easy. Because there were numberless objects remaining to be discovered and named in the region beyond the orbit of Neptune, and recognizing that the new body together with Pluto (discovered in the 1930s) were only the first and second of these, its astronomical characterization as a true 'planet' of our solar system was in doubt. This was so even though this new body, already nicknamed Xena after the television warrior princess, was about the same size as the existing Pluto, and identical in astronomical category.

The public, and the astrologers too, were fond of little Pluto, previously known as the outer-most member of the solar system, and school children had been memorizing it for years as part of the litany of planet names. Mike Brown, the discoverer of Eris, confidently considered this new celestial body to be even more important than Pluto, and was the 'tenth planet' for which astronomers had long been searching. Eris was slow to be discovered because although it was the same size as Pluto, even possessing a similar satellite configuration with one major moon, for the past century and a half Eris has been much farther out. Eris was only finally discovered through better astronomical techniques in our century. She was found quite near to her aphelion, or greatest distance from the sun. Her extremely eccentric orbit makes its orbital period a little over twice that of Pluto, taking 556 years to completely circle the Sun.

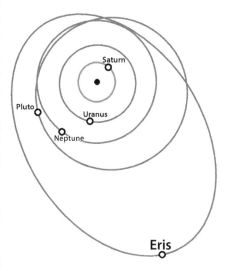

Nevertheless the IAU, in a controversial move, decided to officially designate this next planet of the solar system a "dwarf" planet, and to reclassify Pluto to this same category.

This decision caused considerable controversy and consternation almost everywhere. Debates sprang up within the astronomical community over Pluto's reclassification. When the Hayden planetarium in New York decided to modify its sculptural representation of the solar system to disallow the former ninth planet, many people were confused and disappointed. The official name that this new tenth planetary body was given, whether planet or dwarf, was turning out to be very significant in the furor of her coming because that name was Eris – in Greek myth the Goddess of Discord and sister of the God of War.

When this designation was made, creating a new astronomical category of 'dwarf planet', it presented a problem for astrologers as well as astronomers. The question became whether this latest member of the solar system, the first in the 21st century, would represent a new major archetype in Western Astrology just as had the discoveries of Uranus, Neptune and Pluto in the centuries before it. Thus in astrological circles, standards were also being overturned but from a different angle. Even though his astronomical designation had changed, there was no way that the established astrological symbolism of mighty Pluto – small in size but powerful in effects – would be dropped.

In the seven or more decades since its discovery, Pluto has come to represent the deep interior realm of human desire nature, largely unconscious, and the important area of death and rebirth. Pluto was seen as symbolizing deep transformation as a natural process, as well as sexuality. Wherever it touches the natal chart, there lies the potential for enormous change. This is true for aspects within a natal chart and, in the case of a transiting, or passing influence, such a Plutonian contact represents a climactic year of powerful metamorphosis for whatever natal factor is involved. Western astrologers have had the universal response that these demonstrated delineations, shown to be true over decades of practice, would be no different with the alteration of Pluto's official astronomical designation.

But what now, of Eris? Occupying the same astronomical category as Pluto, would it prove to be just as powerful in charts? Astrologers who disregarded the new planet because it was not considered by a majority of one section of the astronomical community to be a fully-fledged planet like Uranus and Neptune, were missing the point. Eris was still a complete match with Pluto, entirely similar in size and placement and representing the next step in planetary nomenclature even though officially a 'dwarf planet,' in fact a planet! This is especially so since the name Eris arises out of the same tradition of the Roman and Greek pantheon of gods and goddesses that had already supplied names for the other outer planets discovered in recent times, beginning with the discovery of Uranus in the eighteenth century, Neptune in the nineteenth, Pluto in the twentieth , and now Eris in the twenty-first.

Thus, I was captivated by the idea that the investigation into the astrological archetype of Eris would lead to vitally important results for modern Western Astrology. I began with her mythology. Just as the mythology of the gods had helped in initially informing astrologers as to the nature of the earlier planetary archetypes, what clues would the mythology of goddess Eris provide?

The Mysterious Connection Between Name and Astrological Function

The question arises as to why the name of these astronomical bodies might indeed matter. In other words, as Shakespeare famously inquired, "what's in a name?" Well, it turns out, quite a lot. As those who work with astrology already acknowledge and recognize, the name of newly discovered planetary bodies represents a strong clue as to their astrological function.

This gets into the question of how and why astrology works. That it does work can be demonstrated. For a remarkably complete exposition of the subject matter of astrology I recommend Richard Tarnas' landmark work *Cosmos and Psyche*, published in 2006. I could also recommend the software that I created, TimePassages. This astrology program puts up text for each chart feature. I created it with the specific purpose of demonstrating that astrology works, by allowing anyone who would like to take an unprejudiced view of Western Astrology their own access to the traditional meanings of factors in the chart: planets (including the Sun and Moon) houses and signs.

The issue for our times is, what does this fact – that astrology does work – tell us about the universe in which we live? Most importantly, that it is a far more magical universe than consensus thinking gives credit to. To again quote Shakespeare, it must mean that there are indeed "more things in heaven and in earth than are dreamt of in [our] philosophy", if by our philosophy we imply the scientism that currently prevails in this early part of this paradigm-changing 21st century.

Astrology gives us a unique view of the human condition and of the specifics of a particular person's innermost dynamics. For more information and a list of references about astrology and how it works, see http://www.astrograph.com/learning-astrology/books.php – which gives specialized meanings of the existing planetary archetypes of Western astrology and their combinations. Incidentally, the way that astrology does work, in concordance with the mythology of 'planets' such as Venus, Mars and the Moon, also seems to discount physical cause and effect as being in any way responsible for the power of the astrological archetype. I am referring to such notions as emanations of hitherto unknown 'rays' from astronomical bodies, or gravitational or magnetic influences; theories which do not hold water because these planetary energies work on a symbolic level. However, how can this be? How can the name that is chosen for an astronomical body, in this case Eris, come to stand for its meaning in the astrological chart? It is a truly mystical connection that exists, as has been proved time and time again, over the past 350 years, as these more recent Western planetary archetypes have come to light in modern times.

If we take a look at the mythology of Eris, the idea of potentially violent struggle comes to mind as well as the ideal of the vital feminine warrior fighting for a just cause. Eris was named after the Goddess of Strife and Discord, who willingly accompanied her brother Ares (in Latin, Mars), the God of War, into the battle. The new planet was originally designated 2003 UB313, and was nicknamed Xena, after the warrior princess of popular television culture. We will also want to take a look at the events surrounding this discovery and naming period of 2003–2006. Combining these ideas, the archetypal image comes to the fore of a militant feminism that does not shrink from violence.

In preliminary investigations of the Eris astrological archetype, there is also to be considered a Plutonian element of deep inner process. When Pluto was found in the 1930s, its discovery introduced some dark notions regarding the human condition, of a depth and a power that were previously unacknowledged. It stands to reason that so also will the discovery of Eris, a cousin to Pluto by astronomical category, and in every other way. Eris is found even farther out into the dark void at the edge of the solar system and therefore partakes of the same symbolism. We have grown as a culture through our understanding of the astrological Pluto, and so too will we grow as we come to integrate the Eris archetype into modern astrological understanding.

The astrology of Eris seems to be related to the no-holds-barred fight for continued existence that is fundamental in all natural processes, and for making a stand for what one believes, even if violence is involved. As the sister of Mars, Eris willingly sought the battle. The struggle for survival is a side of nature that is quite harsh; and this struggle is a fundamental part of the human condition as well, for we are still half animal. Nature can be viewed in a rosy light, as it was in the hippie movement of the Sixties,

Bambi drinking from a little stream; but underlying this beauty is the possibility of sudden death at any moment, since all of nature's children need to eat. Eris is related to this principle of necessary harshness in nature to achieve a life-enhancing goal – and to the concept of the female warrior that embodies it – and especially to the feminist struggle for survival rights in a patriarchal society.

In the charts that follow, I will introduce the glyph that I designed for Eris with the help of my son, Asia Seltzer. This was circulated amongst the astrological community as a provisional glyph and is now gaining acceptance. This glyph, with a small circle above a downward arrow, is a combination of the glyphs for Pluto, Mars and Venus, as seems fitting for the sister of Mars and the astrological cousin of Pluto.

The first set of charts that came to mind as I began this research were the feminists of the twentieth century. They were struggling to right the wrongs done in the name of patriarchal culture not only to themselves as women, but to nature and to the ideal of communal coexistence among the peoples of a potentially peaceful and beautiful Earth.

And some were more involved with violence than others. Andrea Dworkin is one such feminist. In her day she was a standard-bearer for the struggle of women for equality, and did not shy from pursuing an extremely candid means to that end if necessary, speaking out against violence as a method of masculine control. As a young woman, she also was physically abused by her husband.[1]

It was fascinating to see that Eris is indeed prominent in her chart – standing alone in one half of the available 180 degrees and therefore the focus of a Bucket (or Funnel) pattern. It stands across from the rest of her planets and directly opposed to the Libra planets in her eighth house of evolutionary change, including Neptune directly on the cusp of that house representing the idealism of her fundamental position toward necessary change and her activist focus on sexual power issues and pornography. Her chart is given in Chapter 2, Fig. 2-14.

Another feminist from the Sixties who is philosophically and intellectually prominent and is also sometimes associated with very direct and radical action in pursuit of societal goals is Angela Davis. See chart on the next page. In Davis's chart we can again observe a strong Eris, aspecting all five of her personal planets, as well as Uranus, Neptune and Pluto. Closely square the Mercury/Venus midpoint, Eris makes a close parallel to Mercury and to Venus and is contra-parallel to Saturn and Uranus. Notice that her

☉ ♒ △ ♂♊ / ♅

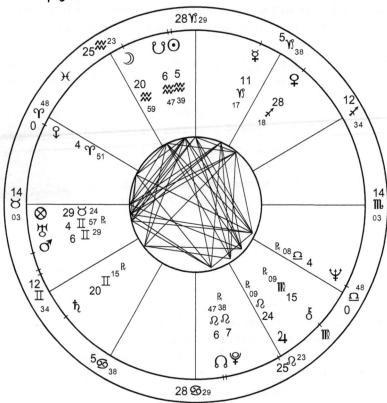

Fig. 1-1 Angela Davis, January 26, 1944, 12:30 PM CWT,
Birmingham, Alabama, USA

Sun trine Mars and Uranus is mediated by Eris at the midpoint. This lends an edge to the stand that she is willing to take in support of her idealistic and forward-thinking, even revolutionary, agenda. During the violent Sixties, Davis was accused of involvement in the courtroom abduction of Judge Harold Haley in an attempt to free her lover, Black Panther leader George Jackson, from San Quentin prison. This incident resulted in the deaths of Jackson's younger brother and three others, including the judge. Although her politics mellowed with maturity, earlier in the Sixties Angela Davis had made the statement: "The only path of liberation for black people is that which leads toward complete and radical overthrow of the capitalist class."[2]

The last example that I would like to include in this introductory chapter is Jane Fonda. Although not initially feminist, Fonda's life definitely demonstrates a radical and activist bent.

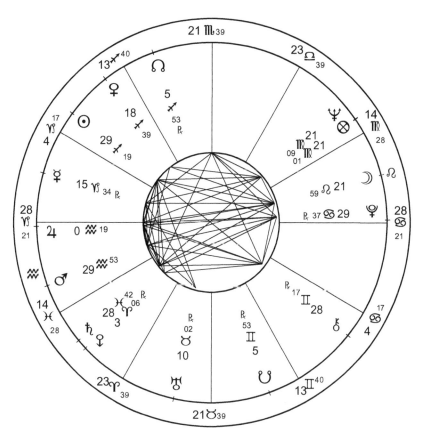

Fig. 1-2 Jane Fonda, December 21, 1937, 9:14 AM EST,
New York, New York, USA

Jane Fonda's chart reflects her life. Jupiter near her Ascendant symbolizes the good fortune that has followed her in her chosen careers; the Moon
in her seventh house of relationship, and Pluto directly on her descendant,
reflect the co-dependence of her early years when she came under the influence of powerful men like director Roger Vadim. Her difficulty with her
father while growing up, documented most precisely in her brother Peter
Fonda's autobiography *Don't Tell Dad*, is indicated by her Sun square Saturn
and opposed to Chiron, while her active imagination and iconic film career
is shown by the strongly placed Neptune in her eighth house. Adding to the
picture is Eris, which is parallel Mercury, Venus and the Sun, with a contra-
parallel to Pluto, exact to within a tenth of a degree. Eris is also conjunct
Saturn, and thus constitutes an important piece of her father complex. With
Saturn as Fonda's chart ruler, we would expect to see her develop a strongly

iconoclastic persona as she matured. Indeed that has proven to be the case. She played the rebel in her role as an anti-war protester in the late '60s and early '70s, famously allowing herself to be photographed behind the sights of an enemy anti-aircraft gun. Her vocal, defiant and radical opposition to the war highlights the basic idealism of evolved Eris as a force for change and in opposition to the existing patriarchal establishment.

As these charts have shown, and as client work over these past two years has also demonstrated to me, the Eris archetype has a consistent theme of taking a stand for oneself, violent if necessary, and of being very sure of oneself in the face of pressure to conform. Just as with Pluto, there are positive manifestations as well as the more compulsive and relatively un-evolved activities that can also be associated with this archetype. Jane Fonda has been a positive force for good in the world, and a steady moneymaker. Over the course of her life she has been a strong voice for physical fitness, having produced a series of exercise videos, as well as a champion of the underdog, including the Viet Cong, and this is consistent with a strongly placed Eris in the second house of body, resources and finances, and in conjunction with Saturn. In speaking of two of her father's films, *12 Angry Men* and *The Grapes of Wrath*, Jane Fonda had this to say: these films "in-stilled in me my father's values and made me care about the underdogs of the world, and showed me that films can make a difference." Earth-oriented Saturn represents a powerful connection with the physical world, and also implies a sense of justice, being exalted in Libra.

In the course of several years of research, I have seen hundreds of charts that show a powerful correlation between Eris and taking a strong stand for oneself, radical and even violent if necessary. These people can be a handful, especially when young and relatively unevolved. Later they become a strong force for advancing what they see as necessary and good, both in terms of social ideals and for what has come to be regarded by them as their soul purpose.

Notes
1. See Dworkin *Heartbreak*, p. 119; Dworkin, *Letters from a War Zone*, pp. 103, 332. Also see *Life and death: unapologetic writings on the continuing war against women*.
2. From a speech in 1968 when Ms. Davis joined the Communist Party. Quoted in her bio on marcuse.org: URL http://www.marcuse.org/her-bert/scholaractivists/AngDavisBioBib88.htm.

2

The Erisians – Further Chart Examples

The woman's perspective is like the dark side of the moon: it always exists,
but it is never exposed, at least not in my culture.

Ang Lee[1]

As I have already indicated, the astrological archetype of Eris is logically important because new discoveries in the solar system have historically been significant for Western astrology. This was true in the late 18th century when the discovery of Uranus expanded the number of planets beyond Saturn – the last of the classic seven planets, including Sun and Moon, known to the ancients. This began to change things in Western astrology, especially when augmented by the discovery of Neptune in the 19th and Pluto in the early 20th century. During the revival of Western astrology in the 1960s and 1970s, humanistic and holistic astrologer Dane Rudhyar referred to these three 'outer' planets as the "ambassadors from the galaxy". Work with these powerful archetypal energies continues to this day and has come to be of <u>fundamental importance in characterizing the new psychologically-centered model for modern Western astrology.</u>

Now with the naming of Eris in the fall of 2006 we have discovered what is essentially the tenth physical planet. The astronomical category has been revised to 'dwarf planet' but this is something of a quibble. The operant word here is planet – and indeed the newly named dwarf planets from the Kuiper Belt, also called TNOs or Trans-Neptunian Objects, of which Eris is only the first, are spherical and do orbit the Sun, the basic definition of the term 'planet' in astronomy. The discoverer of Eris, Mike Brown, asserted that when he was working up his data, he was excited to find the tenth planet that astronomers had long sought.

In any case this new body is identical in size and section of the sky to Pluto, and modern Western astrology has no intention of dropping small but powerful Pluto from the set of psychological archetypes useful in delineating charts, which tacitly admits the importance of these other new planets as well. As of 2012 there were three such bodies to be officially named, including Makemake and Haumea, these last two refreshingly named after

Polynesian creation gods and goddesses. It is beyond the scope of this present work to explore these last two archetypes more fully, but no doubt they will repay further study.

In examining the newly named Kuiper Belt objects, or planetary TNOs, Eris deserves a special place for several reasons. One is its status as the first of these objects to be named and given planetary designation; another is the origin of its name – like the other existing astrologically significant archetypes, Eris is named from the Greek and Roman pantheon of gods and goddesses. Still another reason is the close similarity of Eris to Pluto, both in size and shape, general location of orbit, and other characteristics. We are looking at an object exactly akin to Pluto, only a bit further out, especially at aphelion, and with a more eccentric orbit angled to the plane of the ecliptic. Otherwise we are looking at a twin of Pluto in the sky. Eris by its very nature, and the nature of its discovery, is bound to be of significance in Western charts.

Having come to this theoretical conclusion, the detective work begins to determine its exact significance and to explore this new archetype in detail. When I began to characterize Eris as feminine warrior energy based on the mythology of Eris, sister to the god of War, and found evidence for that characterization, it was a good start to this research, but it was only the beginning. What remains is the most exciting part of the journey.

Now that we have a preliminary idea of the Eris archetype, let's take a look at a few more charts. In doing so we will be checking out the initial conception – feminine warrior for important soul purpose – in the context of a larger body of evidence, and also getting a more specific look at what nuances of the archetypal meaning might show themselves.

Since the feminine warrior is an implicit factor in the view that we have of Eris, one of the first charts that I looked at was that of Angelina Jolie, who has embodied the female warrior for much of her film career. In her first major film, *Foxfire*, and in 1999's *Hackers*, Jolie played rebel activists, and starred as the quintessential female warrior in *Lara Croft: Tomb Raider*. She also played female James Bond characters in *Mr. and Mrs. Smith*, *Salt*, and the 2008 hit-man action adventure flick, *Wanted*. As this book was in its final stages, in mid-2014, she starred in the film *Maleficent*, the story of the dark witch in *Sleeping Beauty*. At one time Jolie had herself tattooed with the Chinese characters for Death and Courage. I was interested in seeing where Eris would be found in her astrological map.

In Jolie's chart, we find that her Pluto-Mars opposition is made more pronounced by the presence of the the Moon, her chart ruler, in an elevated

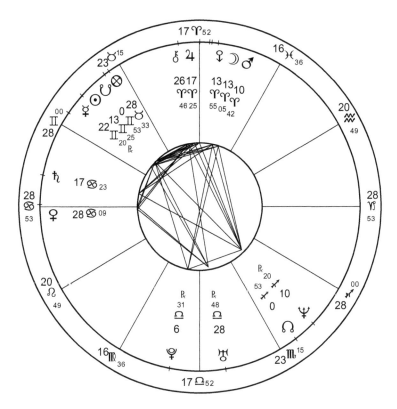

Fig. 2-1 Angelina Jolie, June 4, 1975, 9:09 AM PDT,
Los Angeles, California, USA 34N03 118W15

position close to the Midheaven and conjunct Mars within 3 degrees. Additionally we find Eris in partile (same degree) conjunction with this Moon position. Only Jupiter, very near the tenth house cusp, is more elevated than Eris. Jupiter is displayed in the tenth house, an optional feature of the TimePassages astrology software used to create these charts.

Along with Jupiter, elevated Eris-Moon represents the potential for dealing with the public, leading to success in professional life, and for being a warrior in so doing – entirely fitting for the roles Angelina Jolie has played as a feminine warrior figure and as the most visible and highest paid actress of her generation. And in that high-profile career she has played with remarkable distinction a female killer, displaying a ruthlessness that would more normally be associated with a male role. For myself, as researcher, it was extremely gratifying to find such immediate confirmation of her connection to the Eris archetype. A more in-depth look at Ms. Jolie's chart appears at the beginning of Chapter 10.

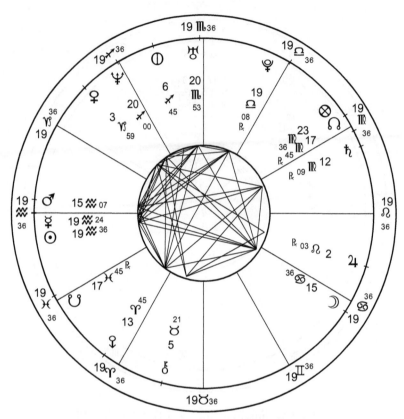

Fig. 2-2 Zhang Ziyi, February 9, 1979, Sunrise Chart,
Beijing, China 39N55 116E25

Powerful Feminine Warriors in Film

Another pair of woman warriors from recent movie fame, actresses Zhang
Ziyi and Michelle Yeoh, have each portrayed martial arts fighters in many
films, most famously *Crouching Tiger, Hidden Dragon*, and, for Zhang Ziyi,
House of Flying Daggers and *Rush Hour 2*. Unfortunately the time of birth for
neither of these talented artists is known – we have only their solar charts.

Ziyi's chart also displays a strong Eris. We can see that Eris mediates
between her Mars-Moon inconjunct, being sextile Mars and roughly square
the Moon, depending on her actual birth time, and thus emblematic of
a feminine warrior energy. Her Sun-Mercury conjunction makes close
aspects to the three major outer planets, and Eris also has powerful outer
planet connections, being trine Neptune, opposite Pluto and bi-quintile
Uranus, as well as inconjunct Saturn. Incidentally, we are using the term
'inconjunct' throughout this book as referring to the 150-degree aspect;
for the 30-degree aspect, also at times called an inconjunct, we will use

12

the term 'semi-sextile.' With these strong outer planet connections to Eris, her warrior persona, she could be expected to bring a spiritual component to her screen roles as indeed she has exemplified in *Crouching Tiger, Hidden Dragon*. Ziyi is considered one of the best actors of her generation. She is also a famous beauty, and no stranger to screen portrayals of deep emotional wounding. Eris is parallel to Chiron, the Wounded Healer, and therefore participates in her Venus-Jupiter-Chiron inconjunct-trine-square formation. She has chosen roles that have a difficult or hurt side to them, such as in *Crouching Tiger* and in portraying the wounded central character of *Memoirs of a Geisha*.

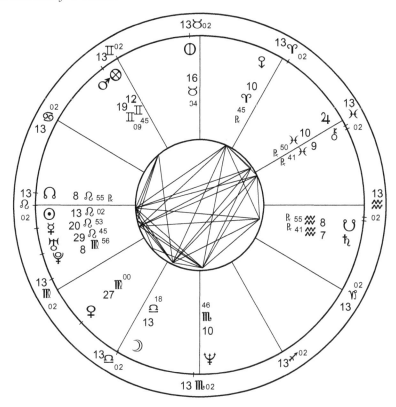

Fig. 2-3 Michelle Yeoh, August 6, 1962, Sunrise Chart,
Ipoh, Malaysia 4N35 101E05

Like Zhang Ziyi, Michelle Yeoh also brings a mystical and transformational coloration to her martial arts roles, as seen perhaps most clearly in her spiritual warrior portrayal in *Crouching Tiger, Hidden Dragon*. Eris is prominent in her solar chart, with the outer planet connections that we have seen in Zhang's chart.

Eris is inconjunct to Pluto and in exact inconjunct to Neptune (to the minute) so that their sextile forms a yod to Eris, which is precisely semi-sextile to her Jupiter, semi-sextile within one degree to Chiron in conjunction with Jupiter, and sextile to Saturn. She therefore displays similar outer-planet connections to Eris as with Zang Ziyi. Eris is also trine and contra-parallel to the Sun, closely contra-parallel to Mercury, and likely opposite her Moon.

Another example of a spiritual warrior, in a masculine actor this time, comes from a film of the Sixties, *Lawrence of Arabia*. That screen epic catapulted the young Peter O'Toole to stardom with his searing portrayal of T. E. Lawrence as a spiritual warrior for the Arab cause during World War I. As represented in the movie, his real goal was the recognition on the world stage of the Arab peoples and their needs, and even though he was a European, he fought for them with his last ounce of energy. In the movie

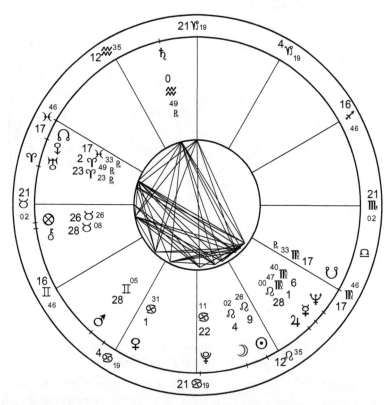

Fig. 2-4 Peter O'Toole, August 2, 1932, 12:15 AM GDT,
Wicklow, Ireland 52N59 6W03

portrayal, O'Toole conveyed the character of a man dedicated to that cause, and so attracted to violence and danger that he could not resist it. He was also beloved of the Bedouin brethren he led and was thought by them to have magical powers to escape the bullets of his enemies.

The chart of Peter O'Toole, for whom we do have a reliable time of birth, is shown on the previous page. O'Toole has Eris in aspect to no fewer than nine planets including Chiron; in trine with Sun and Moon, square Venus, out-of-sign square plus close contra-parallel with Mars, widely sextile Chiron, closely bi-quintile Jupiter, sextile Saturn and inconjunct Mercury and Neptune. There are several close aspects, particularly to his Mercury, his Venus, which is his chart ruler, and the Moon. With his Eris located in the twelfth house this rebellious warrior energy might have been elusive in his personal life and more something that he could play out in fantasy, as was indeed the case with his acting. His character in more than four dozen subsequent films was not war-like, although he could rage with the best of them; reference for example his bravura turns in *The Ruling Class*, playing the part of Jack the Ripper, and in *The Lion in Winter*, playing a feisty King Henry II.

Incidentally, the chart of T. E. Lawrence also shows a strong Eris. The speculative time of 2AM for Lawrence's birth gives a chart with Eris elevated near the Midheaven. His data is August 16, 1888 at Tremodoc, England, time speculative: "Thomas Edward, according to his mother, was born in the small hours of the 16th of August, 1888, Tremodoc; he was registered as born on the 15th by his father."[2]

Eris also makes many aspects to T. E. Lawrence's personal planets; to the Sun and Moon, Mercury, Mars, Saturn, Uranus and Neptune, although these are not particularly close aspects. Most featured is the yod formation to his Eris from a close Mercury-Uranus sextile, and it is worth noting that he was a renowned philosopher and writer, the author of *The Seven Pillars of Wisdom*. In researching Eris I have often noticed that it seems to amplify whatever natal factor it touches; in this case his philosophical and writerly Mercury-Uranus sextile.

Violent Filmmakers and Directors
The Eris placements of the filmmakers who brought these characters to the screen are also interesting. The director of *Mr. and Mrs. Smith*, the violent vehicle for Brad Pitt and Angelina Jolie, was Doug Liman. His solar chart follows.

In Liman's chart, Eris is widely trine the Sun, sextile the North Node, sesquiquadrate Mercury and Venus, opposite Mars, and inconjunct Uranus and Pluto, while being in close bi-quintile to Neptune. His chart therefore exhibits a strong Eris. He would be a rebel by nature and one who needs to act true to his soul purpose, likely bringing a form of spiritual engagement

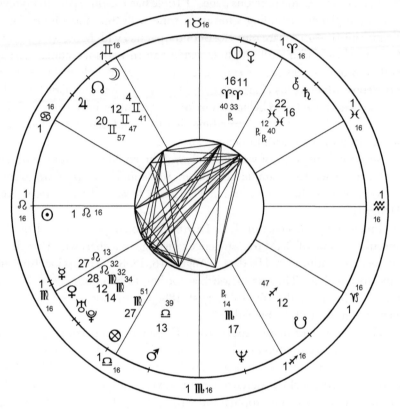

Fig. 2-5 Doug Liman, July 24, 1965, Sunrise Chart,
New York, USA 40N43 74W00

to his film-making. This theory is borne out by his choices, and also by a recent interview in Rolling Stone magazine in which he remarks, regarding his 2014 film *Edge of Tomorrow*:

I also really wanted to make a film with a strong female character. In the action genre, that's really rare – you have Sigourney Weaver's take on the ass-kicking heroine, and that's sort of it. I thought, this is a chance to really put this front and center. I'd done it before – I'd argue that *Mr. and Mrs. Smith* is more about Angelina Jolie's character, who is a better spy than Brad Pitt's character – and I kept thinking, it'd be great to look at this story from the female perspective. You have this person who was a great warrior, who had a power and lost it; the world is counting on her to save it and she's unable to do it.

He has also been in trouble for speaking out on the set. "He has no filter when it comes to being honest," the film's co-star, Emily Blunt, is quoted as saying in the same Rolling Stone piece.[3]

Another chart we could look at would be that of the director of *Crouching Tiger, Hidden Dragon*, Ang Lee. Lee's solar chart displays the same outer planet emphasis that we observed in the charts of his female stars. Uranus is elevated, conjunct Jupiter and square the Sun and Neptune, while Pluto participates by semi-sextile and sextile. As with many of Lee's projects, the film broke existing standards and was definitely of a mystical and spiritual bent. In his chart we find Eris singular by hemisphere as well as square the

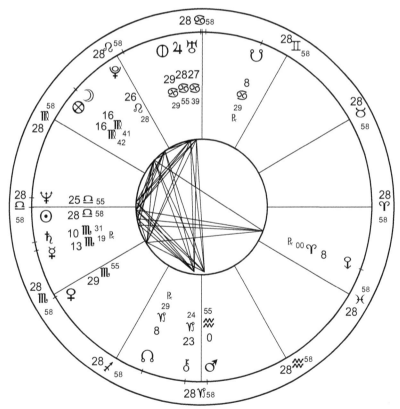

Fig. 2-6 Ang Lee, October 23, 1954, Sunrise Chart,
P'ing-tung, Taiwan 22N40 120E29

nodal axis, therefore quite strong by placement. Additionally, Eris is bi-quintile and closely parallel Mercury and inconjunct Saturn, confirming my suspicion that Eris would be a powerful feature in this chart.

The chart of the filmmaker Peter Jackson, who brought the *Lord of the Rings* trilogy to the screen in often-brutal detail, is also of interest to us here. He has made horror films, and in *Heavenly Creatures*, based in New Zealand in the 1950s, two teenage girls create an intense fantasy world and form an obsessive bond, which results in them murdering one of their mothers. In his 2005 remake of *King Kong* there was also considerable violence, almost as a motif running through the movie. His chart is below.

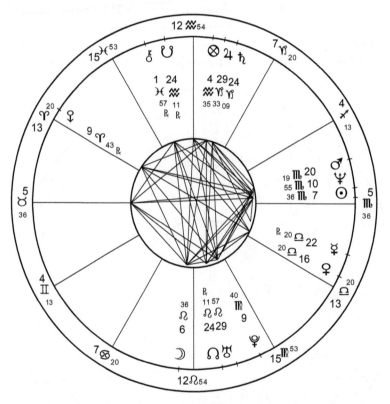

Fig. 2-7 Peter Jackson, October 31, 1961, 6:45 PM NZT, Wellington, New Zealand 41S18 174E47

In Jackson's chart Eris is closely inconjunct both Pluto and Sun/Neptune forming a yod to Eris. Widely opposite Venus, Eris is trine and closely contra-parallel the Moon, quintile Jupiter, and parallel Mars. In a common characteristic of these filmmakers' charts, Eris is in close aspect to Neptune, which rules images and film-making. In the nearly exact inconjunct from Eris to Pluto we can see the darkly violent energy that he has displayed in so many of his films.

Another example of a violent filmmaker is Luc Besson, the French director of a little movie with a female assassin called *La Femme Nikita*, that went on to become famous as the first of a new genre. Besson also made *The Fifth Element* in a Sci-fi mode with a different kind of woman warrior. We have his birth time.

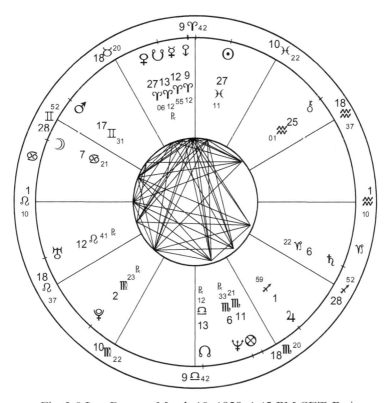

Fig. 2-8 Luc Besson, March 18, 1959, 1:45 PM CET, Paris,
France 48N52 2E20

I was fascinated to see that in Besson's chart Eris occupies an extremely elevated position, being entirely coincident with his Midheaven, in addition to being conjunct Mercury and the Moon's South Node in the tenth house. In fact no fewer than seven planets are in close aspect. Eris is square the Moon, trine Uranus, bi-quintile Pluto, inconjunct Neptune, square Saturn and semi-square Chiron. Eris is also widely trine to Jupiter and closely contra-parallel to the Moon and to Uranus.

Another violent filmmaker, David Lynch, made *Blue Velvet* and *Wild at Heart* in the 1990s, and the mysterious Hollywood fantasy *Mulholland Drive* in 2001. These films have strong female characters and use violence as a motif. We have his birth time. Eris is in the fifth house of artistic production, and in close opposition to Neptune. Additionally, Eris is trine Pluto and closely inconjunct the Moon within 12 minutes of a degree. Eris is also parallel the Sun and Venus.

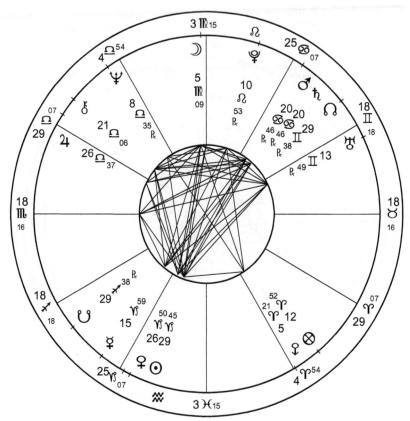

Fig. 2-9 David Lynch, January 20, 1946, 3:00 AM MST, Missoula,
Montana, USA 46N52 114W00

To bring a few more filmmakers into this set of examples, let's consider the chart of Quentin Tarantino who made the notorious and very violent *Kill Bill* films, released in two parts in 2003 and 2004.

Kill Bill featured a female warrior protagonist ('the bride') who seeks violent revenge for the murder of her entire wedding party. Tarantino also made brutally graphic classics like *Reservoir Dogs* (1992) and *Pulp Fiction*

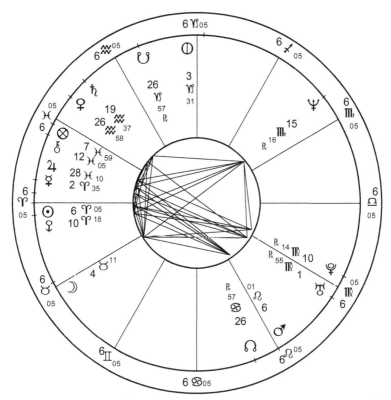

Fig. 2-10 Quentin Tarantino, March 27, 1963, Sunrise Chart, Knoxville, Tennessee, USA 35N58 83W55

(1994). Even though we do not have his actual time of birth, his chart represents yet another example of a strong Eris: conjunct the Sun, trine Mars, semi-sextile Chiron, semi-square Venus and parallel Saturn. In addition to these aspects, just as in these last several examples of violent filmmakers, he also has Eris in close aspect to Neptune, planet of images and film-making; in this case it is closely bi-quintile.

The chart of Uma Thurman, the female lead in *Kill Bill* and *Pulp Fiction*, also demonstrates a strong Eris. Uma was named after a Hindu goddess, and is the daughter of Buddhist theologian Robert Thurman and Nina von Schlebrugge, who was a famous model. Uma is intelligent and has a strong spiritual side to her personality, but in her early days had issues with self-confidence as well as her body image.[4] Her chart exhibits a strong Eris, with Eris conjunct Chiron, sextile Mars, semi-sextile Saturn and opposed to Uranus, and also closely contra-parallel the Sun and Saturn, and septile the Moon. All these aspects indicate that she comes equipped with a sense of

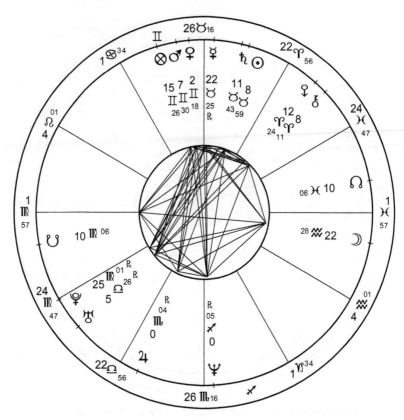

Fig. 2-11 Uma Thurman, April 29, 1970, 1:51 PM EDT, Boston, Massachusetts, USA 42N21 71W04

what her purpose in life could be, and that there might be a painful struggle on her part in order to achieve it.

Finally, there are the charts of the Wachowski siblings Lana and Andy, who made the rather fierce *Matrix* trilogy of films, plus *V for Vendetta*, *Ninja Assassin* and more recently *Cloud Atlas*, a somewhat brutal portrayal of a spiritual subject, namely reincarnation and karma. Their two charts are given below, and it is striking how strongly Eris sits in both of them.

Andy Wachowski represents another example of a violent filmmaker and like Tarantino has Eris in close aspect to Neptune, a sesquiquadrate within half a degree. Eris is also shown to be a strong influence in general, being square his Sun-Mercury conjunction, conjunct Saturn – his Sun ruler, closely bi-quintile Jupiter within a degree, precisely parallel Mars, and in exact sesquiquadrate with Venus, ruler of his Solar Chart Midheaven.

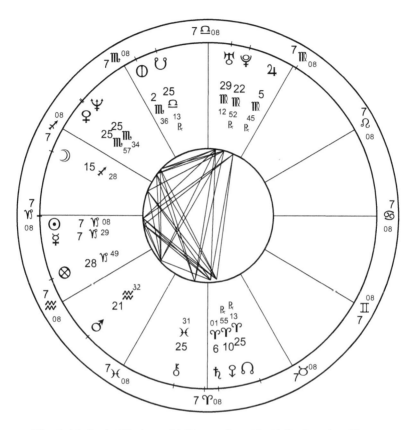

Fig. 2-12 Andy Wachowski, December 29, 1967, Sunrise Chart,
Chicago, Illinois, USA 41N51 87W39

In Lana's chart, the Eris-Neptune aspect is not a sesquiquadrate, as in Andy's chart, but instead an extremely close bi-quintile, within a few minutes of a degree. Eris and Neptune are also parallel within 20 minutes of arc. In Lana's chart, Eris is even more strikingly central, career-wise, being located in her tenth solar house, in partile square with Mercury, square Venus, in partile inconjunct with Uranus, and inconjunct Pluto as well. Given the closeness of these aspects, and, in view of the spiritual theme and edgy revolutionary tenor of their movies, as reflected in the strong emphasis on the Uranus-Pluto conjunction of the Sixties indicated by her Eris placement, it may well be that Lana is the creative genius of the pair.

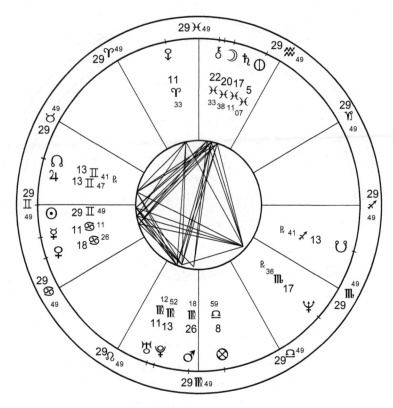

Fig. 2-13 Lana Wachowski, June 21, 1965, Sunrise Chart, Chicago, Illinois, USA 41N51 87W39

Feminists

After investigating the female warrior role in movies, and the filmmakers who portrayed them, I turned my attention to the charts of feminists. I had already noticed that Gloria Steinem's Sun was closely conjunct Eris, and it is logical that women who found it vitally necessary to fight for their rights in a male-dominated society would represent a breed of feminine warrior. In this struggle for equality they would be motivated by a deep need – characteristics I had come to recognize as part of the Eris archetype.

One of the figures I first examined was the chart of extreme feminist Andrea Dworkin. She is particularly strong in her rejection of female stereotypes, and could be considered aggressively violent in her rebellion and in her feminism. As mentioned in Chapter 1, her chart exemplifies a very strong Eris placement, being solo in the eastern hemisphere of her chart and roughly opposed to nearly all the rest of her planets. Among personal

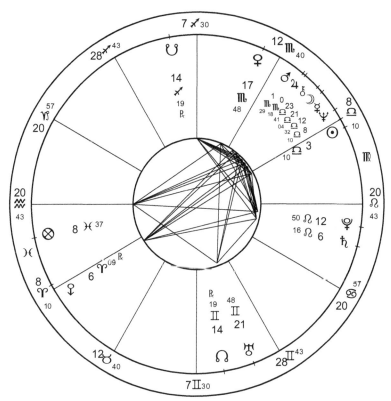

Fig. 2-14 Andrea Dworkin, September 26, 1946, 5:03 PM EDT,
Camden, New Jersey, USA 39N56 75W07

planet aspects, Eris is particularly closely opposed to her Sun in the seventh
house of relationship, within 3 degrees, and her Neptune, precisely on the
eighth house cusp, within 2 degrees. Eris is thus a demonstrably powerful factor in her personality, and indicative of her penchant for difficult
partnerships. Dworkin's Eris is also nearly exactly in a trine aspect to her
Saturn. I have seen repeatedly that strong combinations of Eris and Saturn
have shown themselves to be associated with the personality of someone
who prominently speaks truth to power. For example, Marianne William-
son, who proposed a Department of Peace for the American government
and has continuously spoken out against injustice, has the opposition.
I then looked more closely at the chart of Gloria Steinem, a woman whose
name came to be synonymous with the feminist movement of the late Sixties and early Seventies.

In Steinem's chart, Eris participates in a triple conjunction with Sun and
Mars, giving a powerful oomph to her ability to make things happen. This

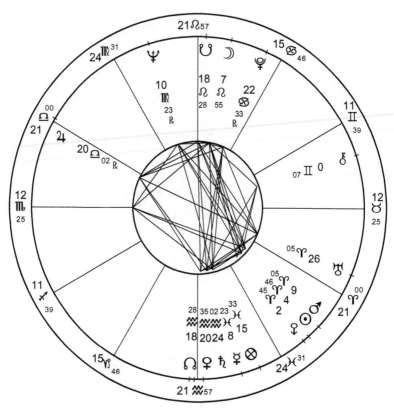

Fig. 2-15 Gloria Steinem, March 25, 1934, 10:00 PM EST,
Toledo, Ohio, USA 41N40 83W33

is also a possible clue to her longevity as an author and speaker. As of 2014
and in her 81st year, she is still active in this arena. The Sun is well connected in Steinem's map, being trine the Moon and aspecting both Ascendant
(bi-quintile) and Midheaven (sesquiquadrate) which with the participation
of Eris makes for a powerful personality and a natural leader. Eris also
sextiles Chiron, indicating problems with father (because Sun-Chiron) and
a familiarity with suffering along the way to her ascendancy in the leadership of the women's movement, as her biography indicates. Her quote that
"Most American children suffer too much mother and too little father"
could have been a pronouncement on her own early life, since her mother
suffered from depression, forcing Steinem to be her own caretaker, and she
was separated from her father after her parents divorced during her childhood.

Another feminist of the Sixties was Betty Friedan, whose 1963 publication of *The Feminine Mystique* started the Sixties' feminist ball rolling. In her
chart, shown on the next page, we once again find a very strong Eris.

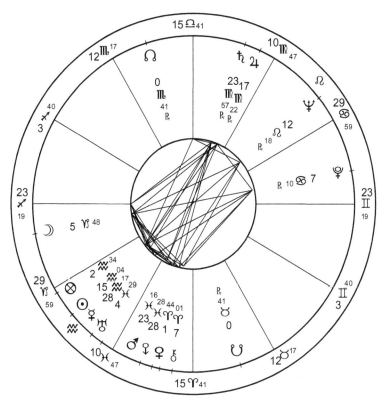

Fig. 2-16 Betty Friedan, February 4, 1921, 4:00 AM CST, Peoria, Illinois, USA 40N42 89W35

In Friedan's chart, Eris aspects every personal planet, being square to the Moon, semi-square to the Sun, in exact semi-sextile to Mercury and conjunct Mars and Venus, positioned right between their wide conjunction. Her Eris also mediates her Sun-Neptune opposition by semi-square and sesquiquadrate, and is opposite Saturn. We can see from this placement that she uses her warrior-like battling spirit to fight for something she truly believes in (Eris); issues of justice would predominate (Eris-Saturn), and she might use her writing (Eris-Mercury) and her media presence (Eris-Neptune) to achieve these aims. She had a characteristically warrior-like presence whether in support of her cause or going through daily life. Her biographer (her husband) Carl Friedan had been quoted as saying:

> She changed the course of history almost single-handedly. It took a driven, super aggressive, egocentric, almost lunatic dynamo to rock the world the way she did.[5]

Indeed it seems a natural fit, feminine warrior Eris and the iconic figures of the women's movement. Going back to the very beginning of it, one of the first writers to become recognized for the work of redressing the balance of inequality was Mary Wollstonecraft, the 18th century author of *The Vindication of the Rights of Women* and the mother of Mary Shelley. Strikingly she also has a close Sun-Eris aspect in her chart, a sesquiquadrate within a third of a degree. Her chart and a fuller commentary appear in Chapter 3.

To take a look at a few more examples, Lucretia Mott was an American woman born just as Mary Wollstonecraft was coming into prominence; she became a noteworthy figure in the women's rights and abolitionist movements, and later helped found the American Anti-Slavery Society in 1833. After the Civil War, she was the first president of the American Equal Rights Association that advocated universal suffrage. She too is in possession of a strong Eris. Her chart data is referenced in Appendix B.

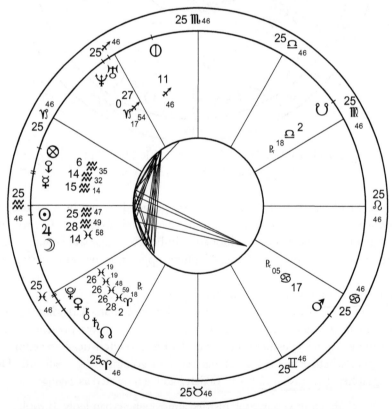

Fig. 2-17 Susan B. Anthony, February 15, 1820, Sunrise Chart, Adams, Massachusetts, USA 42N37 73W07

A triumvirate of important figures in the 19th century women's movement were Susan B. Anthony, Lucy Stone and Elizabeth Cady Stanton. The latter co-founded the first women's rights conference in Seneca Falls, NY, in 1848 along with Lucretia Mott. Lucy Stone was another prominent American abolitionist and suffragist of the period. Susan B. Anthony, equally prominent, went on to found the American Equal Rights Organization and the National Women's Suffrage Association. She died in 1906, before women received the right to vote, but declared that she saw it as inevitable.

These three women exhibit the characteristically strong Eris that we find in all these charts. For Susan B. Anthony, Eris is in almost exact conjunction with Mercury, inconjunct Mars, widely conjunct the Sun, and mediates by midpoint the important Uranus-Saturn square – which is actually Uranus-Neptune in square with Pluto, Venus, Chiron and Saturn. This quadruple conjunction is close to the Moon's North Node; and we find Eris in semi-square to both ends of this powerful square and stellium configuration.

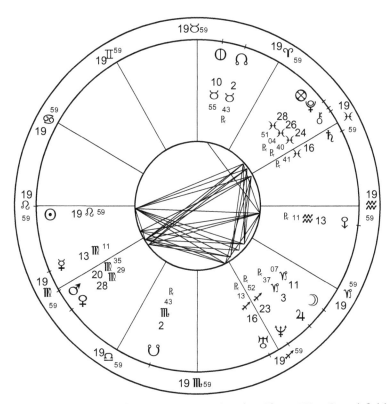

Fig. 2-18 Lucy Stone, August 13, 1818, Sunrise Chart, West Brookfield, Massachusetts, USA 42N14 72W08

For Lucy Stone, Eris is opposite the Sun, semi-square Pluto, and participates in the Saturn-Uranus square by being sextile Uranus and widely semi-sextile to Saturn. Eris is also found in close aspects to the other personal planets in her chart, being bi-quintile Mars, in close sesquiquadrate to Venus, and inconjunct Mercury to the minute of a degree. Regarding this last aspect, she was a prolific writer on a wide range of women's rights, so that the extremely close aspect from Eris to her already strong Mercury (opposite Saturn and conjunct Mars) makes perfect sense.

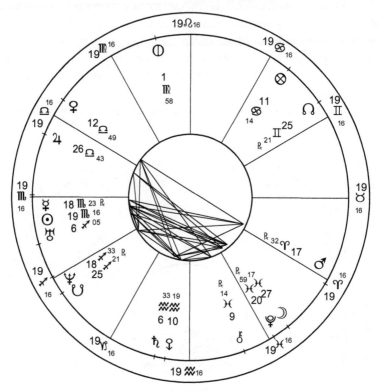

Fig. 2-19 Elizabeth Cady Stanton, November 12, 1815, Sunrise Chart, Johnstown, New York 43N00 74W22

In the case of Elizabeth Cady Stanton, her chart contains Eris in conjunction with Saturn, widely square the Sun, semi-square the Moon, trine Venus, exactly sesquiquadrate the North Node, sextile Uranus, septile Neptune and in semi-sextile to Chiron. Many of the charts of leaders of the feminist movement have an Eris-Chiron aspect, perhaps indicating the degree to which they were aggrieved by the inequality of the time.

As I went on to examine more than twenty charts of notable feminists of the 19th and 20th centuries, I found that all contained similar indications of a strong Eris. The birth data for these charts and the details regarding their Eris placements are summarized in Appendix B.

Iconic Rebels on the Music Scene

The last few charts that we will look at in this early survey are those of rock stars. Like feminists and revolutionaries, musicians often represent a radical point of view that comes through clearly in their work. An example is Bruce Cockburn, who shares his activism as well as a strong romantic presence in his body of work. He expressed his rage against the military atrocities that he witnessed in Guatemala in the 1980s with the song *If I Had a Rocket-Launcher*. The meaning of the title is that he would take violent action, at least in imagination, against the helicopter-based paramilitary actively engaged in killing innocent civilians. Cockburn went on to express

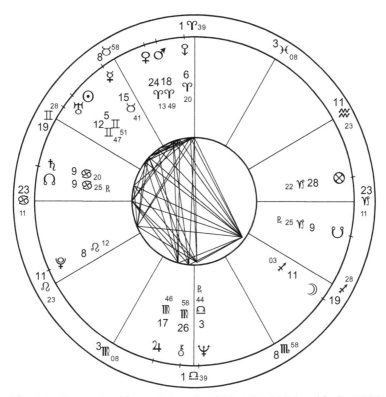

Fig. 2-20 Bruce Cockburn, May 27, 1945, 8:50 AM (rectified) EWT, Ottawa, Canada 45N25 75W42

a philosophical and spiritual activism in such songs as "Southland of the Heart" and "The Burden of the Angel/Beast". He also wrote "Tie Me at The Crossroads (When I Die)", an ironic reflection on life and death.

His rectified chart, by astrologer and fan Nathan Elderkin is given on the previous page. The rectification is based on the supposition of a Cancer rising chart, with angular Neptune. It is interesting that this rectification also puts Eris at the top of the chart. Eris is sextile and contra-parallel the Sun and square to Saturn. No matter what his actual time of birth, one striking feature is his Eris-Pluto trine, echoed as well by a possible Eris-Moon trine, all in fire signs, to make a Grand Trine in his chart. Eris to Pluto represents his activism, while Eris to Moon his romantic streak. The presence of the strong Eris-Saturn square indicates someone who would fight for the rights of the underdog, as indeed Cockburn has done many times, often travelling to Third World countries to do so.

Since Cockburn is known for his profoundly poetic lyrics, as well as his musicianship, one would expect to see Mercury-Neptune in aspect. In this case, without Mercury-Neptune directly, we have Eris in a novile or 40 degree aspect to Mercury and opposite to Neptune, bringing these planets together and thus making sense for the chart of a world-renowned singer-songwriter who writes such deep and beautiful lyrics. For an example, see these lines quoted in Chapter 7 from "The Burden of the Angel/Beast".[6]

Another singer, Ani DiFranco, was an early candidate for a strong Eris in my thinking because she is an activist, even somewhat militant in her approach. Her sunrise chart is given on the facing page.

DiFranco has Eris closely inconjunct her Mercury-Mars conjunction in the twelfth solar house and inconjunct Venus, forming a yod to Eris. She also has Eris conjunct Chiron, opposite Uranus and sesquiquadrate Neptune. Eris is widely opposite her Sun-Pluto conjunction. It is interesting that while there is no direct Mercury-Neptune aspect in her chart, which would be a standard signature for such a powerful and adept singer-songwriter, as with Bruce Cockburn's chart, Eris closes this gap by being in aspect to both her Mercury and Neptune.

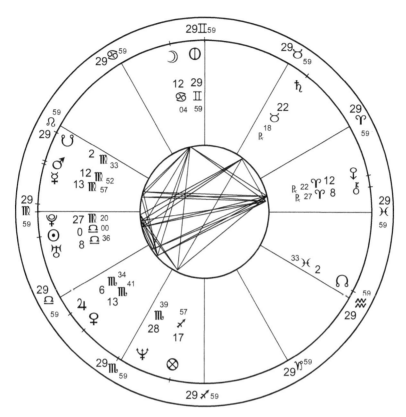

Fig. 2-21 Ani DiFranco, September 23, 1970, Sunrise Chart, Buffalo, New York, 42N53 78W53

Yet another singer-songwriter from the same generation also exhibits a powerful feminist streak, extremely articulate lyrics and a good musical sense, and also exhibits strong Eris-Mercury and Eris-Neptune aspects. Feminist, lesbian, and Native American activist Amy Ray has been part of the dynamic duo known as The Indigo Girls since the late 1980s. Her solar chart is overleaf.

Amy Ray has Eris in exact conjunction to Mars, accounting for her somewhat masculine qualities as a singer, sextile Venus, and in wide conjunction to her Sun and to the Moon at sunrise, as well as in close inconjunct aspect to Pluto, giving her a strong and volatile personality. She has been an outspoken voice for women's rights since she began writing and singing. She also has Eris in exact semi-sextile to Mercury and in exact bi-quintile to Neptune, as befits an accomplished singer-songwriter.

Her partner in song, Emily Saliers, born eight months earlier, has similar Eris aspects. Her solar chart is given on the following pages.

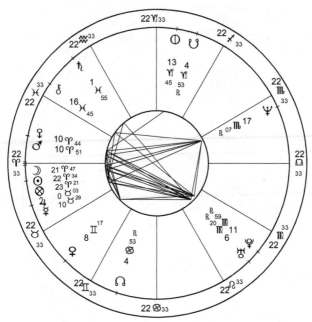

Fig. 2-22 Amy Ray, April 12, 1964, Sunrise Chart,
Decatur, Georgia, USA 33N46 84W18

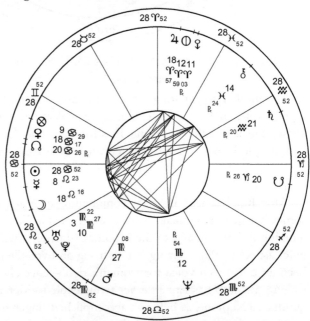

Fig. 2-23 Emily Saliers, July 22, 1963, Sunrise Chart,
New Haven, Connecticut, USA 41N18 72W56

Emily Saliers has Eris conjunct Jupiter and widely trine the Sun Amy Ray, she has Eris in close inconjunct with Pluto. Her Sun/Moon point at about 8 Leo 30 is conjunct Mercury, assuming that she was born in the morning or early afternoon, with Eris in trine. She writes extremely poetic lyrics in support of causes that she cares about, social progress and gay recognition, so the Eris-Mercury trine is entirely appropriate symbolism. Since Eris is also inconjunct Ms. Saliers' Neptune, Eris participates in her Mercury-Neptune connection, as we have seen with many of these notable singer-songwriters.

The radical feminist singer, Tori Amos, was initially well-known for softer and quieter songs, although her line "never was a cornflake girl" might have given fair warning that she was singing from her own unique voice.

When I took a look at her chart, and her Eris placement, I knew that she had the signature of a feminist: Ms. Amos has a strong Eris placement,

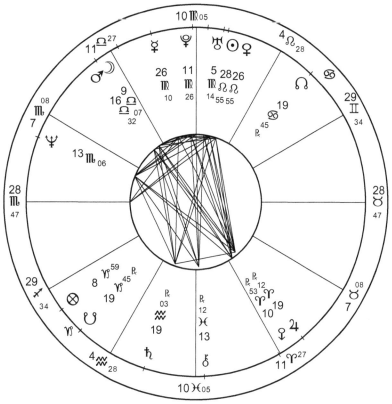

Fig. 2-24 Tori Amos, August 22, 1963, 1:10 PM EST, Newton, North Carolina, USA 35N40 81W13

35

being widely conjunct Jupiter, closely opposite Moon, opposite Mars, sesquiquadrate Sun and closely sesquiquadrate Venus, septile and closely parallel Saturn, in close bi-quintile to Uranus (being less than half a degree) and inconjunct both Pluto and Neptune, making a yod to Eris. It is the number of these aspects and the closeness of many of them that make for an extremely strong Eris configuration in her chart.

A few lines from a recent online blog post at *Music News* will give a good idea of who she is.

> Just over twenty years ago Tori Amos became the first well-known female singer-songwriter to speak up about her own experience of sexual assault, in her 1991 song *Me and a Gun* (it was inspired by a rape that occurred when Amos was 21). At the time, it was shocking. It was even criticized by some as being self-indulgent and attention-seeking (Jesus wept). A few years later she co-founded RAINN, the Rape Abuse and Incest National Network, which provides a free help line in the US that connects callers with their local rape crisis centre. It would be impossible to estimate how many women have been directly encouraged to report rape by Amos's actions.
>
> The singer celebrates her 49th birthday today, so it's an apt time to salute her potency. Since the release of debut *Little Earthquakes* twenty years [ago?], she has brazenly tackled topics that many writers avoid: Christian patriarchy, sexuality, gender, guilt, shame, miscarriage and motherhood, couched in her swelling, filigreed piano rock and sometimes sweet, often acerbic vocals. She pulls up the music industry on its sexism and patriarchal structure without fear; a vanguard, paving the way for female artists to be received equally to men.[7]

In all these charts, I found a prominent Eris as the indicator of a rebellious and activist personality; one who pursues their life quest and soul purpose in order to change the world around them – either through direct action or through the inspiration of their art.

Notes

1. www.brainyquote.com/quotes/authors/a/ang_lee.html
2. Richard Aldington, *Lawrence of Arabia*, 1955, p. 25.
3. www.rollingstone.com/movies/news/no-tomorrow-doug-liman-on-the-blockbuster-that-almost-broke-him-20140606.
4. Talksurgery, May 15, 2001, accessed August 16, 2010; referenced in her Wikipedia article.
5. Ginsberg L., 'Ex-hubby fires back at feminist icon Betty', *New York Post*, 5 July 2000 – quoted in Betty Friedan's Wikipedia page.
6. Bruce Cockburn, "Burden of the Angel/Beast" from *Dart to the Heart*, written by Bruce Cockburn, used by permission of Rotten Kiddies Music, LLC.
7. www.nme.com/blog/index.php?blog=1&title=happy_birthday_tori_amos_we_need_your_ou&more=1&c=1&tb=1&pb=1

3

A Deeper Look at the Eris Archetype

Surely something resides in this heart that is not perishable –
and life is more than a dream.

Mary Wollstonecraft[1]

As we have discovered, the Eris archetype partakes of a powerful desire to act, to do something; those with a strong Eris are activists, feminists, revolutionaries. They are those who can, when they need to, make something happen at all costs, using a radical approach if necessary. The necessity to act comes from a deep place inside which could be characterized as a sense of soul purpose.

This seems to be in line with the nature of Eris as an outer planet, just like Pluto. Eris has the same depth, so that when we identify Eris as the archetype of the Spiritual Warrior, we understand this summons to warfare to be in response to the most profound soul-level need on the part of the person. It is almost literally do or die.

The case histories in previous chapters demonstrate this theme again and again; the women's movement, or the struggle for the civil rights in the U.S., was no casual exercise in power politics, but a deep response to an abiding need.

A more in-depth example will be helpful here. Let's look again at the chart of Mary Wollstonecraft, one of the very earliest leaders of the nascent 18th and 19th century women's movement. Her groundbreaking work *The Vindication of the Rights of Woman*, published in 1792, was one of the first few trickles of what later became a flood of feminist activity.

There are several important things to notice about this chart, including the aspects made by a prominent Eris, in the context of the locomotive planetary pattern, which could also be considered a bucket or a funnel shape with a focus on Neptune. Eris is the planetary leader of this pattern. I have found in my research that Eris tends to create an emphasis on the planet or planets being aspected, and in this chart there are several such emphases. Eris is conjunct Pluto and square Uranus, emphasizing the Pluto-Uranus square in Wollstonecraft's chart. Eris is closely semi-sextile Jupiter

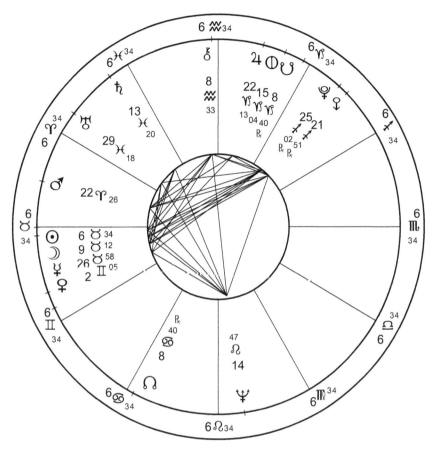

Fig.3-1 Mary Wollstonecraft, April 27, 1759, Sunrise Chart,
London, England 51N30 0W10

and trine Mars, thus emphasizing her tight Jupiter-Mars square, and finally, Eris is semi-square Chiron and closely sesquiquadrate the Sun, emphasizing her strong natal Sun-Chiron square.

From the strengthening of Mary Wollstonecraft's Pluto-Uranus square by Eris, we would expect her to be a born revolutionary, and perhaps one who would sympathize with the ideals of the French Revolution, which came to pass in the years of her maturity. Indeed this was the case, since she wrote and published a rebuttal to Edmond Burke's defense of the French monarchy, *Reflections on the Revolution in France*, almost as soon as it was released in late 1790. The French Revolution was marked by the Pluto-Uranus opposition of 1787-1798 (using the 15-degree orb that astrologer Richard Tarnas recommends; see his *Cosmos and Psyche*). The Eris combination with

Pluto and Uranus is of course a generational aspect shared by her peers, although few of her immediate contemporaries would have had the striking Sun, Mars, Jupiter and Chiron aspects to add to the generational aspects included in the archetypal mix.

With the added emphasis from Eris on her Jupiter-Mars square, Wollstonecraft would have likely been a risk-taker with a strong tendency to travel, especially in the context of harrowing or militant situations. Indeed, she went to France at the height of the revolution, in December 1792, about a month before Louis XVI was guillotined. While visiting there she decided to commit to a man who was an uncertain prospect and became totally enamored of him. She became pregnant, had his child and came to a somewhat perilous state, being alone and the mother of an infant in the middle of a revolution. She was able to return to London but the experience with the father of her child was difficult and depressing, and she attempted suicide twice, once about a year later and again a year after that, on her return from Sweden and Norway. After returning to London, she had embarked on another hazardous business trip to Scandinavia, traveling with her young daughter and only a maid for support.

Finally, the Chiron-Sun square indicates difficulties with her father, which would have been greatly magnified by the Eris aspects. Her father is described as abusive and the root cause of some of the suffering that she experienced.

Since Eris is so powerfully configured in Wollstonecraft's chart, we would expect it to show up in the chart of the man that she obsessed over, the father of her first child, born out of wedlock in May of 1794. The father's name was Gilbert Imlay, and he was born in New Jersey on February 9th, 1754, with Eris conjunct Pluto and sextile the Sun. He also has Eris square the Moon, if born before late afternoon, and closely septile Venus, suggesting that any woman he was attracted to would be strongly Erisian, as was the case.

It will be interesting to examine the transits to Mary Wollstonecraft's chart for the period of her most intense writing and life events, which would include her swift publication on November 29th, 1790 of the rebuttal to Edmond Burke in response to his paper (published on November 1st, 1790.) This shot her into public prominence, as did the subsequent publication of her revolutionary tract that explored women's rights, *The Vindication of the Rights of Woman*, early in 1792, and then the life-changing trip to France when she met Gilbert Imlay, from December 1792 to the spring of 1793. We have the following set of transits for November 29th, 1790, when she published her first widely read treatise, the rebuttal to Edmond Burke's *Reflections* (see chart, Fig. 3-2.)

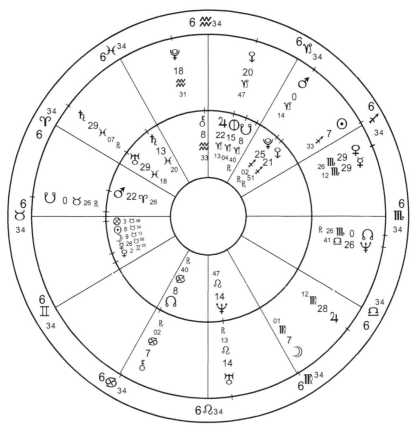

Fig 3-2 Mary Wollstonecraft, Transits for Monday, Nov 29, 1790, 12:00 PM GMT

As the Uranus-Pluto opposition was drawing closer to exact, Eris had moved almost one full sign on from its original position and was beginning to conjunct natal Jupiter, and to square Wollstonecraft's natal Mars, highlighting her close natal Eris-Mars and Eris-Jupiter aspects. Her elevated Jupiter in the ninth solar house of publishing could be considered an important factor in the events of November 1790 when she shot into greater prominence through her published writing. Further, transiting Uranus was exactly on her Neptune, while Mars had just reached its square with transiting Saturn, itself in close conjunction with her natal Uranus by the time of publication; the Uranus factor indicates the revolutionary nature of this event, and as well its suddenness. The presence of Eris in these transits makes sense because this revolutionary outlook represented a deep soul-level commitment for her.

Mary Wollstonecraft was working on and getting ready to publish *The Vindication of the Rights of Woman*, her most important work, in the fall of

1791. During this time she had transiting Eris exactly conjunct her Jupiter and square her Mars, both within a quarter of a degree. The final work went to the publisher in early January, with Eris still mere arc-minutes of a degree away from conjuncting her natal Jupiter in her ninth solar house of publishing and semi-sextile to her natal position, while Pluto by transit was also sextile. Again, it is no surprise to see Eris so hugely implicated in these transits for Mary Wollstonecraft; this was her life's work that has echoed down through the centuries.

In the transits for her departure to revolutionary France, around December 15th, 1792, transiting Eris was at 22 Capricorn 49, still at a semi-sextile aspect to its natal position, and closely conjunct her natal Jupiter, and squaring natal Mars – these transits being descriptive as well of a trip to a dangerous war zone. Transiting Uranus, at 23 Leo 30 was, within arc-minutes of a degree, exactly trine Pluto/Eris at 23 Sagittarius 30 in her natal chart, an indication of the suddenness of unfolding events, and the revolutionary fervor that gripped her during this time in her life, so soon after the publication of *The Vindication.*

For the next few months, as she pursued her fated romance with Gilbert Imlay and conceived their child, events that were to dramatically challenge and ultimately change her life, Eris drew closer to an exact semi-sextile with her natal Pluto. Eris stationed there the week of her 34th birthday in late April, 1793. Transiting Pluto on this date was sextile to her natal Pluto within 14 minutes of a degree, with Eris at the exact midpoint, semi-sextile to each, symbolic of the extent of the impact upon her of these transformative life events.

Albert Einstein

Another example chart that I chose more or less at random is a well-known one. The chart of Albert Einstein throws additional light on the Eris archetype from a different angle than we have been exploring thus far. Einstein was not known to be a strong advocate for feminist rights, although politically he was left-wing all his life and supported the rights of the underdog. We do have his birth time.

There are two interesting things about the Eris placement in Einstein's chart. One is its elevated position in the tenth house, close to the MC; the other is the close square with the Moon. This latter is the only major aspect that Eris makes to any personal planet, although it is semi-sextile Venus, quintile Pluto and septile Chiron. This is at first glance a startling result in the chart of the greatest physicist of the 20th century, when we might have expected Mercury, Uranus, or a combination of Jupiter and Uranus to be

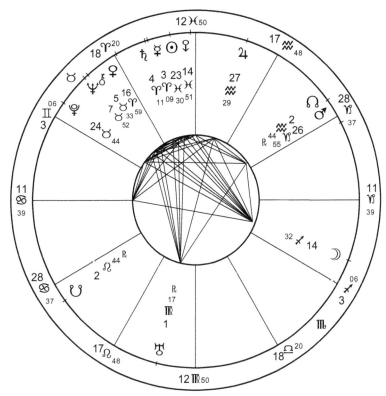

Fig. 3-3 Albert Einstein, March 14, 1879, 11:30 am LMT,
Ulm, Germany 48N24 10E00

more prominent. Indeed there is that emphasis in Einstein's chart, having nothing however to do with Eris. Uranus is singular in the first quadrant opposite his Jupiter, and is inconjunct his Saturn-Mercury conjunction in the tenth house.

But what are we to make of this Eris-Moon emphasis? It would seem that Einstein had other qualities than would appear in the broad outline of his scientific influence. A closer look reveals that the Eris emphasis to his Moon makes perfect sense. His strong Moon, singular in the second quadrant, trine Venus and empowered by the Eris square, reveals a man who adored women; the love of home and family was an important part of his makeup. He also loved music – and he was a virtuoso on the violin.

Einstein's biography reveals that he had an extremely close relationship with both his parents, and was very comfortable socially. He was attractive to women. His principle biographer, Albrecht Folsing, quotes a fellow student's description of Einstein at the age of seventeen:

grey felt hat pushed back over the silky mass of dark hair, he strode along with vigor and assurance... Nothing escaped [his] acute gaze... Whoever approached him was captivated by his superior personality... Unconfined by conventional restrictions, he confronted the world spirit as a laughing philosopher, and his witty sarcasm castigated all vanity and artificiality.[2]

Einstein was never without a female companion from the age of 16 until just a few years before his death at 76. At that early age he had a close involvement with the 18-year-old daughter of his host family in Switzerland where he had emigrated to prepare for a higher course of education at the Swiss Federal Polytechnic. A few years later, his early marriage to Maleva Maric made him the young father of two boys, to whom he was devoted as long as the marriage lasted. The couple separated in 1912, the year of his emotional involvement with his cousin Elsa, who became his second wife as soon as the divorce was finalized. After Elsa's death in 1936, Einstein's sister Maja lived with him until she herself passed on in 1951.

Although the Eris placement in Einstein's chart does not directly aspect his intellectual planets, it does color his academic achievement since its prominent conjunction with his Midheaven reveals a person with the personal strength to pursue his own thinking, even as an outsider to the world of universities and the scientific establishment of his day. His greatest discoveries were made working virtually alone, and publishing in scientific journals, while at the same time holding down a full-time job as an examiner in the Swiss patent office. He was in his own words "an impudent Swabian" as well as being Jewish in a time of prevailing anti-Semitism. He was thus in the period of his ascension the quintessential maverick, and an outsider with a complex relationship to authority, and this gives us further insight into Eris as symbolizing a back-up-against-the-wall nature, taking a strong and uniquely individual stand for oneself, and resenting any outside authority. In this there are some similarities to a Pluto tenth house placement.

Consonant with the strong Eris-Moon square lighting up his Sagittarius sixth house, his warrior-like courage and stubbornness was coupled with a natural grace of personality and a good heart. He was a confirmed pacifist all his life. His legacy for today's world goes far beyond his tremendous contribution to physics and mathematics, and includes many pithy sayings, among them:

> Imagination is more important than knowledge.
> You cannot simultaneously prevent and prepare for war.

Common sense is the collection of prejudices acquired by age eighteen.

Two things are infinite: the universe and human stupidity; and I'm not sure about the universe.

To punish me for my contempt for authority, fate made me an authority myself.

Whoever undertakes to set himself up as a judge of Truth and Knowledge is shipwrecked by the laughter of the gods.

The most beautiful thing we can experience is the mysterious. It is the source of all true art and all science. He to whom this emotion is a stranger, who can no longer pause to wonder and stand rapt in awe, is as good as dead: his eyes are closed.

It is my conviction that killing under the cloak of war is nothing but an act of murder.

※ Any man who can drive safely while kissing a pretty girl is simply not giving the kiss the attention it deserves.

How on earth are you ever going to explain in terms of chemistry and physics so important a biological phenomenon as first love?

There are only two ways to live your life. One is as though nothing *aut Caesar* is a miracle. The other is as though everything is a miracle. *aut nihil*

A human being… experiences himself, his thoughts and feelings as something separated from the rest... a kind of optical delusion of his consciousness. This delusion is a kind of prison for us. Our task must be to free ourselves from this prison by widening our circle of compassion to embrace all living creatures and the whole of nature in its beauty.[3]

As these quotations and the earlier description of the seventeen-year-old science student reveal, Einstein had a philosophical outlook and a strong personality that allowed him to take full advantage of his intellectual gifts to push the scientific model of the physical world into new territory. For this he was justifiably lauded and honored. In later years, with his wild and rebellious hair style, he became one of the most recognizable figures in the world, iconic as scientist and savant. It all began in his early years just before and during the time he spent in the patent office in Bern.

His creative process was also unusual. In a description of Einstein's *Miraculous Year: Five Papers That Changed the Face of Physics*, edited by John Stachel, a reviewer writes:

Stachel's discussion of Einstein's creative process is equally illuminating. Einstein's creativity seems to have required periods of solitude interspersed with interaction – not collaboration – with peers. His way of thinking was highly non-verbal, and rested on strongly developed physical intuition. This physical intuition, as Stachel emphasizes, was 'visual and muscular.' Hence Einstein's frequent use of gedanken or thought experiments, the most famous of which is no doubt his image of 'chasing after a light ray at the speed of light.' But such insights, no matter how profound, are useless unless translated into mathematics and the written word, and for this task Einstein depended on so-called 'sounding boards' with whom he would discuss his various ideas, digesting his visual and kinesthetic concepts into a form accessible to others.[4]

And this fits together nicely with his strong Moon. An intuitive and non-verbal method of visualizing (Moon in Sagittarius) replaced a more conventionally academic use of logic, deriving new descriptions of the physical universe and, in the end, mathematical ones. It was equally fundamental to Einstein's creative process that he interact with peers for purposes of feedback or mirroring, and that, as an important component of his investigative experience, also correlates with the Moon, symbolizing relationship and fellowship.

The timing of the original burst of insights that made his reputation brings up a good example of the effect of transiting Eris on his chart. Eris started in his natal map early in his tenth house, but two decades later it was its transit to Einstein's tenth house Sun that accompanied the crucial beginnings of his world-wide reputation. The date range is from 1899 to 1909, with twelve exact hits beginning in June of 1901 and a direct hit in February 1905 and a retrograde hit that was also a station to direct motion in mid-December 1905. This last took place within less than one minute of a degree to his natal Sun. These are the very years that Einstein was formulating his breakthrough theories. Letters from 1899 reveal the beginning of the thought process that would lead to the special theory of relativity.[5] In 1901 his first academic paper, 'Conclusions from the Capillarity Phenomena', was published. The year of 1905, when Eris was directly on his Sun degree, is referred to as his annus mirabilis (miracle year) when he published a bumper crop of papers that eventually reconstituted the foundations of modern physics. There were five groundbreaking papers including his thesis and comprising the photoelectric effect, Brownian motion, special relativity, and the equivalence of mass and energy, from which he received international attention and the respect of the academic world, and eventually the Nobel Prize. By 1909 he had quit the patent office and been appointed to a professorship at the University of Bern.

This association of strong natal and transiting Eris with those who fight the lonely battle to defy existing convention – and as well the timing of their work to establish a new paradigm of science or social structure – is not limited to the chart of Albert Einstein. See Appendix C for a list of eighteen such paradigm-shifters through modern western history, beginning with Nicolaus Copernicus.

Another side of Eris is reflected in the full story of Einstein's parenting. Although he was a good father – at least while his marriage lasted – to his second and third children, both boys, Hans Albrecht, and Eduard, he abandoned his first child, a daughter born out of wedlock (he stated in letters that he most wanted a son). This daughter of his courtship was discarded, probably put up for adoption, and very likely on his decision.[6] It is possible that his parents' objections were a factor. Another issue was his provisional employment status at the time, which in conservative turn-of-the-century Switzerland could have been jeopardized by an illegitimate child. The job at the patent office was the breath of life to him, giving him a decent salary and time for research. In any case he was able to move coldly and decisively to put the child up for adoption, which was extremely depressing for Maleva. The Eris archetype, so closely tied to Einstein's Moon, therefore coloring his mothering or nurturing behavior, shows a capacity for ruthlessness when called for, submitting to a greater need, in this case for his work. It has a deep drive to pursue an overarching purpose. The Eris archetype, like that of Pluto, is a two-edged sword that can create difficulties as well as strength.

This latter concept is echoed in Einstein's story of his own development, definitely, and defiantly, marching to the beat of his own drum, no matter what, and is summed up in his quotation cited above: "To punish me for my contempt for authority, fate made me an authority myself."

There is the difficult side of the strong stand for oneself that Eris demands, as Einstein's life illustrates in some of its features. There is also the ability to claim one's destiny, similar to the product of Jung's developmental process, which he termed the route of 'individuation.' In his more evolved development, Einstein showed this strongly individualistic streak, and the power to claim his own unique dharma, that made him what he is known for to this day: simply the most influential thinker in the subject matter of physics that his remarkable century ever produced.

Notes

1. Mary Wollstonecraft, from letter written in 1796; *Letters Written during a Short Residence in Sweden, Norway and Denmark* (1796). A longer quote containing the passage cited:

> It appears to me impossible that I should cease to exist, or that this active, restless spirit, equally alive to joy and sorrow, should only be organised dust — ready to fly abroad the moment the spring snaps, or the spark goes out which kept it together. Surely something resides in this heart that is not perishable, and life is more than a dream.

2. Fölsing, Albrecht. *Albert Einstein: A Biography*, translated from the German by Ewald Osers, Viking, New York, 1997, p. 39.

3. www.goodreads.com/author/quotes/9810.Albert_Einstein and http: //rescomp.stanford.edu/~cheshire/EinsteinQuotes.html

4. www.oxonianreview.org/issues/5-1/5-1foster.html))

5 *Albert Einstein: A Biography*, p. 62

6. *Albert Einstein: A Biography*, p. 114.

Part II

Literary Exemplars:
Melville, Lawrence and Blake

Here are three important literary figures that reveal the Eris archetype in greater depth. For Melville, examining the natal and transiting configurations of Eris gives us additional information about his character, his connection to the whaling industry, and the writing of *Moby Dick*. The discussion continues with the figure of D. H. Lawrence, who embodies the Eris energy in a very specific way, as demonstrated also by his chart, which has an extremely prominent Eris. William Blake represents another iconic figure in Western literature that fully personified the Eris archetype.

4

Herman Melville and the
Quest for Vengeance

It is better to fail in originality, than to succeed in imitation. He who has never failed somewhere, that man cannot be great. Failure is the true test of greatness.
Herman Melville[1]

There are various classics of literature that attempt to reveal the seamy underside of our common humanity, of blood lust and the implacable will of the hunt. Herman Melville's iconic tale of the hunting of the Leviathan is one. Melville's creation of *Moby Dick* not only documented the nineteenth century whaling industry, but also the dark forces within man that drive him to kill for profit and to seek vengeance. The story serves as an example of the struggle for the resources of the natural world represented in the hunt – either by natural predator or by man – as well as the single-minded quest for a deeply desired outcome, namely Ahab's monomania as he pursues his revenge against the White Whale. Melville's masterwork thus reflects an important piece of the Eris archetype.

The connection between the violent side of Eris and natural process is fascinating. Violence is, after all, an integral part of the natural world, a means to an end. There can be moreover a spiritual component to such dire and drastic action, even among the two-leggeds. Native Americans used to bless the spirit of the animal that they killed, and they killed only for necessity – in order to eat. Western civilization has gotten away from that concept, and the more 'civilized' cultures are decidedly less civilized in this regard, killing for sport in nature, and in relation to their fellow man for retribution, for terrorizing, or even in a twisted form of selfish pleasure. One way of thinking about this is that the civilizing progression, in its attempts to dissociate from primitive emotions and ways of life, such as the natural world's rule of 'kill or be killed', has lost connection with natural process. Moderns, by denying and repressing these natural urges, cause them to go underground. These natural urges therefore become toxic and are acted out in a less-than-conscious manner.

In *Moby Dick*, considered by the time of the early twentieth century an American classic novel, a young man, who is in some sense everyman, ships on a whaling vessel out of Nantucket with a crew of many different nationalities, as Melville himself once did. The circumstances of the voyage are described in loving detail, including many particulars of the way the hunt for whale oil was then conducted, giving a celebration and an important chronicle of a lost period of history in the years just before the first oil wells were put into service.

Whalers were after whale oil, and the specialized substance ambergris, used in perfume. The hunt for this oil, which at the time provided the most common lighting for homes, was every bit as intense as the hunt for fossil fuel in today's society. Once the whaling ships had spotted their target, the seamen would put out in smaller boats to chase down Leviathan and harpoon it, violently killing the whale for the sake of its valued resource. Most of the carcass would be discarded after the oil had been rendered from the blubber. This treasure, stored in barrels and worth a small fortune, would be carried back to homeport after a year or even two at sea.

Melville signed on with the whaling industry during the last stages of its heyday when he was at the age of 21. He set sail out of Nantucket on January 3rd, 1841, and later said that his life began at this time. After spending 18 months at sea, he deserted in the South Seas. Ten years later, having established a reputation as a novelist on the basis of lighter works, such as *Typee*, the story of his sojourn as a deserter in the Tahitian islands, he was moved to celebrate the industry. And celebrate it he did. Chapter after chapter detailed the men and their equipment and techniques that enabled them to pursue and slay these fantastic creatures – the very largest of mammals, many times the size of a man.

Beyond providing descriptions of the whale fishery, Melville's novel is famous in its literary rendering of the iconic tale of Captain Ahab and his lost leg, and his implacable lust for revenge against the white whale that took it, the symbolic "Moby Dick" of the book's title. Ironically, the symbolism of the color of the whale, being white, brings up the counter to this color, black. This part of Melville's story is where he brings in the depths of the psychological in his characterization of what would now be regarded as shadow material. The vengeance that Ahab seeks issues from a deep well of darkness within him, as emblematic of the human condition in general. Ultimately, the obsessive hunting of the white whale, accompanied by the novelistic symbolism of the multi-racial crew, and Fedallah, the dark Asian leader of the captain's own boat, and symbolically his shadow, becomes an entirely figurative story of the fruits of dark and buried passion.

Fedallah was calmly eyeing the Right Whale's head, and ever and anon glancing from the deep wrinkles there to the lines in his own hand. And Ahab chanced to stand, that the Parsee occupied his shadow; while, if the Parsee's shadow was there at all it seemed only to blend with, and lengthen Ahab's.[2]

In the book's ending, by a reversal of fortune, the whale takes down the ship, and all are lost except the lone narrator. Ahab throws the last harpoon, and is dragged down in a final fury of mingled spite and maniacal intent.

The following discussion of the Eris archetype in the context of Melville's classic owes a debt to Richard Tarnas, who in his seminal work, *Cosmos and Psyche*, discussed Melville's connection to conflict in the natural world, and in the whaling industry, in synchronicity with the conjunction of Saturn and Pluto observed both at Melville's birth and again at the time of the writing of *Moby Dick*.

In his section on this Saturn-Pluto combination, for which Tarnas assigns an orb of 15 degrees for its period of significance, he brings to light the amazing correlation of Saturn-Pluto with the time periods of Melville's birth and the subsequent writing of *Moby Dick*, thirty-two years later when Saturn and Pluto were once again in conjunction, and with the only two recorded instances of a whale attacking and sinking a whale ship (in 1820 and 1851).[3]

In Tarnas' view, this combination of planetary archetypes is appropriate because Saturn with Pluto represents conflict, contraction and confrontation within the darker side of one's nature. This shadowy side is presented within the tale more specifically by Ahab's lust for vengeance against the whale that took his leg. This dark side of nature is also portrayed by the violent course of the natural world of kill or be killed; and by the allegorical completion wherein the whale becomes in turn an agent of revenge for the hunting and 'harvesting' activity of man against beast.

A look at Melville's chart reveals the powerful presence of all the outer planet archetypes, including Eris.

We can see that Eris is strong in Melville's chart, being elevated and conjunct Jupiter, in his tenth house of career and outer manifestation. The Eris-Jupiter conjunction opposes his Sun in the fourth house of family. Melville was a strong family man for most of his adult life and had a markedly private side to his personality. Ironically, he did not become famous overnight with the publication of his masterwork, but instead lived on in relative obscurity. The fate that eventually overtook him was to become one of the most well known literary figures of his era. It was not until decades

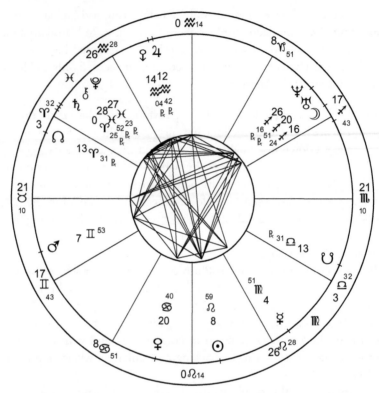

Fig. 4-1 Herman Melville, August 1, 1819, 11:30 PM LMT,
New York, USA 40N43, 74W00

after his death that his work, including the posthumously published *Billy Budd*, became better appreciated and even idolized by critics.

His chart reveals a powerful combination of Pluto with other outer planets, in close conjunction with Saturn and in square with Uranus and even more closely with Neptune. Pluto is in extremely close conjunction with Chiron, symbolizing deep psychological wounding, very appropriate for the tale of dark desire for revenge arising out of the deep wounding exhibited in physical form by the twisted figure of Ahab.

The imagery of dark psychological forces represented by Pluto, and the sea, as symbolized by Neptune, would seem appropriate given the subject matter of his most deeply psychological writing and its setting. Indeed, the square between Neptune and Pluto is quite close, about a degree away from exact. His chart ruler, Venus, is trine Pluto and inconjunct Uranus and Neptune, with also a contra-parallel between Venus and Neptune to within a few minutes of a degree.

We also note that the Jupiter-Eris conjunction near the top of his chart mediates the extremely close Neptune-Pluto square, because it resides near their midpoint. Recalling that the Eris archetype so aptly describes the whaling industry with all its violence, we can see the appropriateness of this symbolism to Melville's masterwork; it was this correspondence that stimulated me to seek out the influence of Eris in his chart.

Jupiter represents expansion and spiritual congruence; it represents the happier and more optimistic side of our human condition in contrast with dour and limited Saturn. The archetypal combination of Eris with Jupiter is plainly indicated in his writing – a joyous way of speaking with regard to the most violent of activities, suffusing them with an over-riding spiritual significance:

Ka-la! Koo-loo! Howled Queequeg, as if smacking his lips over a mouthful of Grenadier's steak. And thus with oars and yells the keels cut the sea. Meanwhile Stubb retaining his place in the van, still encouraged his men to the onset, all the while puffing the smoke from his mouth. Like desperadoes they tugged and they strained until the welcome cry was heard, "Stand up Tashtego! – give it to him!" The harpoon was hurled... the same moment something went hot and hissing along every one of their wrists. It was the magical line. An instant before, Stubb had swiftly caught two additional turns with it round the loggerhead, whence by reason of its increased rapid circlings, a hempen blue smoke now jetted up and mingled with the steady fumes from his pipe.[4]

His exuberance for the task of chronicling this violent way of life can be clearly seen in this celebratory language. The strongly Jupiterian nature of his masterpiece is also shown by the sheer size and the range of styles of the classic that he produced.

Another quote, in this instance in the voice of Melville's dark hero, Ahab, serves to demonstrate the almost Shakespearean nature of Melville's examination of the depths of the human condition; in this regard it is interesting to note that Shakespeare himself had strong Uranus, Neptune and Pluto. The following relates as well to that fight to the finish so characteristic of the Eris archetype. The fight could be for principle, or as here, for darker motives of implacable and dire resolve being brought to bear:

Am I cut off from the last fond pride of meanest shipwrecked captains? Oh, lonely death on lonely life! Oh, now I feel my topmost greatness lies in my topmost grief. Ho, ho! From all your furthest bounds pour ye now in, ye bold billows of my whole foregone life, and top this one piled comber of my death! Towards thee I roll, thou all-destroying but unconquering whale; to the last I grapple with thee; from hell's heart I stab at thee; for hate's sake I spit out my last breath at thee. Sink all coffins and all hearses to one common pool! And since neither can be mine, let me then tow to pieces while still chasing thee, though tied to thee, thou damned whale! Thus I give up the spear![5]

When I examined the transiting positions of Eris at two of Melville's important life events, namely his setting sail on the whaler *Acushnet*, when he said his life began, and the period of writing *Moby Dick* and sending it off for publication, I came upon significant configurations.

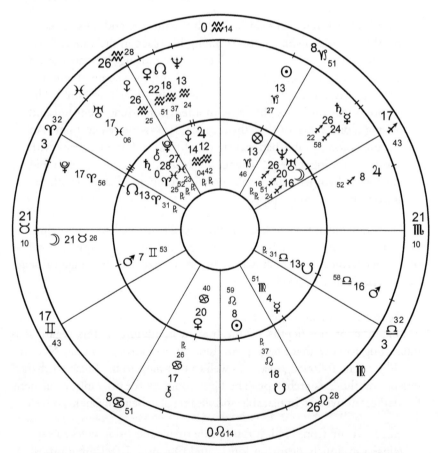

Fig. 4-2 Herman Melville, Transits for Sunday, January 3, 1841, 5:00 PM EST

On January 3rd, 1841, when Melville set sail on his adventure, transiting Eris had moved to 26 degrees of Aquarius – exactly sextile his natal Neptune and semi-sextile natal Pluto, within a degree. Transiting Saturn at 26 Sagittarius 20 was exactly conjunct natal Neptune – practically to the minute – and square natal Pluto, and as well making an exact sextile to transiting Eris. Meanwhile Neptune had moved by transit to his tenth house, and was in conjunction with his natal Jupiter-Eris combination there, exactly conjunct their midpoint within 2 minutes of a degree of arc. These configurations show that while Saturn, Neptune and Pluto are integral to Melville's character and subject matter, Eris is also extremely significant in helping to delineate them more closely. This fits well with Melville's project, since in going to sea at age 21 he was unwittingly setting the stage for the literary work that would occupy the rest of his life, culminating in *Moby Dick*. His personal mission to expose the violent struggle against the natural world for essential resources represents a major theme of the Eris archetype, as we are coming to understand it.

The planetary combinations that figured in the astrology of Melville's birth were also prominent during the events surrounding the creation of *Moby Dick*, namely Saturn-Pluto and Uranus-Pluto. As indicated above, Melville's birth was coincident with a Saturn-Pluto conjunction, very nearly exact, and also with Neptune and Uranus in square with Saturn/Pluto. His masterwork was truly begun during the summer of 1850, and finished nearly a year later.

The book was a departure from his earlier crowd-pleasing fiction; this time he expressed a vision that was deeply symbolic in his horror-fraught chronicle of vengeance in the whaling industry, the book that was destined to become a classic of early American literature. Melville meticulously describes the hunting down and sacrificing of these huge and intelligent beasts; he serves up a glorified examination and celebration of the whaling industry given in extraordinary detail, and includes the monomania of Ahab and the revenge of the whale, when the hunted becomes the hunter.

When he came to the writing of his masterpiece in July and August of 1850, Melville abandoned his earlier writing style to focus on deeper and darker themes. The chronology of his writing process is very interesting, especially in light of outer planet transits. Up until July of 1850, he was engaged in writing a chronicle of the whale fishery much like his earlier, more popular, works: *Typee, Omoo, Redburn* and *White-Jacket*. "Dollars damn me," he wrote in a letter, referring to this activity of pumping out popular fiction, "I write these books of mine almost entirely for lucre – as a wood-sawyer saws wood."[6]

He made a similar reference to the early stages of his writing of *The Whale*, which later became *Moby Dick*, and his editor commented on the earlier version as a "romantic, fanciful, most literal & most enjoyable presentment of the Whale Fishery."

In July 1850 he was presented with a copy of Nathaniel Hawthorne's *Mosses from an Old Manse* and its dark vision inspired him to write a review – based partly on his recent dipping into Shakespeare's tragedies, notably *Hamlet* and *King Lear*.[7] In the course of writing this now-famous review/essay on Hawthorne and Shakespeare, published on August 17th, his passion for his subject matter returned and he apparently resolved to write the book in a way that more nearly matched his inner vision.[8] A year later, in August of 1851, the revisited and revitalized manuscript was completed.

The turn-around of July and August 1850 was marked by Uranus and Pluto in nearly perfect conjunction in trine with his natal Neptune and hinting at Shakespearean themes – the great depths of passion that represent the true picture of the human condition – that so occupied him at that time. They were to be joined by Saturn in a triple conjunction before the year of his labor was over. At this time also, transiting Neptune and transiting Eris opposed his natal Mercury, representing writing, each within 2 degrees so that their midpoint matched almost perfectly. It is interesting to note that the July 9th New Moon exactly conjoined his chart ruler, Venus, while at this same time transiting Mars, in conjunction with his Mercury, opposed transiting Eris exactly and while the North Node of his destiny opposed his natal Eris.

On August 7th when Melville was completing his Hawthorne essay and presumably contemplating the massive change in direction of *Moby Dick*, there was a solar eclipse that opposed his natal Eris within a degree (see chart in Fig. 4-3). Finding this eclipse, so precisely positioned, at just the time that Melville's major shift was likely occurring, convinced me that I had been on the right track in seeking the Eris archetype in connection with his classic monumental tale of vengeance and the hunt for the whale.

This dramatic New Moon and Solar Eclipse was accompanied by a triple conjunction of Mars, Venus, and Jupiter squaring his Neptune-Uranus conjunction in late Sagittarius, while transiting Pluto-Uranus still trined natal Neptune. Neptune and Eris still opposed Melville's Mercury, with the transiting Neptune-Eris midpoint only 30 minutes away from an exact opposition.

By the time he sent the manuscript off to England on September 10th, 1851, Eris had moved closer, with the transiting Neptune-Eris midpoint again just minutes away from an exact opposition to natal Mercury. Eris

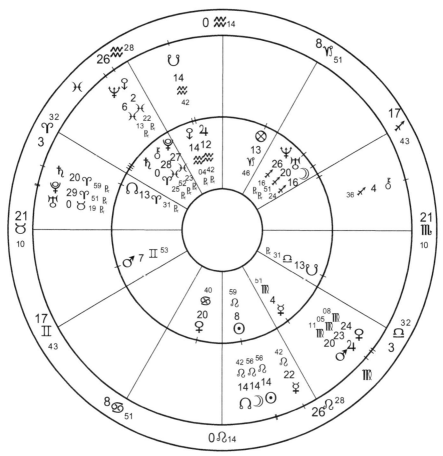

Fig. 4-3 Herman Melville, Transits for Wednesday, Aug 7, 1850,
4:34 PM EST

had stationed just slightly more than one degree away from opposing his
Mercury on May 30th as Melville was in the fervor of completion.

The fact that Eris by transit was in combination with transiting Neptune
and in exact connection to Melville's natal Mercury – during the writing of
this American classic of the high seas – contributed greatly to confirming
my sense that Eris is an appropriate archetype for his underlying themes
of violence, monomaniacal fixity of purpose, and the eventual implacable
destruction by the whale of its hunters, in symbolic retribution for an entire
species.

Notes

1. Melville, Herman. 'Hawthorn and His Mosses' from *The Literary World*, Aug 17th and 24th, 1850.
2. *Moby Dick*, p. 384.
3. Tarnas, Richard. *Cosmos and Psyche*, pp. 237-241.
4. *Moby Dick*, p. 284.
5. ibid pp. 571-572.
6. Charles Olson, from the article entitled 'Call Me Ishmael' p. 24, reprinted in *Modern Critical Interpretations: Herman Melville's Moby-Dick*, ed. Harold Bloom, 1986, Chelsea House Publishers.
7. 'Historical Notes' in *The Writings of Herman Melville Vol. Six*, ed. Harrison Hayford, 1988, Northwestern University Press, p. 622.
8. The extent to which Melville was inspired by his reading of Hawthorne may be judged from the following quote from his essay, published in the *Literary Review* of August 1850:

> "To what infinite height of loving wonder and admiration I may yet be borne, when by repeatedly banqueting on these Mosses, I shall have thoroughly incorporated their whole stuff into my being, – that, I can not tell. But already I feel that this Hawthorne has dropped germinous seeds into my soul. He expands and deepens down, the more I contemplate him; and further, and further, shoots his strong New-England roots into the hot soil of my Southern soul."

5

D. H. Lawrence – Violent Iconoclast of Holy Vision

Kill when you must and be killed the same: the must coming from the gods inside you or
from the men in whom you recognize [them].

D. H. Lawrence[1]

We now come to another important exemplar of the Eris archetype, iconoclast and novelist D. H. Lawrence, whom many consider one of the most important figures in 20th century English letters.

D. H. Lawrence is well known as a novelist, short-story writer, a poet far ahead of his time, and a fearless explorer of sexuality and its unbridled expression in literature. But few are aware of the fundamental fierceness of his character and how much he struggled with the political establishment of his day, which was still emerging from the repressive Victorian era. He fought hard all his life for the right to freely voice his opinions, however avant garde and morally inappropriate they might be. He therefore represents another example of a powerful Erisian personality: he fought, and fought to the death, in response to an inner calling, and was able to make his stand for what he truly believed, against all odds.

The above quotation is one example of his stated creed, voiced at the age of 37. The gods that Lawrence refers to here were his so-called "dark gods" – not necessarily the Christian ones.

Early on in my research on the new planet I had chanced to come across the following paragraph from Lawrence's novel *Kangaroo* and identified indications of a strong Eris presence:

> He had come to the end of his own tether, so why should he go off in tantrums if other folk strayed about with the broken bits of their tethers trailing from their ankles. Is it better to be savagely tugging at the end of your rope, or to wander at random tetherless? Matter of choice! But the day of the absolute is over, and we're in for the strange gods once more. "But when you get to the end of your tether you've nothing to do but die" – so sings an out-of-date vulgar song.

But is it so? ... Anything is better than stewing in your own juice, or grinding at the end of your tether, or tread-milling away at a career. Better a "wicked creature" any day than a mechanical tread-miller of a careerist. Better anything on earth than the millions of human ants.[2]

Since I had already suspected a strong Eris in Lawrence's chart I was gratified to find it.

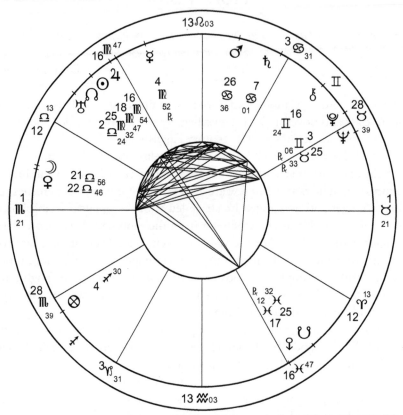

Fig. 5-1 D. H. Lawrence, September 11, 1885, 9:45 AM GMT, Eastwood, Nottinghamshire, England 53N01 1W18

Not only does Eris stand apart, singular in the more private northern hemisphere of Lawrence's chart, but it is also on the fifth house cusp of artistic creativity and in exact opposition to his Sun-Jupiter conjunction in Virgo. Eris makes a close square to Chiron, so that Chiron is in a nearly perfect T-square with Sun/Jupiter and Eris. With Eris so prominent in Lawrence's chart, he is an excellent exemplar of the archetype.

Like Melville, Lawrence has an aspect between Jupiter and Eris, in his case the opposition, exact to within 20 minutes of arc. And like him, he would spend his life work to glorify elements of fierce natural process, over and above the rationality of conditioned response and normative thought as represented by the bulk of human society. Hear Lawrence in praise of the whale:

> They say the sea is cold, but the sea contains
> the hottest blood of all, and the wildest, the most urgent.
>
> All the whales in the wider deeps, hot are they, as they urge
> on and on, and dive beneath the icebergs.
> The right whales, the sperm-whales, the hammer-heads, the killers
> there they blow, there they blow, hot wild white breath out of
> the sea!
>
> And they rock, and they rock, through the sensual ageless ages
> on the depths of the seven seas,
> and through the salt they reel with drunk delight
> and in the tropics tremble they with love
> and roll with massive, strong desire, like gods.[3]

As I began a further study of Lawrence's work in search of Eris, other characteristic quotes then came to light, indicating his identification with the deeply unconscious places of the spiritual warrior within. To give a few examples, among many:

> [on finding a German motto on a wooden heart "the world belongs to the courageous"]
> That was the motto to have on one's red heart: not Love or Hope or any of those aspiring emotions: "The world belongs to the courageous." To be sure it was a rather two-edged motto just now for Germany [in the 1920s]. And [he] was not quite sure that it was the "world" that he wanted. Yes, it was. Not the tuppenny social world of present mankind: but the genuine world, full of life and eternal creative surprises, including of course destructive surprises, since destruction is a part of creation.[4]

Then from a telling short story called "The Ladybird," written slightly before *Kangaroo*, and published in 1923; Lady Daphne in conversation with Count Dionys asks him, "How did you succeed in being happy?" And he answers:

"How shall I tell you? I felt that the same power which put up the mountains could pull them down again – no matter how long it took."

"And was that all?"

"Was it not enough?" … "Ah you are bored," he said. "But I – I found the God who pulls things down especially the things that men have put up… I have found my God."

"The God of destruction" she said, blanching.

"Yes – not the devil of destruction, but the god of destruction. The blessed God of destruction. It is strange… but I have found my God." …

"With my heart I will help while I can do nothing with my hands. I say to my heart: Beat, hammer, beat with little strokes. Beat, hammer of God, beat them down. Beat it all down."

"Beat what down?" she asked harshly.

"The world, the world of man. Not the trees – … nor those chattering sorcerers, the squirrels – nor the hawk that comes. Not these… the world of man, Lady Daphne" – his voice sank to a whisper. "I hate it." …. "I believe in the power of my red, dark, heart. God has put the hammer in my breast, the little eternal hammer. Hit – hit – hit! It hits upon the world of man. It hits, it hits!" …

He stood before her with his teeth set together, his black eyes leaping thin flames upon her, like a little demon.[5]

We can see in this paean to the internal 'God of destruction' a self-revealing symbol of Lawrence's own attitude: the ruthless and if necessary ultimately destructive attitude toward a world of falseness to which he can no longer allow himself to be a part. In this he was very much affected by the horror of World War I and the perceived hypocrisy of conventional attitudes at that time, as we shall see. He was influenced as well by the mindless industrial poisoning of natural beauty that he saw all around him as he was growing up in the midlands area of Great Britain, infected by coal mining. It was in his last major literary work, toward the end of his life, that he expressed this feeling most succinctly. From *Lady Chatterley's Lover*:

The car ploughed uphill through the long squalid straggle of Tevershall, the blackened brick dwellings, the black slate roofs glistening their sharp edges, the mud black with coal-dust, the pavements wet and black. It was as if dismalness had soaked through and through everything. The utter negation of natural beauty, the utter negation of the gladness of life…[6]

D. H. Lawrence's very being was bound up with the Eris archetype, as is clearly shown in his philosophy, his literary art, and its synchronistic placement in his chart.

Although it would be in relationships that his passion for violent struggle most clearly arose, in fact it colored every aspect of his career. His life-long opposition to social norms that he found so stultifying, restrictive and out of date, is indicated in the passage from *Kangaroo*. This is not fighting for the fun of fighting, or violence for the sake of violence, but rather for a life-affirming cause. It is this sense of life affirmation for which we most remember Lawrence today.

The archetype of violent will to achieve a necessary and organic need arises in his personal life as well as in his writing. His first major novel, *Sons and Lovers*, published in 1913, made his reputation. It was highly autobio-graphical, revealing the situation he grew up with – an unhealthily close connection with his mother, as he explores the possibilities of young love. The novel describes his own feisty nature, which comes out in his relation-ship with the fictional Miriam, based on his real-life friend Jessie Chambers. In the following paragraph he describes how he was with her, teaching her algebra, which she had trouble understanding:

> "Do you see?" She looked up at him, her eyes wide with the half-laugh that comes of fear. "Don't you" he cried. He had been too fast. But she said nothing. He questioned her more, then got hot. It made his blood rouse to see her there, as it were, at his mercy, her eyes dilated, … she was poring over the book, seemed absorbed in it, yet trembling lest she could not get at it. It made him cross. She was ruddy and beautiful. Yet her soul seemed to be intensely supplicating. The algebra book she closed, shrinking, knowing he was angered; and at the same in-stant he grew gentle, seeing her hurt because she did not understand. … So the lessons went. He was always either in a rage or very gentle.[7]

In the next paragraph he relates how he threw a pencil in her face and then apologized. So too, years later, Lawrence would treat his wife Frieda. He met and eloped with her in 1912, in a whirlwind romance after his mother died, and he never left her until he left his own body nearly 18 years later. Ill all his life, Lawrence died young, at 43, from tuberculosis.

From the accounts of many witnesses he would rage and storm at this most important person in his life, sometimes committing small acts of vio-lence like striking the cigarette out of her mouth. He once threatened her with a fireplace poker, with which he subsequently swept the tea things to oblivion. And yet, consistently, the storm would soon pass and he and they would be happy with one other again as though nothing had happened. It was just his way. In spite of his outbursts they really loved each other. After his death, Frieda Lawrence was able to say: "What he had seen and felt and known he gave in his writing to his fellow men, the splendor of living, the hope of more and more life, ... an heroic and immeasurable gift."

This streak of domestic violence in Lawrence is echoed in many of his fictional relationships; these are portrayed as fierce struggles, almost to the death, for dominance. Note that in Lawrence's chart, Eris stands in opposition to his Sun, symbolizing relationship with the other. It is interesting to see how this opposition plays out in the novels, in combination with the struggle for making one's own self-expression paramount that is characterized by the soul warrior archetype of Eris.

It seems there is a deep need for mastery and control – the same sense of dire purpose that drives the tigress to hunt for the food she needs for her family to survive – and this can manifest wherever close interpersonal relationship calls it forth, when there is that degree of closeness.

The exploration of this theme in Lawrence, of a deep struggle for mastery, is characteristic of his best work. The unconscious struggle for power in relationship is perhaps most clearly exemplified in his classic early novels *The Rainbow* and *Women in Love*.

In *The Rainbow*, written in 1913-14 after his fateful meeting and elopement with Frieda, three important male-female relationships are described. The first is between Tom Brangwen, a rural 19th century farmer, and Lydia, a foreign woman, a Pole, whom he meets and marries and brings to his farm, called the Marsh. The second is between her daughter Anna and her beau, when she in her turn becomes engaged to Will Brangwen, a cousin of Tom. Ursula Brangwen is the fruit of this union, one of the two sisters whose story continues in *Women in Love*. The final pairing with which the novel ends is between Ursula and her early lover, a military man named Skrebensky. The depth of unconscious process within these various relationships, almost wholly inarticulate to the characters involved, is revealed by Lawrence as narrator; as with Tom and Lydia:

> she was aware of a heat beating up over her consciousness. She sat motionless and in conflict. Who was this strange man who was at once so near to her? What was happening to her?[8]

Or, again,

> A daze had come over his mind... somewhere in his body, there had started another activity. It was as if a strong light were burning there,

and he was blind within it, unable to know anything except that this transfiguration burned between him and her, connecting them, like a secret power.[9]

Lawrence's description of unconscious process in lovemaking can be couched in terms that speak directly to the war-like hunt of natural process, as here, describing the love relations between Anna and Will Brangwen as a hawk, hunting:

> And she loved the intent, far look in his eyes when they rested on her… she wanted his eyes to come to hers, to know her. And they would not. They remained intent, and far, and proud, like a hawk's, naïve and inhuman as a hawk's. So she loved him and caressed him and roused him like a hawk… he came to her fierce and hard, like a hawk striking and taking her… she was his aim and object, his prey. And she was carried off, and he was satisfied, satiated at last.
>
> Then immediately she began to retaliate on him. She too was a hawk. If she imitated the pathetic plover running plaintive to him, that was part of the game. When he, satisfied, moved with … a half-contemptuous drop of the head, unaware of her, ignoring her very existence, after taking his fill of her and getting his satisfaction of her, her soul roused, her pinions became like steel, and she struck at him. When he sat on his perch glancing sharply around, with solitary pride, pride eminent and fierce, she dashed at him and threw him from his station savagely, she goaded him from his keen dignity of a male, she harassed him from his unperturbed pride, till he was mad with rage, his light brown eyes burned with fury, they saw her now, like flames of anger they flared at her and recognized her as the enemy…[10]

In passages such as these, Lawrence distinguishes unconscious reactions from more superficially conscious and socially conditioned thought. As many critics have noted, this is a distinguishing feature of his prose, these telling descriptions of his characters' nonverbal reality, in ways that they would be unable to articulate for themselves. Like Freud and Jung before him, he was in his own way exploring the dark unknown part of the psyche, available only peripherally to more ordinary rationality.

If Eris represents natural process within humankind, it also represents the deep drive that emanates out of the unconscious. The Eris in Lawrence's chart is opposed to his rationality, as represented by the Sun and Jupiter, and and is antithetical as well by its archetypal nature, representing an irrational element out of the depths of unconscious process that in the end proves to be, for him, far more powerful than the socially accepted notions of behavior that were prevalent in his own day. With Jupiter involved, and in square with Chiron, Lawrence was motivated to celebrate these darker places within the psyche that represented an all-important drive on the part of his central characrers.

In another part of *The Rainbow* involving love as battle, and in the midst of nature, we come to the climactic love scene of the novel, although it is failed love that is depicted. With Skrebensky and Ursula:

> And she seized hold of his arm, held him fast, as if captive, and walked him a little way by the edge of the dazzling, dazzling water. And there in the great flare of light, she clinched hold of him, hard, as if suddenly she had the strength of destruction, she fastened her arms round him and tightened him in her grip, whilst her mouth sought his in a hard, rending, ever-increasing kiss, till his body was powerless in her grip, his heart melted in fear from the fierce, beaked, harpy's kiss. ... He led her to a dark hollow.
>
> "No, here," she said, going out to the slope full under the moonshine. She lay motionless, with wide-open eyes, looking at the moon. He came direct to her ... She held him pinned down at the chest, awful. The fight, the struggle for consummation was terrible. It lasted till it was agony to his soul, till he succumbed, till he gave way as if dead, and lay with his face buried ... as if he would be motionless now forever, hidden away in the dark, buried...
>
> He looked up. Her face lay like an image in the moonlight, the eyes wide open, rigid. But out of the eyes, slowly, there rolled a tear, that glittered in the moonlight as it ran down her cheek.
>
> He felt as if the knife were being pushed into his already-dead body.[11]

After this, they part. She returns home and tells her people that her engagement is broken off, meditates over what finally had transpired, and slowly becomes whole again. As the novel ends, she references the rainbow of its title.

The entire thrust of *The Rainbow* is toward an over-arching concept of life and still more life, in response to what Lawrence perceived as the deadening and stultifying effect of modern industrialized culture. He would take this exploration even farther in his next novel, in some sense a sequel to *The Rainbow*.

Continuing the examples from Lawrence's earliest writing, we come to what is considered perhaps his most important work, *Women in Love*. It is set just after World War I. It involves again the character of Ursula Brangwen, along with her sister Gudrun. There are two relationships that are explored in depth; one between Rupert Birkin (a substitute for Lawrence himself) and Ursula, and another between Gerald Critch, a factory owner, and Gudrun.

In the first part of the book, Gerald makes the conquest of a woman called Pussum, in bohemian London. It is interesting to witness Lawrence in his characteristic perception as he relates the beginnings of the sexual act – the flirtation between a man and a woman – and simultaneously reveals the man's underlying impulses and that part of these unconscious currents of emotion that can be a form of violence:

> "How long are you staying?" She asked him.
>
> "A day or two," he replied. "But there is no particular hurry."
>
> Still she stared into his face with that slow full gaze which was so curious and exciting to him. He was acutely and delightfully conscious of himself, of his own attractiveness. He felt full of strength, able to give off a sort of electric power. And he was aware of her dark, hot-looking eyes upon him. ...
>
> She appealed to Gerald strongly. He felt an awful, enjoyable, power over her, an instinctive cherishing very near to cruelty. For she was a victim. He felt that she was in his power, and he was generous. The electricity was turgid and voluptuously rich, in his limbs. He would be able to destroy her utterly in the strength of his discharge. ...
>
> They talked banalities for some time.[12]

Later we see the tables turned against Gerald, with the under-layer of violence implicit in the sexual act now displayed on the part of Gudrun, toward him:

> She looked at him inscrutably.
>
> "You think I'm afraid of you and your cattle, don't you" she asked.
>
> His eyes narrowed dangerously. There was a faint domineering smile on his face.
>
> "Why should I think that?" he said. She was watching him all the time with her dark, dilated, inchoate eyes. She leaned forward and swung round her arm, catching him a light blow on the face with the back of her hand.

"That's why," she said, mocking.

And she felt in her soul an unconquerable desire for deep violence against him. She shut off the fear and dismay that filled her
conscious mind. She wanted to do as she did, she was not going to
be afraid.

He recoiled from the slight blow on his face. He became deadly
pale and a dangerous flame darkened his eyes. For some seconds he
could not speak, his lungs were so suffused with blood, his heart
stretched almost to bursting with a great gush of ungovernable emotion. It was as though some reservoir of black emotion had burst
within him, and swamped him.

"You have struck the first blow," he said at last, forcing the air
from his lungs, in a voice so soft and low, it sounded like a dream
within her, not spoken in the outer air.

"And I shall strike the last" she retorted involuntarily.[13]

Here once more we see that it is the deep unconscious and essentially
wordless process of the lovers' psyches that Lawrence exposes, together
with this theme of implicit underlying violence as one modality of passion-
ate relationship.

In another scene, between the Lawrence-figure, Birkin, and an old lover
of his, Hermione Roddice, the war between the sexes becomes overt:

A terrible voluptuous thrill ran down her arms – she was going
to know her voluptuous consummation… she knew it was upon her
now, in extremity of bliss. Her hand closed on a blue, beautiful ball
of lapis lazuli that stood on her desk for a paperweight. She rolled it
round in her hand as she rose silently. Her heart was a pure flame in
her breast, she was purely unconscious in ecstasy. …

Then swiftly, in flame that drenched down her body like fluid
lightening, … she brought down the ball of jewel stone with all her
force, crash on his head.[14]

In a reflection back upon the sort of blow that Lawrence himself was
capable of striking, it is of extreme interest to note that the character of
Hermione was based in a very recognizable way on Lady Ottoline Morrell,
a well-known figure in early 20th century British artistic and liberal circles.
She had once bestowed upon Lawrence, as a gift, a paperweight made of
lapis lazuli.

In another example of the body's powerfully deep process coming to
light in Lawrence's prose, with Ursula's experience of Birkin, he describes

these depths of mysterious energy in a way relating to the lower chakras and the Kundalini energy of the spine, without specifically saying so:

> He stood there in his strange, whole body, that had its marvelous fountains, like the bodies of the Sons of God who were in the beginning. There were strange fountains of his body, more mysterious and potent than any she had imagined or known, more satisfying, ah, finally, mystically-physically satisfying. She had thought there was no source deeper than the phallic source. And now, behold, from the smitten rock of the man's body, from the strange, marvelous flanks and thighs, deeper, further in mystery than the phallic source, came the floods of ineffable darkness and ineffable riches.[15]

It is a vast sea of unconscious energy that he documents, below volition, together with a primal urge for mastery, through violence if necessary, in order to achieve the willed objective. And this depiction of the depths of unconscious passion and the need to achieve it exemplifies the Eris archetype.

Lawrence often focuses on women as central characters in his fiction, and this, too, fits with the Eris archetype of feminine warrior energy; a strong warrior impulse, not merely to conquer for reasons of dominance, but based on a deep and abiding need to survive, at any cost, and to nurture one's soul-level intention.

He struggled to describe an urge for independence and mastery in terms of his female characters, in the context of turn-of-the-century society when women were so dominated by the power of the surrounding patriarchy, and when their self-concept was changing radically all through the years leading up to the 1920s. Lawrence achieved this aim more than any of his contemporaries. You might almost suppose that he was a woman writing in disguise. In a letter written in 1913, he remarked: "It seems to me that the chief thing about a woman – who is much of a woman – is that in the long run she is not to be had. She is not to be caught by any of the catch-words, love, beauty, honour, duty, worth, work, salvation – none of them – not in the long run." He would come to celebrate this kind of woman in his best-known work, *Lady Chatterley's Lover*.

In this last major novel of the Lawrencian canon, written during his final years, he takes up his cause, which includes the cause of woman's emancipation, in more poetic form. He expresses the loss of natural beauty of the landscape to the dirty horror of industrialism, and the loss of deep purpose and perspective on the part of run-of-the-mill members of modern Western society, together with a more feminine viewpoint that opposes these excesses.

The novel opens with Connie, the Lady Chatterley of the title, in a state of vague discontent, with a husband who is in his own world and apart from her, both because of a kind of intellectual snobbery while living by mental pursuits – he is a writer – and because having served as an officer in the First World War, he has come home in a wheelchair, without the ability to satisfy her sexually. At first she tells herself it does not matter, but in time she comes to recognize how thoroughly alienated she has become, an alienation that is symbolic of the dystopia represented by modern industrial society spreading across the landscape as well as the culture. The coal-mining district where Lawrence grew up had gone through terrible changes and a strongly descriptive passage in the novel, referenced earlier, details how the modern industrial world of coal has laid waste to the natural beauty of the landscape:

> The car ploughed uphill through the long squalid straggle of Tevershall, the blackened brick dwellings, the black slate roofs glistening their sharp edges, the mud black with coal-dust, the pavements wet and black. It was as if dismalness had soaked through and through everything. The utter negation of natural beauty, the utter negation of the gladness of life, the utter absence of the instinct for shapely beauty which every bird and beast has, the utter death of the human intuitive faculty was appalling... Connie sat and listened with her heart in her boots, as Field was filling petrol. What could possibly become of such a people, a people in whom the living intuitive faculty was dead as nails ...?

> ... Tevershall! That was Tevershall! Merrie England! Shakespeare's England! No, but the England of today, as Connie had realized since she had come to live in it. It was producing a new race of mankind, over-conscious in the money and social and political side, on the spontaneous, intuitive side dead, but dead. Half-corpses, all of them: but with a terrible insistent consciousness in the other half. There was something uncanny and underground about it all. It was an underworld. And quite incalculable. How shall we understand the reactions in half-corpses? When Connie saw the great lorries full of steel-workers from Sheffield, weird, distorted smallish beings like men, off for an excursion to Matlock, her bowels fainted and she thought: Ah God, what has man done to man? What have the leaders of men been doing

to their fellow men? They have reduced them to less than humanness; and now there can be no fellowship any more! It is just a nightmare…[16]

The deadness that Connie finds in her own marriage and in the social swirl that surrounds her at her husband's inherited estate, called Wragby, is in vital contrast to what she encounters in the wood nearby, another part of the grounds that includes a shed occupied by Sir Clifford's gamekeeper, Mellors, where baby pheasants are being bred.

> "There!" he said, … She took the little drab thing between her hands, and there it stood, on its impossible little stalks of legs, its atom of balancing life trembling through its almost weightless feet… But it lifted its little head boldly, and looked sharply round, and gave a little 'peep!'
> "So adorable! So cheeky!" she said softly.
> The keeper, squatting beside her, was also watching with an amused face the bold little bird in her hands. Suddenly he saw a tear fall onto her wrist. …
> And suddenly he was aware of the old flame shooting and leaping up in his loins, that he had hoped was quiescent forever. He fought against it, turning his back to her. But it leapt, and leapt downwards, circling his knees.[17]

In the love-making scene that follows, it is interesting to note that Lawrence has abandoned his earlier style of describing the unconscious responses of the participants, often in struggle against one another, and of which they remain barely aware. Instead he chooses to depict the lovers' interactions through dialogue, and through descriptions of the physical intimacy between them in more graphic detail than was currently permissible in popular fiction, thus causing quite a stir when this, his final work, was eventually published.

> "Shall you come to th' hut?" he said, in a quiet, neutral voice.
> And closing his hand softly upon her upper arm, he drew her up and led her slowly into the hut, not letting go of her until she was inside. Then he … took a brown soldier's blanket from the tool chest, spreading it slowly. She glanced at his face as she stood motionless.
> His face was pale and without expression, like that of a man submitting to fate.
> "You lie there!" he said softly; and he shut the door, so that it was dark, quite dark.

With a queer obedience, she lay down... she quivered as she felt his hand groping softly yet with queer thwarted clumsiness, among her clothing. Yet the hand knew, too, how to unclothe her where it wanted. ... with a quiver of exquisite pleasure he touched her warm soft body, and touched her navel for a moment in a kiss. And he had to come in to her at once, to enter the peace on earth of her soft quiescent body. It was a moment of pure peace for him, the entry into the body of the woman.[18]

At the time, describing this kind of behavior was unusual even between liberated lovers. It was almost impossible in a serious work of fiction. The critics and the bowlderizers wailed. Still Lawrence refused to censor himself and published the book in a limited edition in Italy. In an essay he wrote for the second edition, called 'A Propos of *Lady Chatterley's Lover*', Lawrence described what he thought that he was up to:

The body's life is the life of sensations and emotions. The body feels real hunger, real thirst, real joy in the sun or the snow, real pleasure in the smell of roses, or the look of a lilac bush, real anger, real sorrow, real love, real tenderness, real warmth, real passion, real hate, real grief. All the emotions belong to the body and are only recognized by the mind. ...

How different they are, mental feelings and real feelings. To-day, many people live and die without having had any real feelings – although they have had a 'rich emotional life' apparently, having showed strong mental feeling. But it is all counterfeit. ...

Never was an age more sentimental, more devoid of real feeling, more exaggerated in false feeling, than our own. Sentimentality and counterfeit feeling have become a sort of game, everybody trying to outdo his neighbor.

... especially in love, only counterfeit emotions exist nowadays. We have all been taught to distrust everybody emotionally, from parents downwards, or upwards. ... So there goes love, there goes friendship; for each implies a fundamental emotional sympathy. And hence, counterfeit love, from which there is no escaping.

And with counterfeit emotion, there is no real sex at all. Sex is the one thing you cannot really swindle... Sex lashes out against counterfeit emotion, and is ruthless, devastating against false love.[19]

He goes on to state, more or less directly, his creed:

All this is glossary, or prolegomena, to my novel *Lady Chatterley's Lover*. Man has little needs and deeper needs. We have fallen into the mistake of living from our little needs, till we have almost lost our deeper needs in a sort of madness. There is a little morality, which concerns persons and the little needs of man; and this, alas, is the morality we live by. But there is a deeper morality, which concerns all womanhood, all manhood, and nations, and races, and classes of men. This greater morality affects the destiny of mankind over long stretches of time, applies to man's greater needs, and is often in conflict with the little morality of the little needs. … the greatest need of man is the renewal together of the complete rhythm of life and death, the rhythm of the sun's year, the body's year of a life-time, the greater year of the stars, the soul's year of immortality. This is our need, our imperative need. It is the need of the mind and soul, body, spirit and sex: all. It is no use asking for a Word to fulfill such a need. No Word, no Logos, no Utterance will ever do it. The Word is uttered, most of it. We need only to pay true attention. But who will call us to the Deed, the great Deed of the seasons of the year, the Deed of the soul's cycle, the Deed of a woman's life at one with a man's, the little Deed of the moon's wanderings, the bigger Deed of the sun's, and the biggest, of the great still stars? It is the Deed of life we have now to learn; we are supposed to have learnt the Word, and, alas, look at us. Word-perfect we may be, but Deed-demented. Let us prepare now for the death of our present 'little' life, and the re-emergence in a bigger life, in touch with the moving cosmos.[20]

In the end of the tale, it is Connie's gradual recognition of what she really needs as a human being that dictate her choices. She lets Clifford know that she has found something more important to her than the existing marriage and upper class social position that she has with him, as strange as that decision might seem. And she allows her inheritance to sustain both herself and her man, although this is something that Mellors has difficulty in accepting. She leaves Clifford and goes to live with family in Scotland, to prepare for her presumed eventual union with her real lover.

In all his writing, Lawrence is working for not only expressing a language of the body, over and against the meaningless use of spoken language that fails to express real emotional content, but also for describing the choices that this deeper understanding might entail, being real and present in emotional terms.

In bringing the bodily emotions and desires to light that are beyond conscious understanding Lawrence in all his work expresses that which was beyond the overt understanding of his times. He also stated, "We are, today, as human beings, evolved and cultured far beyond the taboos that are inherent in our culture."[21]

The Eris archetype refers to the deep and underlying unconscious parts of ourselves, just as Pluto does. With Eris we find that a strong deed comes alive almost of itself to defend and to promote the desired result, choosing violent means, if necessary. In *Lady Chatterley's Lover*, written at very nearly the end of Lawrence's short life, the inherent violence that he once demonstrated is no longer evident; instead we find a quiet assurance on the part of his central character, a feminine character, to leave behind all social normative behavior in the accomplishment of her need for authenticity.

Notes
1. *Studies in American Literature*, p. 17.
2. *Kangaroo*, p. 149.
3. *Poetry in English*, p. 555.
4. *Kangaroo*, p. 150.
5. "The Ladybird" from *The Fox/ The Captain's Doll/ The Ladybird* pp. 186-187.
6. *Lady Chatterley's Lover*, p. 152.
7. *Sons and Lovers*, pp. 187-189.
8. *The Rainbow*, p. 37.
9. ibid p. 38.
10. ibid p. 151.
11. ibid pp. 444-445.
12. *Women in Love*, p. 65.
13. ibid pp. 170-171.
14. ibid p. 105.
15. ibid p. 314.
16. *Lady Chatterley's Lover*, p. 152.
17. ibid pp. 114-115.
18. ibid p. 116.
19. 'A Propos of *Lady Chatterley's Lover*', pp. 7-9.
20. ibid pp. 24-25.

6

William Blake: A Unique Sense of Mission

Tyger, Tyger, burning bright
In the forest of the night
What immortal hand or eye
Dare frame thy fearful symmetry?

William Blake

In our deeper investigation of the Eris archetype we now come to another major figure in English literature and also in the medium of visual art, William Blake. Although Blake lived and created in 18th and early 19th century England, from the period of the American and French Revolutions and their aftermath, his work retains relevance for our modern times that perhaps no other artist from his era can claim. His vision found renewed popularity during the 1960s, a tumultuous decade characterized by the Uranus-Pluto conjunction; this corresponds to Blake beginning his most profound work during the Uranus-Pluto opposition of 1789–1797 (which also signaled the timing of the French Revolution). He himself was born in 1757 under the preceding square alignment between Uranus and Pluto.

Beyond the revolutionary Uranus-Pluto square in his chart, Blake is also extremely significant as an exemplar of Eris. Eris in Sagittarius is just a degree away from Pluto and in exact square, almost to the minute, with Uranus, and is located in his fifth house of artistic production (See chart, Fig. 6-1).

Eris emphasizes the combination of Uranus and Pluto while at the same time showing up as a powerful factor in its own right, being widely conjunct his Sun and inconjunct his Moon, trine Mars and Neptune, and in exact semi-sextile to Venus. Venus in conjunction with Chiron aspects Uranus by close sextile and Eris by exact semi-sextile, bringing an additional meaning of art and relationship, and of suffering, as indicated by Venus-Chiron, to the symbolism of the powerful Uranus-Pluto-Eris combination. Mars in Leo brings an extra dose of passion to the picture, because it is trine Pluto-Eris and inconjunct Uranus. In the figure of William Blake we thus have another artistic and powerfully iconic representation of the Eris archetype.

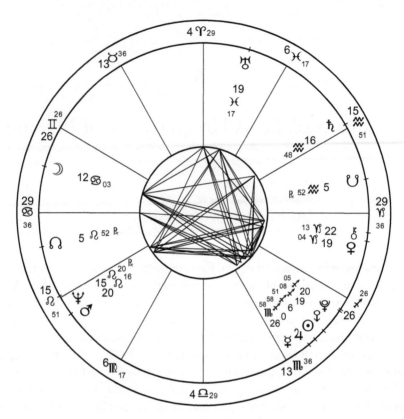

Fig. 6-1 William Blake, November 28, 1757, 7:45 PM LMT, London,
England 51N30 0W10

Like Lawrence, Blake was a man ahead of his own era and his extraordinary
value would only come to be appreciated with the passage of time. Blake
was totally unique as an artist, an extraordinary figure who towers above
anyone else of his period. As with Lawrence, Blake's work would become
more fully accepted during the period of the revolutionary 1960s. The
psychedelic movement is closely aligned with Blakean vision, as expressed
in the quote from his seminal illustrated work *The Marriage of Heaven and
Hell*: "If the doors of perception were cleansed, every thing would appear
to man as it is, infinite." This phrase was the source of the title of Aldous
Huxley's treatise on the psychedelic experience "The Doors of Perception"
as well as the name of the iconic 1960s' rock-n-roll band: The Doors.

Blake's Uranus-Pluto archetypal combination, further emphasized
by Eris, implies that the revolutionary period of the 1960s would be the
strongest modern echo of his thought. His work represents a frank and

brutally honest presentation of the fundamental aridity of a purely rational approach to life. He felt that the modern era emphasized a one-sided mental development at the expense of man's emotional nature. In another chime with the licentious Sixties Blake represents human sexuality as an aspect of spiritual yearning. In this he was a forerunner to the major thrust of Lawrence's work.

In another interesting parallel with D. H. Lawrence, Blake clearly saw how the modern industrial era fostered neglect of an important side of life. Like Lawrence, he deeply and passionately mourned the terrible consequences of the factory approach. Compare his artistic statement with that of Lawrence from *Lady Chatterley's Lover*, a century later, regarding the industrialization that was beginning to corrupt the English landscape. From *Blake's Songs of Experience*:

> I wander thro' each charter'd street,
> Near where the charter'd Thames does flow.
> And mark in every face I meet
> Marks of weakness, marks of woe.
>
> In every cry of every Man,
> In every Infants cry of fear,
> In every voice: in every ban,
> The mind-forg'd manacles I hear.[1]

And from Blake's epic illustrated poem *Milton* (where Jerusalem stands for Spirit):

> And was Jerusalem builded here
> Among these dark Satanic Mills?[2]

From his final epic poem, *Jerusalem*:

> And saw every minute particular, the jewels of Albion, running down
> The kennels of the streets & lanes as if they were abhorred.
> Every Universal Form, was become barren mountains of Moral
> Virtue; and every Minute Particular hardened into grains of sand;
> And all the tenderness of the soul cast forth as filth & mire,
> Among the winding places of deep contemplation intricate
> To where the Tower of London frowned dreadful...[3]

Although Blake is today considered one of the greatest of English poets and painters, in his own era he was so out of step with the normal run of his culture that he was almost universally thought to be mad. At his death he was buried without honors in a pauper's grave. His genius was nevertheless recognized by Wordsworth who said: "there is no doubt that this poor man was mad; but there is something in the madness of this man which interests me more than the sanity of Lord Byron or Walter Scott." This characterization of Blake as a madman was due in part to an abrupt temper and an iconoclastic manner of sticking to his own way of looking at things, as with Lawrence.

A strong Eris can exhibit a penchant for using violence as a means of solving personal problems, and Blake was known to have an aggressive temper upon occasion. Just as with Lawrence and Frieda, this sometimes showed up in Blake's relationship with his ever-devoted wife, Catherine. Referring to a dispute between Catherine and his beloved brother, Blake was said to have told his loyal wife "Kneel down and beg Robert's pardon directly, or you will never see my face again!" Even though she felt that she had nothing to apologize for, Catherine did so, saying that she was in the wrong, but Robert reportedly replied, "Young woman you lie – I am in the wrong."[4] In words that could have been used to describe Lawrence, Peter Ackroyd, Blake's biographer, sums Blake up as eccentric, vexatious and contrary, and refers to his "combative behavior even with those who knew him best."[5]

In another incident, when Blake witnessed a woman being knocked about by a man, presumably her husband, he 'fell upon him.' The offender was heard to tell a bystander that he thought, 'the very Devil himself' had flown upon him.[6]

A further incident also deserves mention, which occurred when Blake was still quite young. During what became known as the Gordon riots, at around midnight on June 6th, 1780, Blake was in the crowd and pushed to the forefront of spectators as the gaol was pulled down and the prisoners allowed to escape.[7] He was actually in some danger of being hanged had his presence been reported in what was considered a violent rebellion. It will be informative to examine the transits to Blake's chart at this time for traces of an Eris influence.

Eris does indeed play a strong role in these transits. On the night in question transiting Eris is exactly opposite Blake's natal Moon, his chart ruler, while transiting Uranus and the Sun are opposed to his natal Eris-Pluto conjunction (see chart Fig 6-2 on following page).

Another powerful incident in Blake's early life took place after his marriage when his brother Robert died, early in February 1787. The date is not known precisely although the anecdotal evidence suggests a time about ten

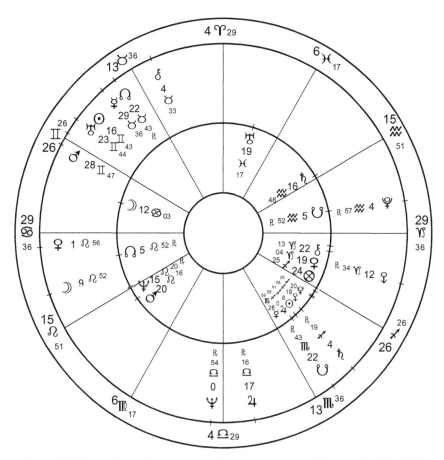

Fig. 6-2 William Blake, Transits for Tuesday, June 6, 1780, 11:55 PM GMT

days or two weeks into February. During this period, Neptune squared his Venus, indicating the spiritual nature of the event, while Uranus opposed his Chiron. The position of transiting Eris for this event is striking, being exactly conjunct his natal Venus within 10 minutes of a degree.

Transiting Pluto is also interesting since it was coming up on a conjunction with natal Saturn in the month following Blake's Saturn Return, with the midpoint of transiting Pluto and transiting Saturn almost exactly conjunct natal Saturn, and with the Sun nearby. The structure of Blake's life-work changed dramatically in the years following his brother's death.

Leading up to the date in question, Blake tended his dying brother without getting any sleep for almost two weeks, and was at his side when he witnessed, according to later accounts, his brother's soul ascending into heaven, clapping its hands for joy. The loss of his brother Robert affected

Blake for the remainder of his life. He continued the use of his brother's sketch book as a kind of journal and work-book which after his own death was found to contain revisions of the later lyrical poems that were subsequently published as *Songs of Experience*, along with ideas, sketches and reactions to his critics and other figures of his times. He continued using and referencing this important workbook, sometimes referred to as "The Rossetti Manuscript" right up to the time of his own death nearly 40 years later.

It was after the event of his brother's passing that Blake created his unique method of self-publishing, by an advanced engraving technique, which he said came to him in a vision as being described by his departed brother. It was a year or two later, in the years 1789 to 1793, that the basis for his longer self-published epics came into being. The most polished of these was eventually to be his last, his masterpiece, *Jerusalem*, which was composed a decade later and not published until 1820 in the years leading up to his death. Taken as a group, these longer self-published poems comprise what critics call his "prophetic works." The longest of these are the epic works *The Four Zoas, Milton* and *Jerusalem*, and these are pre-figured by an odd amalgam of poetry, essay and autobiographical-styled prose that he called *The Marriage of Heaven and Hell*, composed between 1790 and 1793.

Looking at the transits to Blake's chart for this seminal period from 1789 to 1793, we might expect to see Uranus in aspect to its natal position, perhaps also with Pluto and Neptune configured. Then, given the fundamental configuration of Eris in Blake's chart, and the symbolism of Eris in reference to soul-purpose, we might in addition expect to see an Eris factor emerging.

Indeed, we find the Uranus-Pluto opposition that signaled the period of the French Revolution traveling over Blake's chart, with Uranus conjuncting his Neptune and opposing his natal Saturn. Transiting Pluto had stationed conjunct his Saturn at the end of October 1789, while transiting Uranus, not yet directly opposite transiting Pluto, trined his Sun. The most interesting transit for this period might be Eris in conjunction with Blake's Venus and Chiron, located in his sixth house of work and perfection, the house that Dane Rudhyar referred to as "the discipleship to the Higher Self."

As already noted in Blake's natal chart, the close Venus-Chiron conjunction mediates the Uranus square to Pluto and Eris by sextile and by semi-sextile. As Eris began to transit over these points starting in June of 1788, with its conjunction with his natal Venus, it was a transitional time for Blake and his art, as indicated in the foregoing; 1788 was the year that he produced his first illuminated manuscript. This was followed in the fall of 1790 with transiting Eris stationing on the Venus/Chiron midpoint. This is the key timing of his creativity regarding the later works that were illustrated by his own hand and with his own unique methods. Following the conjunctions of transiting Eris with his natal Venus, transiting Eris then conjuncted natal Chiron in April of 1790, the spring that he began work on the artistic departure represented by *The Marriage*. At the time of the mid-April New Moon, the Sun and Moon with transiting Neptune made a T-square to transiting Eris in conjunction with Blake's natal Chiron. Eris went back and forth over his Chiron for the next three and a half years, with exact hits no fewer than seven times – this was the very period of his creation of the rather strange and fascinating work that became *The Marriage of Heaven and Hell*.

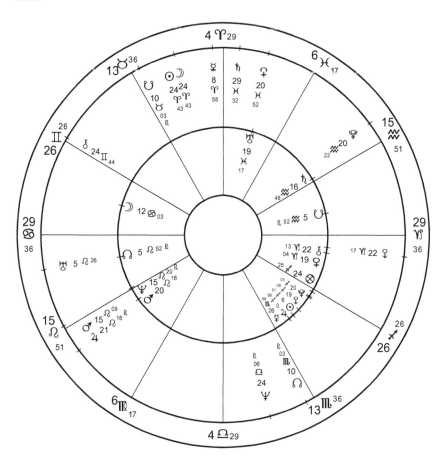

Fig. 6-3 William Blake, Transits for Wednesday, Apr 14, 1790,
12:30 PM GMT

June Singer, noted Jungian author and therapist, has written a book on the correspondences between Blake's thought and that of her mentor, C. G. Jung, entitled *The Unholy Bible*. In this study she examines the prophetic works of Blake's maturity, most notably *The Marriage of Heaven and Hell*. She writes: "Always there have been those who could experience these [dark] forces [of the unconscious] as tremendous powers... Blake was fascinated by this extra dimension of psychic life and he was impelled to write of how it manifested... the raw material of the inner drama is all there."[8]

To astrologers this makes perfect sense, since all three outer planets are so powerfully configured in Blake's chart, and the outer planets represent the darkest and deepest forces of the psyche. We have noted that Eris represents these deeper areas of the psyche as well, in connection with soul-level intention, and also serves to accentuate the area of a chart that it touches. Because Eris conjuncts, squares, and trines Pluto, Uranus and Neptune in his chart, the first two within 1 degree, all three outer planets are greatly emphasized. In his work we can clearly see the power of his Uranus-Pluto square as highlighted by the extreme Eris contact, and as well, in the mighty mythologizing with which he was so intently engaged in his later, prophetic works, a reflection of Eris and Neptune in combination, augmented by Pluto and Uranus.

The Marriage of Heaven and Hell is an illustrated work of some 27 plates (or pages). It is written in an autobiographical style but with fantastical visions that are stated as matter-of-fact experiences. There are also insertions of different kinds of writing, some caustic polemics, some frank discussions of a uniquely integrative point of view in which sin and error are seen as necessary components of the human condition. This idea is summarized in the book's final line, that "Everything that lives is Holy."

An important early section has it that: "All Bibles or sacred codes have been the causes of the following Errors":

That Man has two real existing principles Viz a Body and a Soul.
That Energy, called Evil, is alone from the Body, and that Reason, called Good, is alone from the Soul.
That God will torment Man in Eternity for following his Energies.

Blake goes on to say "But the following Contraries to these are True":

1. Man has no Body distinct from his Soul for that called Body is a portion of Soul discerned by the five senses, the chief inlets of Soul in this age.

2. Energy is the only life and is from the Body and Reason is the bound or outward circumference of Energy.
3. Energy is Eternal Delight.[9]

Blake, by espousing these Contraries, sought to counter the prevailing trend toward rationalism and materialism stemming from the time of the Renaissance that had already gained wide ascendancy in his era as the Industrial Revolution began its march. No wonder his contemporaries so little understood him, and no wonder that in the 1960s the return to Perennial Philosophy found in him a hero.

In *The Marriage*, Blake presents segments of a purportedly autobiographical nature, which he called "Memorable Fancies" one of which serves also as the introduction to his "Proverbs of Hell," those pithy commentaries that mocked the wise sayings of his day with witty and revealing aphorisms. Many of these are still quoted, such as: "The road of excess leads to the palace of wisdom" and "Eternity is in love with the productions of time." This introductory passage begins:

> As I was walking among the fires of Hell, delighted with the enjoyments of Genius, which to Angels look like torment and insanity, I collected some of their proverbs, thinking that as the sayings used in a nation mark its character, so the proverbs of Hell show the nature of infernal wisdom better than any description of buildings or garments.[10]

The Marriage of Heaven and Hell presents a subtle picture of attempting to integrate inner psychic energy, which is conceived as feminine with the mental powers of a more Apollonian nature that he chose to represent as masculine.

Singer states, "Blake's 'torment' consisted in part in the struggle to remain in contact with the flowing stream of creative energy yet to resist being drawn into whirlpools from which the individual may never be able to emerge. One senses … that there alternate in this man the downward pull into senseless spinning of uncontrolled fantasy and the upward thrust of an inner demand for order."[11]

In Blake's natal chart, these factors so eloquently described here by Singer emerge with great power and clarity, especially considering the role of Eris as emphasis of other chart factors. We can see traces of both this downward pull, as represented by Pluto and Eris – illuminated by their square with Uranus and their trine to Neptune – versus the "demand for order" represented by his strongly placed Saturn. In Blake's chart, Saturn is opposite Mars and Neptune, sextile Eris and Pluto, and resides in Aquarius, in quintile to his Sagittarius Sun, the seat of Apollonian reasoning power.

Reviewing the transits to Blake's chart in the period of 1789-1793 when all this was fermenting, we note that the Neptunian archetype was then even more involved since transiting Neptune precisely squared natal Chiron at the beginning of this period. From September 1789 to the spring of 1790, Eris conjuncted Venus, and then Chiron, 3 degrees away from his natal Venus, during the lead-up to his work on the *The Marriage*.

We can see the Chiron archetype revealed in the great sadness that Blake brings to his creation of this philosophically important and apt work. Its very beginning shows the sorrow as well as the rage that was present in his artistic outpouring.

> Rintrah roars and shakes his fires in the burdened air;
> Hungry clouds swag on the deep.
> …
> Till the villain left the paths of ease,
> To walk in perilous paths, and drive
> The just man into barren climes.
>
> Now the sneaking serpent walks
> In mild humility
> And the just man rages in the wilds
> Where lions roam.[12]

Following on from this amazing four-year period of 1789-1793, *Songs of Experience* was published in 1794. This volume included the most famous of Blake's early poetry, "The Tyger", in which we can clearly see the Eris and perhaps also the Chiron archetype. It is worth reviewing this poem in some detail.

The Tyger
Tyger! Tyger! burning bright
In the forests of the night,
What immortal hand or eye
Could frame thy fearful symmetry?

In what distant deeps or skies
Burnt the fire of thine eyes?
On what wings dare he aspire?
What the hand dare seize the fire?

And what shoulder, & what art
Could twist the sinews of thy heart?
And when thy heart began to beat,
What dread hand? & what dread feet?

What the hammer? what the chain?
In what furnace was thy brain?
What the anvil? what dread grasp
Dare its deadly terrors clasp?

When the stars threw down their spears,
And watered heaven with their tears,
Did he smile his work to see?
Did he who made the Lamb make thee?

Tyger! Tyger! burning bright
In the forests of the night,
What immortal hand or eye
Dare frame thy fearful symmetry?[13]

Here we have a paradox on display. How is it possible that a benevolent God, who "made the lamb," could have within his compass the fierce energy to create this terrible wonder? By celebrating the killing machine represented by this most fearful and mighty of hunters and slayers, Blake reveals an aspect of nature that is difficult for civilized men and women to accept, but one that is an integral part of the natural world, and is found within the animal nature of man as well. The Eris archetype represents in part the fierce ability to kill, if necessary, in order to satisfy a deeper need than peace, the need to preserve oneself intact and whole at all costs. Nourished by the meat of the slain, the individual – and the species – survives.

The long 'aye' sound of the vowel in the word "tyger" as Blake spelled it, gives an almost mythic power to the name. Contrast it with the short 'i' of "tigger" as spelled by A.A. Milne in his *Winnie the Pooh* creation, where the self-same beast is rendered friendly and kittenish; exactly the opposite idea. Blake's conception is more realistic, also more terrifying, and represents the Eris archetype precisely: the fierce will to succeed at all costs, by violence if necessary, for the sake of an urgent life-transfiguring goal arising out of a deep instinctual center.

The symmetry referred to in the opening, and also the closing, lines of the poem has a double meaning, additional to the symmetry of the tiger's body. By acknowledging the presence of this violent power at the innermost depths of nature, Blake is alluding to the dark presence of a fierce and even demonstrably evil energy within the psyche of mankind as well. A century later C. G. Jung was to more carefully articulate the compensatory quality of the unconscious, the container for these deeper impulses, that in many ways serve to mirror and provide contrast to the surface layers of the personality. Thus, the symmetry of conscious and unconscious process is also invoked.

As we will see, in his later work Blake created further artistic representations of this sort of fierceness within the psyche of mankind, from the perspective of a feminine war-like figure, which comes even closer to representing the Eris archetype.

We turn now to the complex philosophy that Blake came to portray so eloquently in his later prophetic works, going beyond the lyrical poetry published in *Songs of Innocence* and the subsequent *Songs of Experience*. These early books, displaying the rhymed verse for which he is more popularly known, were overshadowed by his more significant and much longer epic poems, which were also self-published as illustrated works. Beginning in 1789 he started to publish these illuminated manuscripts, from plates made and illustrated by his own hand, and in his own method combining text and illustration in one engraving.

These are serious works in which he takes on his literary purpose as prophet in an almost biblical sense, using the specialized mythology of his imaginative invention. It included figures labeled with his own unique names, such as Urizen, Los and Enitharmon, and features the holy city Jerusalem, which is also a character in his final masterpiece, *Jerusalem, the Emanation of the Giant Albion*.

The theme of this long epic poem might stand for the psychological process of individuation as later set forth by C. G. Jung, as well as a developmental account of human history. In Blake's mythology, his characters are simultaneously historical larger-than-life figures as well as actors in the unfolding dramatic presentation, representing stages in the development of mankind. The central protagonist of *Jerusalem* is Albion, representing everyman (related to the Adam Kadmon of alchemy) as well as a symbolic name for mythic England.

The mythological figures that became the very heart of Blake's poetic visions were laid out in greatest detail in an unpublished work called *The Four Zoas*, or the four "living creatures" of the biblical prophesies of Ezekiel, in which they equally represent the four-fold psychological representation later developed more fully by C. G. Jung, and the four elements of astrological symbolism.

In Blake's mythology, Jungian thinking, feeling, intuition and sensation (Air, Water, Fire and Earth) are represented as Urizen, Luvah, Los and Tharmas. With Blake, only one of these four functions is fully present in fallen man, and that is Reason. This is represented by the figure of Urizen, tyrant and also victim in the stories. There are also four worlds, in increasing level of godliness: The world of Ulro; the world of Generation; the world of Beaula; finally Eden or Heaven on Earth.

Additionally man has his Spectre – which we would today associate with the ego, or the Jungian Shadow; and he has his Emanation, a feminine part, the seat of the finer emotions and the perception of love and family. This feminine side can get split off or not fully recognized, remaining unconscious. In this, Blake anticipated the 20th century discoveries of Freud and Jung.

We have now explored the relationship between the initiation of Blake's most powerful work and the prominent Eris in his natal chart and by transit. We may find further evidence of the Eris archetype by examining the details of his philosophy and his art.

Blake was an iconoclastic thinker who like the biblical prophets of old felt that it was his duty to express home truths to those who had long neglected them. He was clear about this sense of mission when he articulated the final master representation of his philosophy, the work he called *Jerusalem*:

I stood among my valleys of the south
And saw a flame of fire, even as a Wheel
Of fire surrounding all the heavens…

England! Awake! awake! awake!
Jerusalem thy sister calls!
Why wilt thou sleep the sleep of death
And close her from thy ancient walls?[14]

In *Jerusalem*, the full title of which is *Jerusalem: the Emanation of the Giant Albion*, Blake was concerned to awaken his fellow man from the "sleep of Ulro" as he termed modern man's lack of conscious awareness of the fullness of life. To this end he uses the symbolism of the lady Jerusalem – simultaneously holy city and mythological figure – who is the rightful consort (or "emanation") of Albion; the figure of Albion representing mankind, also England, his culture. In the sleep of unconsciousness, the men and women of England have forgotten their rightful place in God's universe, and have substituted reason (symbolized by his character Urizen) for the four-fold unity that includes intuition, sensation, as well as feeling, which could be called love (represented by Jerusalem). This is an entirely similar theme to the work of D. H. Lawrence as described in the previous chapter.

The concept of the feminine in Blake's philosophy is worth greater analysis here, since Eris is a feminine deity. She is an immensely powerful one to be sure, and yet also distinctly feminine, being the sister of the God of War. The exposition of this concept of masculine and feminine, fundamental in Blake's philosophy, will richly repay us as we investigate further.

First it is important to remember that Blake was a man of his times and of his culture-induced training. He thought of women very differently from men; while not exactly inferior, not on an equal footing either. A note from his marginalia reads: "The female… lives from the light of the male."[15]

An example is the way he treated his wife Catherine who was always regarded as his intellectual inferior. An indication of the way the systematic roles of their marriage worked for both of them can be seen in the way that Catherine continued to consult her husband even after his death. On important matters she would simply say "I think I need to consult my husband on that," which she would then proceed to do. It is not known what forms these consultations would take, but after a time she would re-emerge with an answer.[16]

Blake considered the male and the female characters in his mythological writings from very different perspectives. The women are in large part considered to be an "Emanation" of the corresponding male figure; that is to say, to be seen as an emblem for a separate part of the human psyche that can become 'split off' causing all sorts of trouble. He identified this part of the psyche with soul powers – as indeed did Jung a century later.

This is similar to Jung's Anima – also a feminine concept. The description is from a male point of view. For Blake there were different evolutionary paths for men and women, and for women he did not detail these same inner factors, an idea that would need reconsideration in today's era. It is interesting that Blake uses feminine archetypes to convey soul or the feeling and loving element of life. In our own era, C. G. Jung was on the same track when he coined the term 'Anima' for this same subconscious structure (in the male psyche).

In *Jerusalem*, and in Blake's long prose poem *The Four Zoas* (which preceded it), the character of Vala is a central but ambivalent character. She is independent from her male counterpart, Luvah, and is also fundamentally flawed. This is as opposed to the character of Jerusalem, who represents the Emanation of mankind as symbolized by the character of Albion. Her reunion with her male counterpart at the end of the epic signals a return to wholeness; an escape from the fallen state of mankind which is at the very heart of the poem. While Jerusalem is a positive character in Blake's plot, the character of Vala is a difficult one, representing the fallen state of humanity from the feminine angle. In Blake's conception, womankind not only exhibits symptoms of the fall, and their cruelty if anything is even greater than the masculine members, but they also in their fallen state contribute to the male's separation from the divine. Rahab and Tizrah are other names of Vala. Here is Blake toward the end of his vast epic, describing the fallen Vala:

> Then Vala the Wife of Albion, who is the Daughter of Luvah,
> Took vengeance Twelve-fold among the Chaotic Rocks of the Druids
> …
> He saw in Vala's hand the Druid Knife of Revenge & the Poison Cup
> Of Jealousy, and thought it a Poetic Vision of the Atmospheres…
> Here Vala stood turning the iron Spindle of destruction
> From heaven to earth, howling, invisible; but not invisible…
> The knife of flint passes over the howling Victim: his blood
> Gushes & stains the fair side of the fair Daughters of Albion.
> They put aside his curls: they divide his seven locks upon
> His forehead; they bind his forehead with thorns of iron,
> They put into his hand a reed, they mock, Saying: Behold…
>
> Tirzah sits weeping to hear the shrieks of the dying: her Knife
> Of flint is in her hand: she passes it over the howling Victim.
> The Daughters Weave their Work in loud cries over the Rock
> Of Horeb: still eyeing Albion's Cliffs eagerly, seizing & twisting
> The threads of Vala & Jerusalem running mountain to mountain…
> Look! the beautiful Daughter of Albion sits naked upon the Stone,
> Her panting Victim beside her; her heart is drunk with blood…
> He sees the Twelve Daughters naked upon the Twelve Stones,
> Themselves condensing to rocks & into the Ribs of a Man.
> Lo, they shoot forth in tender Nerves across Europe & Asia;
> Lo, they rest upon the Tribes, where their panting Victims lie.[17]

We can compare this depiction of a fierce and cruel feminine archetype with the mythical Eris, who willingly followed her brother, the Greek God of War, into the battle, and "delighted in the groans of the dying."

But if for Blake the feminine could be cruel and terrible in its fallen state, we must remember also that Blake endowed the feminine with the power to release mankind from his one-sided reliance on pure reason, which can never complete him. Just as we saw with Lawrence and his use of female characters to carry the weight of a deeper awareness of the natural world, in Blake the character of Jerusalem, as feminine archetype, is vital to complete his mythic cycle and help to mend the fallen state of man. His song ends with a return to wholeness:

> And every Man stood Fourfold, each Four Faces had, One to the West,
> One toward the East, One to the South, One to the North, the Horses
> Fourfold...
> And they conversed together in Visionary forms dramatic, which
> bright
> Redounded from their Tongues in thunderous majesty, in Visions...
> All Human Forms identified, even Tree, Metal, Earth & Stone, all
> Human Forms identified, living, going forth, & returning wearied
> Into the Planetary lives of Years, Months, Days & Hours, reposing
> And then Awaking into his Bosom in the Life of Immortality.
> And I heard the Name of their Emanations: they are named
> Jerusalem.[18]

To summarize this inquiry into Blakean philosophy with reference to the Eris archetype, we can discern the major features of his thought.

First and foremost, Blake was concerned with the one-sidedness of modern man, his abandonment of the spiritual and feeling part of himself in favor of relying on his reasoning power alone, which Blake symbolized by the weak and tyrannical figure of Urizen. This problem results in war and violence as man – represented in Blakean myth by both male and female elements – fails to demonstrate his love to his fellow man, something that is still perhaps the biggest problem in our own times as well. The bearing of this issue for our current era explains Blake's continuing relevance 200 years after he practiced his art, in strenuous effort to awake his contemporaries.

This is reflected in the strong Eris placement within his natal chart. We can see in Eris the instinctual and feeling side of human nature that counter-balances the purely mental, as well as Blake's own sense of urgency, which is warrior-like in its absolute dire necessity, in order that he might get his soul-oriented message out to the world around him.

The wider perspective constitutes a more earnest spirituality that seeks to prevail against the blindness of the material industrial era of modern history, beginning in Blake's time and continuing today. It therefore represents a wake-up call against what Blake termed "the sleep of Ulro" whereby man but sees "thro the narrow chinks of his cavern".[19]

Another way to see these afflictions and to symbolize them is with Blake's concept of the discarded feminine. He believed that man's so-called

Emanation, or deep soul, was cut off in this modern era and he made this splitting an important piece in his mythology. This fits nicely with the powerful Eris archetype that we find expressed in his chart, since Eris is not only a spiritual warrior but a feminine one as well. In times to come the fight for feminism would be carried out by similar warriors for truth, all of whom, as we have seen in Chapter 2, possessed in significant measure the Eris archetype within their own charts.

Blake represents the consummate rebel, the iconoclast, the challenger of authority. In this his strong Uranus-Pluto square was acted out in his life, as emphasized by the power of Eris to mightily accentuate this rebellious configuration.

In addition to Eris acting on Pluto-Uranus, we can also see Pluto acting on the tight Uranus-Eris square in the sense that Uranus represents a powerful vision of the architecture of the cosmos. Blake represented a new way of seeing the universe around him, the dawning of a set of vastly different ideas, emerging from deep within him, than was current in his day, ideas that would literally shake things up. He felt that consensus ideas of right and wrong were foolishly encapsulated in the accepted thought he challenged, and that instead it was important to remember that "Energy is the only life and is from the Body", with reason being but "the bound or outward circumference of Energy", and that "Energy is Eternal Delight".

As spiritual warrior – the very essence of the Eris archetype – Blake fought on the part of all of us the good fight against blind reason, which he termed "Newton's Sleep", preferring to dwell primarily in the vast unconscious and life-giving power of his inner world. This fecund inner void, whose numinous power Jung was also forced to come to terms with, is part of what Eris symbolizes and represents a deeper sense of order emanating from the instinctual body that is ultimately productive of wholeness.

Notes

1. *The Poetry and Prose of William Blake*, pp. 26-27.
2. ibid p. 95.
3. ibid p. 192.
4. Gilchrist p.59, quoted in Ackroyd p. 83.
5. Ackroyd, p. 327.
6. Wilson, *The Life of William Blake*, p. 215 quoted in Ackroyd p.155.
7. Ackroyd pp. 74-5.
8. Singer. *The Unholy Bible*, pp. 9-10. A fuller quote reads:
   It remained for C. G. Jung to delineate this unconscious entity as a reality with which man could consciously and deliberately attempt to carry

on a dialectical relationship. Consciousness and the unconscious flowed in and out of one another in earlier times as now, but in Blake's day they were not differentiated analytically... [although] there could be, nevertheless, a dynamic relationship between the conscious aspect of man and the dark forces so strange and incomprehensible to him. Always there have been those who could experience these forces as tremendous powers... Blake was fascinated by this extra dimension of psychic life and he was impelled to write of how it manifested...the raw material of the inner drama is all there.

9. *The Poetry and Prose of William Blake*, p. 34.
10. ibid p. 35.
11. Singer. *The Unholy Bible*, p. 77.
12. *The Poetry and Prose of William Blake*, p. 33.
13. ibid pp. 24-25.
14. ibid pp. 230-231.
15. ibid p. 585.
16. Bentley, *Blake Records*, p. 374, quoted in Ackroyd, p. 368.
17. *The Poetry and Prose of William Blake* pp. 211, 218-219.
18. ibid pp. 254-256.
19. *Jerusalem*, plate 1; *Marriage*, plate 14, *The Poetry and Prose of William Blake* pp. 39, 145.

Part III

Philosophical Considerations

This section continues the discussion with a further and deeper delineation of the Eris archetype, and includes a look at the work of several modern exemplars including seminal 20th century psychologist C. G. Jung, and Jungian story-teller Clarissa Pinkola Estés, author of *Women Who Run With the Wolves*.

Part II

Philosophical Considerations

7

Archetypal Characterization

No man chooses evil because it is evil;
he only mistakes it for happiness, the good he seeks.

Mary Wollstonecraft[1]

At this point I would like to summarize the findings of the previous chapters and to present a more thorough characterization of the Eris archetype than I have articulated thus far. First it will be necessary to clear away some underbrush so that the main ideas stand out more clearly.

Different From the Mars Warrior Archetype
As I have demonstrated in the preceding chapters, there seems to be a great deal of evidence for characterizing Eris as a feminine warrior – or spiritual warrior – archetype. I have been asked many times how this differs in any significant way from Mars, and this is an interesting question. There is a clue to be gleaned from the relationship between Eris and Pluto, and from the status of the outer planets in modern astrology.

Pluto has been identified as a higher octave of Mars and sometimes shares the rulership of Scorpio with the god of war, who was called Ares in the original Greek. Some modern astrologers prefer to stick to Mars/ Ares alone as the ruler of Scorpio, especially since Pluto has recently been demoted to 'dwarf planet' status. Newly-named Eris is, in Greek mythology, the sister and companion of Ares, so there is a relationship between all three. Just as Pluto pertains to a deeper level of the psyche than Mars, this logically applies also to Eris, as we are coming to understand her.

Because the potentially violent action – and standing up for oneself – that characterizes Eris, comes from such a profound place and has this soul-purpose depth underlying it, it would never make sense for a person with a strong Eris to act as a mercenary, or commit violence for money or greed as one with a strong Mars might. Just the opposite is true. My research indicates instead a desire to defend the underdog, and to fight for justice over and above self-interest. It is the end to be achieved, and not the violent means to that end, that is truly representative of the Eris archetype.

This relates to deep natural process, as in the animal world. A predator kills to eat, and for the sake of its young; ultimately for the survival of the species. So this natural form is action, potentially violent action, based on ultimate need. Mars fights because he wants to, Eris because she has to.

The Myth of Chaos
In the absence of research and a consensus on the meaning of Eris, many astrologers have seized upon the myth of Eris, also called the 'Goddess of Chaos and Discord', and in particular, one story told about her – 'The Judgment of Paris'. There was a wedding, and Eris was left out. She was upset, and in anger or in the spirit of devilment she rolled a golden apple into the midst of the gathering. It had a description written on it, 'To the fairest', and three of the most beautiful goddesses vied for it. Zeus wisely chose not to act as judge and passed the honor to the mortal Paris, son of the king of Troy. Paris was promised Helen of Sparta, the most beautiful woman in the world, by Aphrodite, if he chose her, and to seal the deal she also dropped her clothes. Paris was hooked; he stole Helen from her husband, and the Trojan War was on. Thus many astrologers have viewed Eris as a sower of chaos.

I would submit that Pluto also is a sower of chaos and discord, owing to the absolute nature of his activity. From the perspective of the home-owner you may have just wanted to adjust the window frame but what you got instead was the wrecking ball. The committed and implacable action of Eris in attaining her aims likewise makes for chaos. Harmony flies out the window when she shows up, full-strength, to adjust an injustice or to fight for her right to survive. Since Eris is portrayed in Greek mythology as the sister and the follower of the War god, she is very naturally labeled 'Chaos and Discord.' Chaos follows war. With Pluto too comes chaos, but this is not the real point. As a wise man once told me, recognizing that the chaos associated with the destructive power of Pluto precedes new birth, do not focus on the chaos, but await the birth.

Similarity of Eris with Pluto
It is fascinating how like twins these two astronomical bodies are. Named from the ancient pantheon of Greco-Roman gods and goddesses, they are both distant planets – in the sense that they orbit the sun – and have each been relegated to 'dwarf' status in the recent IAU decision. They are almost identical in size and occupy a similar position in the solar system beyond Neptune. It is almost as though the discovery and naming of Eris was a setup for us puzzled earthlings to show us that we have further Western Astrological archetypes yet to be explored.

Eris and Pluto as Outer Planets

Could astrologers come to consider for purposes of interpretation that Pluto, while a dwarf, is still a planet? This seems to be the de-facto situation over the seven or more years of the re-classification that took place in the fall of 2006. Perhaps we might consider that in the phrase 'dwarf planet' the operative word is still 'planet'. In this case, Eris, too, is a planet.

Taking the existing outer planets of modern Western astrology, namely Uranus, Neptune and Pluto, all three share a connection with unconscious process; Pluto represents our desire nature at a deep and almost strictly unconscious level; Uranus as deep and instantaneous intuition beyond conscious reason; Neptune as embodying other-dimensional realities and, yes, unconscious process. It seems as though the planets that are farthest out represent those deepest parts of the human psyche, the furthest in. To the dictum of 'as above, so below' must be added 'as furthest out, so deepest within.'

Eris partakes of this same quality. It is a deep need that drives the spiritual warrior. In crusading for soul-purpose, these people reveal their unconscious passion, which might come as a surprise to their more overtly conscious mind. In some cases that we have documented the actual unconscious motivation for their actions might take years to fully elucidate and render into conscious appreciation. We will see this again in a later chapter when we consider the case of C. G. Jung himself, the iconic 20th century figure who explored the unconscious in greater depth than any before him.

Eris by House and in Aspect

How can Eris be distinguished from Pluto, and what is her effect in combination with other natal planets, or by house position? So far, the research seems to indicate a powerful emphasis on the house or the planet thus aspected. Eris seems to facilitate the fullest and most creative manifestation of the particular planet's energies. An example of Eris in combination with Mercury would be James Hillman, who as a noted 20th century psychologist was especially well known for the brilliant articulation of his spoken and written words. He has Eris in close conjunction with Mercury, in his house of fame; see his chart on the following page.

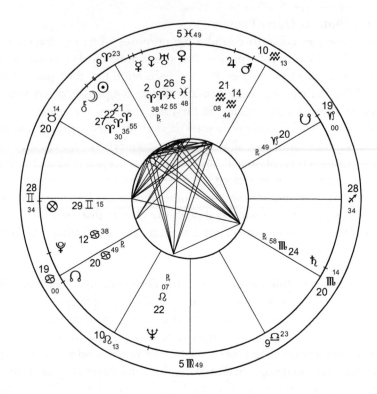

Fig. 7-1 James Hillman, April 12, 1926, 9:08 AM EST, Atlantic City, New Jersey, USA 40N43 74W00

Another pair of writers, Amy Ray and Emily Saliers, the singer-songwriter pair who write and perform as The Indigo Girls, each have strong Eris-Mercury, along with equally strong Eris-Neptune, as befits musicians. Their charts are given in Chapter 2, figs. 2-22 and 2-23. Another example of a nearly exact Eris-Mercury aspect, a semi-sextile, would be Betty Friedan, feminist and prolific author. Her major work, *The Feminine Mystique*, sold over 3 million copies and was crucial for the feminist movement of the early Sixties.

As far as Sun-Eris is concerned, this delineation would be someone who has used their strong personality to push forward to where they feel their work or the society needs to be. Many of the feminists reviewed in Chapter 2 have this aspect, including Gloria Steinem with the conjunction. Another example would be D. H. Lawrence, with his strong opposition between Sun/Jupiter and Eris.

For Eris-Moon we have the likelihood of a softer and more feminine personality, one familiar and partly focused on unconscious process. Both Jung and Freud have Eris-Moon; in the case of Freud he has Eris located in the fourth house of root psychological issues, square the Moon, and in aspect to Pluto, Mars and Venus, as well as the Sun. His chart is below.

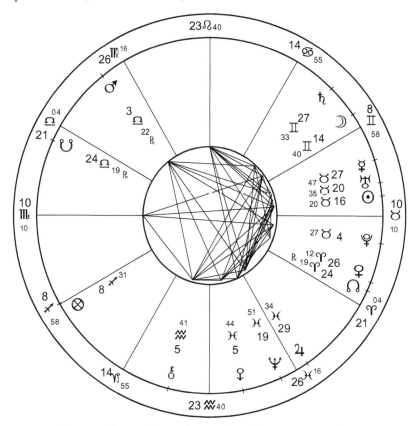

Fig. 7-2 Sigmund Freud, May 6, 1856, 6:32 PM, Příbor, Czech Republic 49N39 18E10

Other examples of Eris-Moon are, somewhat surprisingly, Isaac Newton and Albert Einstein (see Chapter 3) with major partile aspects. These physicists came from left field to overturn the established science of their day. Another with strong Eris-Moon, a partile conjunction, is Masaru Emoto, the disruptive scientist of water, who famously demonstrated that the structure of the crystals that are formed from the water sample as it freezes depend on the quality of positive attention that has been paid to the sample. The Moon in his chart would be important as the ruler of the cardinal Water sign. His chart is given in Appendix C. Then there is Angelina Jolie, whose chart is given in Chapter 2, with the conjunction; Eris and the Moon being also conjunct Mars, who portrays a feminine warrior archetype and is a fiercely protective mother as well as an icon of feminine beauty. The feminine warrior actress Zhang Ziyi who has Eris in square to the Moon and who also has Eris sextile to Mars, is also known for her beauty; another exemplar of Eris-Moon would be Luc Besson, the French director who has specialized in creating iconic female roles in films including *The Femme Nikita* and *Joan of Arc*. (See Chapter 2).

The house orientation of Eris provides emphasis on that house, as in Freud's chart. The fourth house reflects his life-long intention to get to the psychological root of the matter. Also his own household, where he dwelt with his wife and children, and his wife's sister (another significant figure for him) was of prime importance to him in his daily life. Another example of house emphasis would be the chart of Albert Einstein, whose chart is given in Chapter 3. With Eris in the tenth house, he became the most famous scientist in the world.

We can see an example of Eris and Venus in conjunction in the chart of Anias Nin. She was best known for her literary focus on relationships and her life-long extra-marital affair with Henry Miller. Miller himself has a strong Eris position, and the aspect with Venus in her own chart reflects the level of appreciation that she had for the social iconoclast figure that he represented. She also was one of the first to write in praise of D. H. Lawrence, Erisian par excellence, at a time when he was little understood. She led the charge for a change of attitude regarding his work. Other examples of strong Eris-Venus would be Marilyn Monroe, who had Eris in semi-sextile with a prominent Venus-Chiron conjunction, emphasizing feminine allure (Venus) as a powerful factor in her personality. Dustin Hoffman, with a partile square between Eris and Venus involving Saturn, played a male actor playing a woman in the movie *Tootsie*, and insisted on testing his character on the streets of New York to ensure that his portrayal of femininity was an authentic one.

Chiron and the Tree of Life

The discovery of Chiron, an astronomical body officially classified now as a Centaur, took place in 1977, a time period coincident with the rise of alternative medicine and a better understanding of instinctual process and the language of the body. The symbolism of Chiron as a centaur refers back to the animal nature of man. The centaur as half thinking and reasoning man, and half animal, is a telling symbol for the modern much-needed recognition of the language of the body. The rise of somatic forms of therapy followed the decade of Chiron's discovery and continues into the present. Our instinctual side is coming to be acknowledged as an important component of who, at base, we really are.

The Qabalistic Tree of Life represents a rich study for those who desire a more spiritual understanding of astrology. In the Tree of Life diagram, the traditional planets are assigned to different places amongst the Sephiroth or Divine Emanations of which there are ten in number, plus one hidden Sephirah called Daath. There have been many attributions of Pluto to Daath (the Abyss), and this seems to correspond to his astrological archetype as the unconscious portion of the psyche. Some astrologers put Chiron there as well, representing the bodily and instinctual side of our human capabilities.[2] As might be obvious from the forgoing discussion, I believe that Eris, too, could be assigned to Daath. This dark trinity of Pluto, Eris and Chiron, speaks to an important aspect of the human condition that is largely unconscious.

Bruce Cockburn the Canadian activist singer-songwriter, whose chart is given in Chapter 2, has Pluto trine Eris, likely a Pluto-Eris-Moon grand trine, among many other Eris aspects, including an opposition to Chiron. He at times refers to the dual animal/spiritual nature of man:

> Birds of Paradise, birds of prey,
> Here tomorrow, gone today;
> Cross my forehead, cross my palm,
> Don't cross me or I'll do you harm;
>
> Could be the famine, could be the feast;
> Could be the pusher, could be the priest;
> Always ourselves we love the least,
> That's the burden of the Angel/Beast.[3]

One theme of the elucidation of the Eris archetype in our times might therefore be the re-uniting of the dark unconscious material from the deep psyche of humankind with the conscious personality. Can we partake of nature and of natural instinct, that gives each animal the responses that they need to be able to survive as a species, and yet not lose our spiritual side? This might be one theme to ponder as we further dig into the astrological Eris.

The Integration of Man and Nature
As we have seen in these last three chapters devoted to Melville, Lawrence and Blake, there is a special relationship between the astrological archetype

of Eris and the instinctual impulses that commonly arise in nature. The idea of a natural order of 'kill or be killed' echoes throughout all three of these literary figures, in Melville with the glorification of the hunt and the all-consuming quest for vengeance, in Lawrence and Blake in their basic philosophy and in wanting to connect with the natural body in its full functioning and feeling, as opposed to mental concepts or socially sanctioned ones. They view their deep understanding of natural unconscious process as an important and neglected part of human interaction. In essence these writers are telling us that we, as humans lose something when we try to deny our fundamental animal nature.

Both Lawrence and Blake decried the devastation of the natural landscape corresponding to the industrial era, already beginning in Blake's day, a century before Lawrence's "long squalid straggle of … blackened brick dwellings" referencing the coal-mining districts of the English Midlands.

From Blake's scribbled satiric verses: "Great things are done when Men and Mountains meet;/This is not done by jostling in the street." And as to Blake's use of the phrase "Satanic Mills," referring to the factories of his day, this image can be conflated with the modern industrial-era tendency of relying on pure mentality, as opposed to the more instinctual feeling level.

Other exemplars of a strong Eris have a similar bent, although the evidence can be subtle. I am thinking for example of the ending to David Lynch's movie *Blue Velvet*, made in 1986. Lynch has an extremely strong Eris placement, as we have seen (in Chapter 2). In his film, the violence is understated but fully present. At the very end a robin perched on a branch looks sweet, heralding the dawn of a new and more peaceful day. The bird then is shown munching on a large insect in its mouth, reminding us of natural process, and the inherent violence of such process, as we have been discussing. Lynch went on to more fully explore this image, and to make it into something of an environmental manifesto, as well as a depiction of the cycle of violence in nature and human relationships. The opening credits of each episode of his dark TV series *Twin Peaks*, has that same bird appearing, sans insect, but followed by scenes of a factory and an industrial lumber mill – a gnashing of toothy gears. As the opening credits continue, this ugliness is contrasted with delightful scenes of natural beauty, the surroundings of the setting of the series, the rural northwestern town he called Twin Peaks. I was struck by how the industrial scenes stand out like a sore thumb, like the insect in the closing scene of *Blue Velvet*, and for no apparent reason. The industrial motif can be linked to the inherent under layer of violence in the natural setting, and also perhaps to a concern for the devastation of the natural landscape, as described in both Lawrence and

Blake. This is another form of disconcerting recognition of the presence of dark material at the very core of nature – just as the insect was.

The violence inherent in natural process as expressed in human emotion is a major theme for Lawrence, and also Blake, who valued the articulation of unconscious instinctual factors. His line from *The Marriage of Heaven and Hell* still resonates today: "How do we know but every bird that cuts the airy way, is an immense world of delight, closed by your senses five?" Blake also saw Nature as two-sided, with a negative, seductive component. Blake had in his natal chart that conjunction of Eris and Pluto, square Uranus and trine Mars and Neptune, therefore a complex relationship to Eris archetypal issues.

The Discovery Period of Eris: 2003 to the Present

The timing of the discovery of the modern planets has been an interesting correlate to their archetypal meanings, in a way that can help to correct and amplify the myth provided by the naming. The discovery of Uranus in 1781 confirmed the rebellious suddenness of new beginnings by two major revolutions, the American in 1776 and onward, and the French in 1789. We now know that Pluto was opposed to Uranus as well for the latter, a cosmic signature for revolution and personal evolution. When Neptune joined the list of planets in 1846 it was a time of great interest in psychic matters and the occult, especially in America. The origin of the movement called 'spiritualism' is dated from the mid-1840s. When Pluto was discovered, and named after the Roman god of the underworld, its connection with death and rebirth and the darker aspects of human nature, was accentuated by the rise of Nazism a few years later and the use of the atomic bomb, developed in the 1940s and first dropped in 1945.

Because the actual discovery and naming of Eris took place in 2005-2006, from plates developed in 2003, one feature of the global political landscape that stands out was the invasion of Iraq by U.S. forces, in purported response to the events of the American 911 tragedy, beginning a war that lasted from 2003-2011. As is now generally accepted, there were other motives on the part of the U.S. government, not least a perceived dependency on the oil resources of the Middle East, considered vital for its continued economic well being. Viewed in this way, the invasion of Iraq can be seen as a desperate and, in its own way, courageous move on the part of the American elite to preserve its dominance, and indeed its very survival. This makes for a nice fit with the predator impulse of natural process, associated with the Eris archetype as we are coming to understand it, in a life-and-death struggle for the procurement of the resources needed for survival.

At the time of the invasion Pluto was stationing in opposition to U.S. Mars, with Eris in trine to Pluto. (See transit chart in Fig. 7-3.) Two factors are interesting to note regarding the U.S. Eris. They are: the prominence of Eris in the U.S. chart, located in the first house opposed to the Sun and Jupiter, and second, the exact inconjunct aspect to natal Uranus. In accordance with the Uranus aspect we can assign a quality of sudden surprise, and also trickery, to U.S. aggression at times, in defense of itself or to provide what its leaders perceive as vital resources; the Iraq War quest for oil resource being only the most recent example.

Another might be Washington crossing the Delaware River in the dead of night to surprise British troops during the American War of Independence, when freedom from England was just such a vital need for the fledgling colonies.

When the need for Westward expansion was uppermost in the country's mind, the Mexican-American war was fought on a dubious pretext, intending that the territory west of Texas might be gained from the nominal control of a disoriented and distracted state of Mexico. In less than a month, in May of 1846, a skirmish between U.S. and Mexican forces in disputed lands in what is now the southernmost part of Texas was expanded into a declaration of war, so that the rapidity of the American strike capability, as befits Eris in combination with rapid and changeable Uranus, was once again shown. What was finally gained was all the territory westward to the Pacific. Some 50 years afterward, further territorial expansion was sought and quickly gained after the destruction of the U.S. battleship Maine in Havana harbor, considered by some historians to be a 'false flag' event in order to promote war with Spain, ignited the Spanish-American war of 1898. In the treaty ending this war a few weeks later, Cuba, Guam and the Philippines came under American control. It is now known that the 'Gulf of Tonkin' resolution that began the wider Vietnam war in 1964 was also based on a trick, in response to a false announcement of an attack by North Vietnamese vessels on an American destroyer.

As mentioned above the most recent instance of both speed and trickiness in promoting America's vital interests by force of arms was the invasion of Iraq on March 19th, 2003 in symbolic response to the World Trade Center attacks of September 11th, 2001. The campaign used a strategy called 'Shock and Awe' in reference to the suddenness and violence of the attack, and was based on false evidence presented to the world via then-President Bush's 'State of the Union' in January 2003, and, in February, in a presentation before the U.N. by then-Secretary of State Colin Powell.

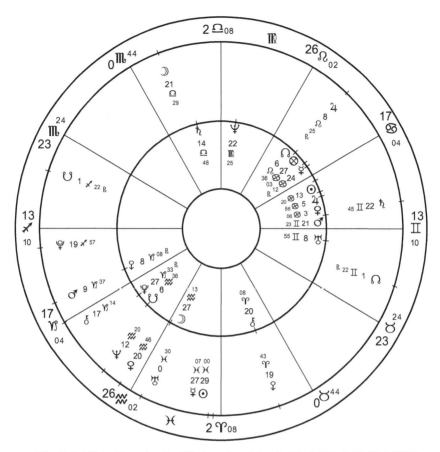

Fig. 7-3 USA, Transits for Wednesday, March 19, 2003, 5:00 PM EST

See the transit chart in Fig. 7-3. One interesting factor is the precise trine alluded to above, between stationing transiting Pluto and transiting Eris, as Pluto opposed U.S. Mars, representing the military. Another is the conjunction of transiting Eris and U.S. Chiron, which lasted (within 1 degree of exact) through to the end of the U.S. occupation in 2010. Eris also stationed retrograde within 2 minutes of a degree on U.S. Chiron in July 2001 just before the September 11th World Trade Center attacks, and remained within half a degree of exact in March 2003. The factor of transiting Eris on U.S. Chiron reflects the extremely painful experience of 9-11 as well as the painful position of American citizens who were again witness to the deaths of foreign nationals and their own young armed services personnel as a result of a strategic war for geopolitical rationale, so soon after Vietnam.

Another huge factor in the current zeitgeist is the environment. The manifold geopolitical issues with curbing modern industrial carbon emissions, which have slowly come to almost universal acceptance as contributors to potential disaster for the entire planet, are also in line with the Eris archetype, since the situation requires courageous activity by the few in the face of strong resistance, in response to an issue of survival.

In today's world, nature is increasingly being destroyed by the mental conception of industrialism without heart, a process that is still going on, and even accelerating, as the stakes grow higher. This is testified to, in the U.S. at least, by the recent failed campaigns against global warming in general and the questionable use of hydraulic fracking to extract the last bit of useable carbon resource. The coming Pluto-Eris square alignment of the end of the current 20-teens decade may well see the climax of this struggle.

Another hallmark of the current political scene, especially in America, is the emergence and high visibility of whistle blowers, heroes to some and traitors to others; journalistic hackers like Julian Assange, who founded Wikileaks, Chelsea Manning, formerly Bradley Manning, the Army PFC who published a video of a brutal U.S. helicopter attack on Iraqi civilians, and former technical assistance worker Edward Snowden, to mention those who have had the most media coverage. Snowden's revelations of U.S. spying – by recording every phone call available to modern technology, including those of German premier Angela Merkel – were panic-inducing for the undercover agents, and brought up the question of his character as publicity-seeker or person of conscience. His case also brings up fundamental issues of a heroic brand of patriotism versus slavishly 'following orders.' That these three individuals all have a strong Eris is perhaps not surprising, as they are all waging what they, at least, consider to be an important fight for principled cause, stand-up young people in their own way, although simultaneously regarded as unwelcome hindrances, or worse, by the existing government.

With Assange and Snowden we have a birth-time. Assange has Eris closely conjunct Chiron, square the Sun, sextile North Node and aspecting Jupiter and Venus. Manning also has Eris in aspect to Chiron, a quintile, considered a spiritually-based aspect, conjunct Jupiter and inconjunct his Mars. With Snowden, Eris stands as his most elevated planet, almost entirely alone in its hemisphere, in the eleventh house of societal contribution, networking and Internet communications. Eris is once more in aspect with Chiron, a close semi-square, and is quintile his Sun, inconjunct his Moon, sextile his Mercury and closely trine his Venus. This last planet rules his twelfth house of imprisonment. All three have Eris-Chiron, and all three have suffered as a consequence of their activism. This is in fact an aspect that they share with another noted whistle-blower, Daniel Ellsberg, who released the Pentagon Papers to the New York Times during the height of the Vietnam war. [4]

Eris Discovery Chart

In the light of these ruminations on the meaning of Eris, it is of interest to review the discovery chart, dating back to January 5th, 2005 at 11:20 AM at Cal Tech in Pasadena, as the photographic plates from past years were being analyzed. Here is the chart.

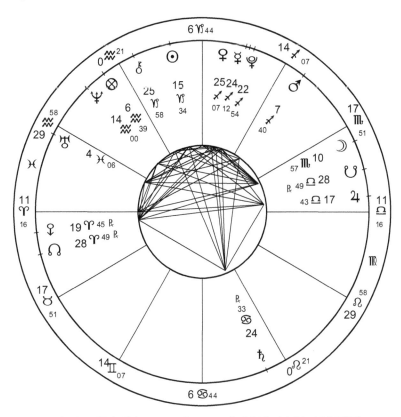

Fig. 7-4 Eris Discovery, January 5, 2005, 11:20 AM PST,
Pasadena, California, USA 34N09 118W09

Let's see what Eris has to tell us, as she makes her way forward into human consciousness.

For one thing, Aries was rising. The birth of this new planet would come to cause much controversy in the scientific as well as in the astrological world. Eris, not being shy, appears in the first house. She is in close trine to Pluto, her astronomical – and astrological – cousin, and in aspect to Chiron. There is a certain painful process that has been associated with this new century, as was revealed in the New Year's chart for the year 2000 that featured an exact Pluto-Chiron conjunction. We might also judge this fact from the prominence of Chiron in this chart, elevated, in the tenth house, in close opposition to Saturn, and forming a T-square to Eris.

Eris as an archetype seemingly participates in some important regard to this painful place that we as a culture find ourselves in. The most pressing issue of all perhaps would be the environmental one, global warming. Any of several issues to do with rising population growth would also be high on the list. With the increased consciousness of our age, the fact that we continue to wage war and use violent means to achieve our ends has become an even greater burden of pain on the collective human psyche than it was in the past.

The prominence of Eris in her own chart, opposite and in close parallel to Jupiter, near the North Node, and moving slowly in the first house, must be reiterated. Eris is close to the farthest-away point from the Sun in her orbit, and therefore moving much more slowly than normal, even for this distant body with her 556-year period. Eris takes about 120 years just to move through the sign of Aries, and this is the sign of Mars, her brother.

Eris is also semi-square to Uranus, patron planetary ruler of Astrology. Uranus is quintile Pluto, bringing their revolutionary combined archetype into this planetary picture, another hallmark of the early years of the new century, that was to be further emphasized in their square aspect beginning in 2012. It is also noteworthy that Saturn, in addition to opposing Chiron, is in close inconjunct with both Venus and Mercury. The triple conjunction of Venus, Mercury and Pluto – in trine with Eris – shows another theme of the Eris archetype: bringing the dark unknown parts of ourselves into the light.

Eris – A planet for our times?

The planetary archetypes of astrology show up when the culture needs them. The early part of the 20th century, the time of the discovery of Pluto, was synchronous with glimpses into our own unconscious depths afforded by Freud and Jung, revealing a vital part of the psyche of each individual that is still, today, barely understood. The culture was, in some important sense, ready to receive this new awareness.

With the depth archetype that is currently emerging in the astrology of Eris, we might wonder what further insights will be revealed that are relevant to our times.

Eris as spiritual warrior reveals the lonely path of the ones who must struggle to articulate a principle that opposes mass consensus awareness. If everyone understands an idea, then a warrior stance is hardly necessary. If the principle is false or entirely idiosyncratic, without basic spiritual truth, then a warrior stance assumes the guise of mere insanity. If, on the other hand, a principled stand for an unpopular cause is vitally necessary for the survival and spiritual evolution of the culture, then the conditions are ripe for invoking the Eris archetype as we are coming to understand her.

Notes

1. From *A Vindication of the Rights of Men*, (1790).
2. Personal communication from Susan Heinz, 2004, who uses it in her work. She is a wonderful teacher and astrologer located in Santa Cruz, California.
3. Bruce Cockburn, 'Burden of the Angel/Beast' from *Dart to the Heart*, written by Bruce Cockburn, used by permission of Rotten Kiddies Music, LLC).
4. The chart data for these whistle-blowers: Daniel Ellsberg April 7th, 1931, in Chicago, Illinois (time unknown). Julian Asssange July 3, 1971, 3:00 PM, Townsville, Australia, listed in AstroDataBank, Rodden Rating: B. Chelsea Manning December 17, 1987, Crescent Oklahoma, USA, Wikipedia reference. Edward Snowden June 21, 1983, 4:42 AM, Elizabeth City, North Carolina, USA, listed in AstroDataBank, Rodden Rating: AA.

8

Jungian Psychology and the Search for Deeper Meaning

All my writings may be considered tasks imposed from within; their source was a fateful compulsion. What I wrote were things that assailed me from within myself. I permitted the spirit that moved me to speak out. … I have been impelled to say what no one wants to hear. For that reason, and especially at the beginning, I often felt utterly forlorn.

C. G. Jung[1]

In our continuing investigation of the philosophical ramifications of the Eris archetype and its representation of deep unconscious process, we now turn to the exemplar par excellence of such process, seminal 20th century psychologist Carl Gustav Jung. It was he who first articulated the concepts of the collective unconscious, the personal unconscious, and the complex. In doing so he made use of the term "archetype" to refer to those contents of the collective unconscious that reveal universal themes, and demonstrated that these themes transcend particular cultures. In many ways his own life reflects the Eris archetype itself, since he was a lonely traveler of his own path, as the above quotation taken from his autobiography reveals.

Jung pioneered the concept and experience of the unconscious. Early in life he detected an unchanging part of his personality that he associated with unconscious process, which he termed "Personality Two." After choosing the field of psychology and completing medical school, he was influenced by Freud, but before that point he had already formed an impression of the value of dreams in revealing hidden parts of the psyche. He had furthered the development of a method, in the so-called word association test, of elucidating unconscious contents which might be hidden from the more ordinary waking awareness of his clients.

At about the age of 32 he became better known in his field and established a mentorship relationship with Freud early in 1907. Freud came to consider the younger man his heir apparent for the burgeoning movement he called "psychoanalysis." Later, after breaking with Freud, Jung was to found his own system that he termed "analytical psychology." Jung was President of the International Society of Psychoanalysis from 1908 to 1914, when he resigned to pursue his own practice, and his own self-analysis on the shores of Lake Zurich.

From about 1912 onwards, Jung, who had become as well known as Freud after several international lectures (notably in America), found himself increasingly disillusioned with the internal politics of the psychoanalytic movement and at theoretical odds with its founder. He was entering a period he described later as a depression, floundering in his professional association with Freud while attempting to get clear within himself on his own psychology. He stated that he felt the need to know himself at deep levels in order to truly be of service to his clients.

He ended his personal relationship with his older mentor at the beginning of 1913. The two years previous to that had been increasingly troubled and he was in a period of breakdown for the next several years. During this time he struggled to discover the layers of his inner world, unlocking a stream of unconscious fantasies and material, which he captured in his private writing project that he called *The Red Book* (only recently published and made available to the general public in 2009). He later stated:

> The years when I was pursuing my inner images were the most important in my life – in them everything essential was decided. It all began then; the later details are only supplements and clarifications of the material that burst forth from the unconscious, and at first swamped me. It was the prima materia for a lifetime's work.[2]

Jung's Philosophy

When C. G. Jung came to describe the results of this private research into the unconscious, he published *Psychological Types*, the monumental early work that first defined his own independent research, giving us the terms extrovert and introvert, as well as the four functions of thinking, feeling, sensation and intuition. This was the first truly independent major instalment of his prolific writings, which eventually comprised the eighteen volumes of his *Collected Works*. His contributions to the field of psychology are too numerous to mention but among them are two that have importance as philosophical underpinnings of modern humanistic Western astrology, namely the concept of synchronicity and the archetype. The first of these, his principle of synchronicity, which Jung defined as an "acausal principle of meaningful connection" between events, such as a flock of birds over a death house, was not published until 1957 toward the end of his life (perhaps because fundamentally unscientific). This underlies our modern understanding of how astrology works, as Richard Tarnas has pointed out in *Cosmos and Psyche*. The synchronistic chime between planetary archetype and life event or the character of the native based on the moment of birth has come to be seen as the best philosophical foundation for the astrological assumption, as summed up in the ancient maxim "as above, so below".

The other important concept for astrology, that of the archetype, was the direct result of both Jung's early experiences as a psychiatrist with psychotic patients, such as with schizophrenia, and his own descent into the depths from 1913 to roughly 1918, which he later termed his "confrontation with the unconscious". He continued to work on *The Red Book* until 1928 when he began his research into medieval alchemy. This formed a foundation for the remainder of his life's work, as eventually published in books such as *Psychology and Alchemy* (1945) and *Mysterium Coniunctionis* (1955).

The idea of archetypal realities or fundamental patterns of psychic functioning that underlie human behavior goes back in Western thought to the Greeks, to their many gods and goddesses that were mythic representations of what they conceived as universal cosmic principles. These were later expanded upon by Plato as ideal forms, and were associated with the then-known planets, just as modern planetary archetypes are today. The concept of numinous astrological and archetypal realities flourished all through the Middle Ages but lost its currency during the so-called Age of Reason that followed the High Renaissance of the 14th and early 15th centuries. Jung was responsible for reviving this vitally numinous and necessary concept, and assigning fresh meaning to it as part of an explanatory theory of human behavior and, in particular, of unconscious process. He felt that archetypes such as Senex, Puer, Mother, Child, Anima and Animus were universal first principles that underlay all important psychological realities, and were best approached not by any form of rational analysis but rather through the means of poetic imagination and the elucidation of dream experience.

One important archetype that Jung came to identify was that of the Hero, which in the perfection of its development would be a universally positive figure, the one who would do the important and perfect deed, perhaps rescuing the maiden, after many trials. In this view there would be no negative elements. Jung saw another side to this archetype however during his dark night of the soul. Before the onset of the First World War, Jung dreamed repeatedly of a great flood that turned red with floating corpses overwhelming the mountain stronghold of his native Switzerland. He feared that he was menaced by a psychosis. When asked what he thought of the political situation of 1913-1914, he replied in an entirely prophetic statement that he saw "rivers of blood." Once the war had started in August 1914, he realized that these dreams had been in response to onrushing world events and also that these visions reflected his growing sense of alienation and uncertainty in his own psychic functioning. He felt he had to dive down into the depths of his unconscious, and began a process of daytime visualization that he referred to as active imagination. In one such session he found an abyss beneath his feet and willingly dove, although with great fear.

> It was during Advent of the year 1913 – December 12th to be exact – that I resolved upon the decisive step. I was sitting at my desk once more, thinking over my fears. Then I let myself drop. Suddenly it was though the ground literally gave way beneath my feet and I plunged down into dark depths. I could not fend off a feeling of panic. But then, abruptly, at not too great a depth, I landed on my feet in a soft, sticky mass. I felt great relief... after a while my eyes grew accustomed to the gloom, which was rather like a deep twilight. Before me was the entrance to a dark cave...³

He began to record the fantasies that he encountered and six days later had an important dream in which he killed the Hero. He dreamed that, together with a small dark person he identified as the Shadow, he stalked and killed Siegfried, a figure out of Wagnerian opera, the tall, blond and blue-eyed representation of Germanic ideal beauty; in form and in action a representation of the Hero. The date of this dream was December 18th, 1913. After this, his fantasies led him to admit the principle of evil as a rejected but profound part of his own unconscious process. He recorded everything in his journals, later transcribed into *The Red Book*. Near the end of his life he gave a poignant description of this crucial dream:

> I heard Siegfried's horn sounding over the mountains and I knew that we had to kill him. We were armed with rifles and lay in wait for him on a narrow path over the rocks.
> Then Siegfried appeared high up on the crest of the mountain, in the first ray of the rising sun. On a chariot made of the bones of the dead he drove at furious speed down the precipitous slope. When he turned a corner, we shot at him, and he plunged down, struck dead. Filled with disgust and remorse for having destroyed something so great and beautiful, I turned to flee, impelled by the fear that the murder might be discovered. But a tremendous downfall of rain began, and I knew it would wipe out all traces of the deed. I had escaped the danger of discovery, life could go on, but an unbearable feeling of guilt remained.

When I awoke from the dream, I turned it over in my mind, but was unable to understand it. I tried therefore to fall asleep again, but a voice within me said, "You must understand the dream, and you must do so at once!" The inner urgency mounted until a terrible moment came when the voice said, "If you do not understand the dream, you must shoot yourself!" In the drawer of my night table lay a loaded revolver...[4]

He pondered once more over the dream's meaning and came to understand that the figure of Siegfried represented a significant part of the German psyche that wished to impose its will on the rest of the world, and that he, Jung, had wanted to do the same. He recognized that this way of the heroic will – identified with the more conscious layers of the personality, or the ego – was no longer possible for him and had to be mercilessly destroyed.

Later as he recorded his subsequent fantasies, he struggled to accept this dark and potentially evil inner part of himself of his own soul's devising. In a typical passage he expressed these fantasies as follows:

I have evidently taken on a completely monstrous form in which I can no longer recognize myself. It seems to me that I have become a monstrous animal form for which I have exchanged my humanity. This way is surrounded by hellish magic, invisible nooses have been thrown over me and ensnare me.

But the spirit of the depths approached me and said, "Climb down into your depths, sink!"

But I was indignant at him and said, "How can I sink? I am unable to do this myself."

Then the spirit spoke words that to me appeared ridiculous and said, "Sit yourself down, be calm."

But I cried out indignantly "How frightful it sounds, like nonsense, do you also demand this of me? You overthrew the mighty gods that mean the most to us. My soul, where are you? Have I entrusted myself to a stupid animal, do I stagger like a drunkard to the grave, do I stammer stupidities like an idiot? Is this your way, my soul? The blood boils in me and I would strangle you if I could seize you. You weave the thickest darknesses and I am like a madman caught in your net. But I yearn, teach me."

But the soul spoke to me "My path is light."

Yet I indignantly answered, "Do you call light what we men call the worst darkness? Do you call day night?"

To this my soul spoke a word that roused my anger: "My light is not of this world."

I cried "I know of no other world."

The soul answered, "Should it not exist, because you know nothing of it?" I: "But our knowledge, does our knowledge also not hold good for you? … Where is security? Where is solid ground? Where is light? Your darkness is not only darker than night, but bottomless as well. If it's not going to be knowledge, then perhaps it will do without speech and words too?"

My soul: "No words."

…

"Come close, I am ready. Ready, my soul, you who are a devil, to wrestle with you. You donned the mask of a God and I worshiped you. Now you don the mask of a devil, a frightful one, the mask of the banal, of eternal mediocrity! … the lust for battle burns in my limbs. No, I cannot leave the battlefield defeated. I want to seize you, crush you, monkey, buffoon. Woe if the struggle is unequal, my hands grab at air. But your blows are also air, and I perceive trickery."

I find myself again on the desert path. It was a desert vision, a vision of the solitary who has wandered down long roads. There lurk invisible robbers and assassins and shooters of poison darts. Suppose the murderous arrow is sticking in my heart?[5]

In the foregoing we can make out some of the components of the Eris archetype. There is a struggle to the death with that part of his personality symbolized by Siegfried; proud, handsome and arrogant. A murderous intent has been invoked in order that his better nature might emerge and prosper. There is also the wordless reliance on depth exploration that D. H. Lawrence described in his novels, and that can be recognized in Blake's later "prophetic" works such as *Jerusalem* – and also in the ravings of Nietzsche's struggle with his soul in *Thus Spake Zarathustra*.[6] Later, near the end of Jung's life, he came to say:

The individual who wishes to have an answer to the problem of evil, as it is posed today, has need, first and foremost, of self-knowledge. That is, the utmost possible knowledge of his own wholeness. He must know relentlessly how much good he can do and what crimes he is capable of, and beware of regarding one as real and the other as an illusion. Both are elements within his nature, and both are bound to come to light in him should he wish – as one ought – to live without self-deception or self-delusion.[7]

Jung thus came to understand this dream as very significant for his life direction at this important time. The struggle going on within his depths was an essential conflict with the egoic portion of his psyche. This has profound implications for the Eris archetype, which at its highest manifestation can be seen as an implacable warrior archetype for the purpose of "slaying the ego," making for an important chime to other feminine warrior mythic traditions – as we will explore in the next chapter.

Jung said that his starting point was to recognize that it was important to live by an active myth, but that he did not yet know what form his own myth might take, and what direction it might lead him. He also felt incapable of helping clients to discover their path when he did not know his own. He emerged out of the years of his lonely struggle as a more whole human being, and this became the focus of his psychology, which he termed the process of individuation.

In June of 1916 a writing project came to Jung almost unbidden, *The Seven Sermons of the Dead*. This was literary rather than scientific, and Jung published it under an assumed name. In this project he identified a god based only in part on the Christian God, in which was compounded a principle of active evil as in the Gnostic philosophy of the first and second century. He gave this god the name Abraxis, which comes out of this ancient tradition. In the mandala that he created around the same time, showing dark and light to left and right, and above, the drawing of a winged spiritual figure, the name Abraxis appears at the very bottom, in the place of the descent into the underworld. He later commented that the nadir of this mandala corresponds to "the lord of the physical world, a world-creator of an ambivalent nature."[8]

Jung later stated that he only stopped working on *The Red Book* when he came into contact with medieval alchemy in 1928 when his friend and colleague, the sinologist Richard Wilhelm, sent him a copy of a text from *Chinese Alchemy, The Secret of the Golden Flower*. He spent the next ten years on alchemical studies producing the notable works *Psychology and Alchemy* and *Mysterium Coniunctionis*, in which there is the principle of a dark god as well as one of light. This too has implications for a deeper understanding of Eris, as do the many references to be found within the works of D. H. Lawrence to his "dark gods." It seems that what is dark and potentially to be shunned by conventional thought – symbolized in large part by Eris – has an important place at the table from the standpoint of the more fully integrated psyche.

Towards the end of his long and productive life work, Jung identified a theme of biblical proportions in his *Answer to Job*, in which he discussed the concept of an unfulfilled deity that, human-like, possessed both dark as well as positive elements.

As the quotation at the beginning of this chapter indicates, Jung operated outside the domain of strictly mainstream thought process for his whole life. As the rest of the culture has begun to catch up to his core ideas, time has softened the knee-jerk opposition that he, like other Erisians, faced in his own day.

Jung's Private Life and the Exploration of His Chart

Invested as he was in this sense of deep purpose, to the exclusion of more ordinary goals such as fame and financial success, Jung pursued his understanding of his own psychology over and above the more ordinary demands of his work in the world. This study led him to the concepts that later evolved into the four functions and the collective unconscious. He felt that he was on a mission, and that his mission involved plumbing the depths of his soul; and he did this all his life. Even in his eighties he was still writing – encouraged by his acolytes to record observations on his long and productive life – and these latter thoughts involved his inner work over and above the usual material for an autobiography, the outer events. From this we might conclude the presence of a strong Eris, as representing the warrior for truth, and for soul-level mission. We also would suspect a strong Chiron, indicative of a healing quest, and of the painful and solitary path of an iconoclast. Not surprisingly, we find them both. See his chart overleaf.

Eris is in Jung's first house and therefore emphasized. It connects with the Moon, by a close sextile, and to the chart ruler, Uranus, by an inconjunct aspect within one degree. We also find the closest aspect of Eris to a personal planet in the trine to Mercury, within mere minutes of a degree. Eris with Mercury reflects a prolific writer and an articulate spokesperson for his or her own personal philosophy, and this Jung certainly was. Much of his alchemical research focused on the god Mercurius, a factor that was intimately connected with the *lapis philosophorum*, the goal of medieval alchemists.

Chiron, symbolic of Jung's role as healer, is opposite Jupiter and in close parallel to Neptune, which it also conjuncts. Chiron is trine Mars and sextile Saturn. An out-of-sign square with the Sun is indicative of a somewhat difficult relationship with his father, as was evidenced in his life. The close opposition of Chiron to Jupiter indicates that the faith of his ancestors was not enough for him, although that doctrinal truth appeared to be so for his father; he had to find his own way through. His father was a Protestant

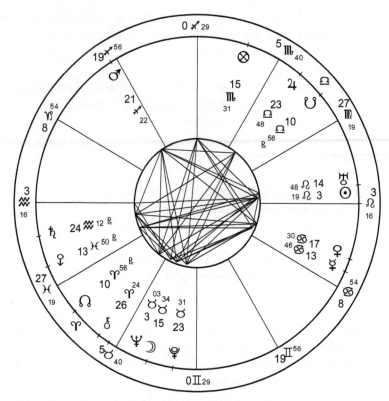

Fig. 8-1 Carl Gustav Jung, July 26, 1875, 7:37 PM LMT, Kesswil, Switzerland 47N36 9E20

minister and although Jung was influenced by the church and the Bible, and in many ways was a man of his time, including its Christian bias, in his maturity Jung did not consider himself a Christian.

In addition to the above aspects, Jung's Eris is trine Venus, widely square Mars, and makes a quintile to Pluto. This latter aspect brings Eris into indirect contact with the Sun, which at 3 degrees of Leo makes a quintile to Pluto as well. It is interesting that Eris connects more directly with the Moon, in symbolic resonance with unconscious process, a powerful life-long factor for Jung. The Moon also represents the mother, and in his autobiography, *Memories, Dreams, Reflections*, is an interesting reference to his mother as possessing what he calls a "natural mind," that only at times came to the surface.[9] A footnote refers to a 1940 lecture in which Jung mentions more specifically what he meant by this concept of "natural mind" as "the mind that says absolutely straight and ruthless things." This resonates with the Eris archetype.

120

That is the sort of mind which springs from natural sources, and not from opinions taken from books; it wells up from the earth like a natural spring and brings with it the peculiar wisdom of nature.[10]

1912-1918 were in many ways the most important years of his life; the time when he was in the midst of his "confrontation with the unconscious" that influenced all his subsequent work. It will be of great interest to examine the transits for this period.

In late December 1911 and into 1912 there was a row with his mentor, Freud, which paved the way for the final split between them over the following year and finalized in January of 1913. Jung's first major work was being published in journal form, which was also his first venture into stating his independent psychology. *Symbols of Transformation* was published in two parts, and angered the older psychologist, Freud, as it departed in significant ways from his own original doctrine. This was particularly true of Part II of *Symbols*, published in April 1912. There were actually difficulties raging between the two men in their correspondence from late 1911 through early 1912.

There were also attacks on Jung, and on psychoanalysis in general, in the Zurich press that escalated after the end of January 1912. In addition to dealing with the attacks, as a spokesperson for the psychoanalytic movement, Jung was also bitten on the hand by a dog, and was unable to write for some time. This was when he was finishing Part II of *Symbols*, the last chapter of which he hesitated to complete. The transiting position of Eris for this period is revealing.

Transiting Eris had recently stationed direct in mid-December, less than a degree away from a semi-sextile aspect with Jung's Chiron, indicating the psychic, professional and even the physical pain that he was going through. Transiting Eris to natal Chiron remained within a 1 degree orb for these years of struggle with his own depths that accompanied the break with Freud and its aftermath and resulted in the creation of *The Red Book*. The first exact hit had been in June 1910, the month that Jung began working with Toni Wolff; Toni later became a fundamental partner in developing his own form of psychology in the years 1913 to approximately 1915, during what might be called his self-analysis. The second took place in April 1911. The third exact hit of transiting Eris to natal Chiron was March 30th, 1912, a month before Jung published Part II of *Symbols*, the work that initiated his break with Freud. This work introduced a different and expanded concept of the term libido – initially coined by Freud as referencing strictly sexual energy. The initial chapters of Part II that brought the expanded definition to bear, followed by later chapters presenting a new concept of the oedipal transformations of childhood, finally set him apart from his mentor, to go his own way entirely. This was another difficult and painful episode for Jung, in keeping with the symbolism of the Chiron archetype, and also important in terms of soul purpose, thus matching superbly with the symbolism of Eris, as this long-term aspect of transiting Eris would indicate.

The Transits of 1911
1911 was Jung's last year of relatively peaceful collaboration with Freud, and it was interesting in several ways.

In late March, his colleague and assistant, Jacob Honegger, committed suicide, which constituted a serious and unexpected challenge for Jung, affecting his own research into mythology in which Honegger had been participating under Jung's direction.

The transits for the day of Honegger's death, March 29th, 1911 are fascinating. In a letter referenced in Sonu Shamdasani's *Dream of a Science*, Jung

> informed [Trigant] Burrow that Honegger had committed suicide after realizing that he had made the wrong decisions and did not sufficiently believe in life. He added that this was a great loss to him, as Honegger was his only congenial friend in Zurich.[11]

The transits that Uranus makes to Jung's natal chart are many: it is coming on to conjunct his Ascendant and to oppose his Sun in another 4 degrees. Uranus is also sextile to his Midheaven. The transits to the angles are approximate, based on Jung's reported birth time of sunset. In an appropriate symbol for the pain of the separation, Uranus also squares his natal Chiron within 2 degrees. The closest aspect Uranus makes is a semi-square to his natal Eris, exact practically to the minute. We can see this as an indication of the suddenness of this untimely passing. With Eris involved, the symbolism could reference Jung's soul purpose, and speaks to the profound meaning that Honegger held, both professionally and personally, in Jung's life, involving Jung's early work on mythology and the collective unconscious.[12] In addition, transiting Eris was making a nearly exact semi-sextile to Jung's natal Chiron, partile and within 20 minutes of a degree.

The Uranus transit to natal Eris was within a degree for the first half of the year, then again at the end of 1911 and the beginning of 1912, exact on June 12th, 1911 and January 10th, 1912. In spring and early summer Jung was in the midst of investigations that were fundamental to his more mature thought. In a letter to Freud on June 12th, 1911, he detailed some of them, including an interest in astrology – ruled by Uranus – which would later become part of his investigation into his principle of synchronicity, and thus an important part of his life's work. He wrote:

> Everything I am doing now revolves round the contents and forms of unconscious fantasies… it seems that in Dementia Praecox you have at all costs to bring to light the inner world produced by the introversion of libido… My evenings are taken up very largely with astrology. I make horoscopic calculations in order to find a clue to the core of psychological truth. Some remarkable things have turned up, which will certainly appear incredible to you…[13]

Examining other long-term transits from the difficult passage at the end of March 1911, we have the trine that transiting Pluto makes to natal Jupiter and natal Saturn, forming a grand trine configuration in Air signs, and indicating transformation of the structure of Jung's life and beliefs. Both of these are about two degrees away, with the most recent exact aspects occurring in 1909. Transiting Pluto is sextile natal Chiron, only half a degree away, which again had an exact hit in the summer of 1909. Jung's contact with Jacob Honegger began in the spring of 1909 with an analysis for an incipient schizophrenia. Finally, Jupiter was in partile trine to both natal Eris and natal Mercury, thus forming a partile grand trine. This activation beautifully articulates Jung's soul-level concerns at this critical time, as exemplified by his writing, the research being conducted by Honegger and his own work on Part II of *Symbols*.

The Jupiter trine to natal Eris was close in February and March, then again one final time during the last ten days of September 1911. On September 22nd after the Weimar conference, which was a great success professionally, and with transiting Jupiter trine to both his natal Eris and his natal Mercury, both within a degree, Jung wrote to Sabina Spielrein that she needed to follow her own star:

> Never forget that under no circumstance should you ever allow yourself to shrink back from an immediate goal which your heart views as true and beautiful. Every time, this will involve a sacrifice of egoism, pride and stubbornness and will appear to you as if you are losing yourself in the process. But only through this mysterious self-sacrifice will you win yourself a new, beautiful form, and thereby become a blessing and a source of happiness for other people.[14]

With Jupiter, Eris and Mercury thus invoked, here is another entirely appropriate chime for the optimistic side of the Eris archetype as we are coming to understand her, speaking as it does to soul purpose commitment at the sacrifice of ego needs.

Transits of December 1912, 1913, and 1914

The December 1911 station direct of transiting Eris in aspect to natal Chiron was followed by mid-December stations in 1912, 1913, and 1914, each closer to the exact contact with natal Chiron. Because Eris moves so slowly, the station was at the same time of year, almost to the day, so that it is quite interesting to review these December time periods as touchstones in Jung's life and work.

In December 1912, around Christmas, or ten days after the Eris station, Jung had one of the seminal "big dreams" of this 1912-1915 period, one most often quoted in the story of how *The Red Book* came into being.

Around Christmas of 1912 I had a dream. In the dream, I was seated in a magnificent Italian loggia, with pillars, a marble floor and a marble balustrade. I was sitting on a gold Renaissance chair; in front of me was a table of rare beauty. It was made of green stone, like emerald. There I sat, looking out into the distance, for the loggia was set high up on the tower of a castle. My children were sitting at the table too.

Suddenly a white bird descended, a small gull or a dove. Gracefully it came to rest on the table, and I signed to the children to be still so that they would not frighten away the pretty white bird. Immediately, the dove was transformed into a little girl, about eight years of age, with golden blond hair. She ran off with the children and played with them among the colonnades of the castle.

I remained lost in thought, musing about what I had just experienced. The little girl came back and tenderly placed her arms around my neck. Then she suddenly vanished; the dove was back and spoke slowly in a human voice. "Only in the first hours of the night can I transform myself into a human being, while the male dove is busy with the twelve dead." Then she flew off into the blue air and I awoke.[15]

Later he declared that this dream opened up for him the possibilities of the projected anima archetype as an actual love interest for himself. He was most likely referring to Toni Wolff, whom he had been close to and who had been helping him with the research for Part II of *Symbols* the previous spring.

In December 1912 came also the concluding episodes of his break with Freud. These were most painful to him, in part because of his difficulties with his own father whose belief system ran counter to his, and who had died when Jung was not yet twenty-one. In early January 1913, the final break came; Jung felt adrift and at sea.

His relationship with Toni Wolff would be an important component of his subsequent descent into his unconscious process for she was the only one who was allowed to see his evolving manuscript, as he continued working with her on his inner fantasy world the next spring. He decided that stimulating the feelings of youth would be especially important, and so he began playing with stones, as he did when he was a boy, building a little town on the shore of Lake Zurich.

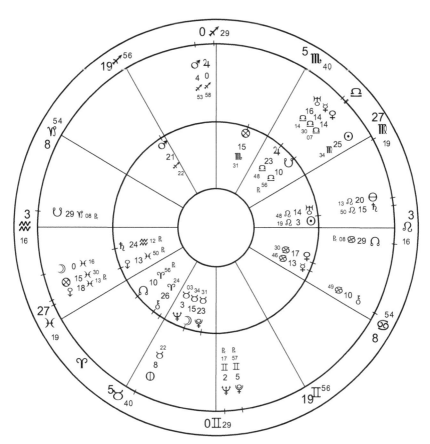

Fig. 8-2 Carl Gustav Jung, Comparison Toni Wolff,
September 18, 1888, 2:30 AM - 50 Zurich, Switzerland

The chart comparison between C. G. Jung and Toni Wolff might be expected to show many Eris contacts, and indeed this is the case. See the chart comparison in Fig. 8-2.

Toni's Eris connects with Jung's personal planets, being exactly sesqui-quadrate to Jung's natal Sun, within a few minutes of a degree, sextile his Moon, square his Mars, and trine his Venus within a degree. Her Eris also makes a close semi-square aspect to his natal Neptune, within one sixth of a degree. The planetary archetype of Neptune is an entirely appropriate one as she helped to guide his stream of fantasies during this crucial period. Jung's Eris is also well-aspected by Toni's planets, since her mid-Libra Mercury-Venus-Uranus conjunction is closely inconjunct his Eris, with Mercury and Venus exact within a degree. Her mid-Leo Saturn is also inconjunct within two degrees forming a yod to Jung's Eris at nearly 14 degrees of Pisces. Toni's Chiron is also in trine to Jung's Eris.

The Transits of December 1913

December 1913 saw the two "big dreams" of the killing of Siegfried. These took place on the night of the 12th and of the 18th. He also began his self-analysis in the months that followed. Toni Wolff was his only confidante, in many ways his second concurrent wife, and obviously a very important person in his life at this time.

In *The Red Book*, Jung transcribed from his journals the following waking fantasy:

> I stand in black dirt up to my ankles in a dark cave. Shadows sweep over me. I am seized by fear but I know I must go in. I crawl through a narrow crack in the rock and reach an inner cave whose bottom is covered in black water. But beyond this I catch a glimpse of a luminous red stone which I must reach. I wade through the muddy water. … I take the stone, it covers a dark opening in the rock. … I place my ear to the opening. I hear the flow of underground waters. I see the bloody head of a man in the dark stream. Someone wounded, someone slain floats there. I take in this image for a long time, shuddering. I see a large black scarab floating past on the dark stream. In the deepest reach of the stream shines a red sun, radiating through the dark water... Deep night falls. A red stream of blood, thick red blood, springs up, surging for a long time, then ebbing. I am seized by fear. What did I see?[16]

Later Jung realized that the corpse was that of Siegfried, whom he actually saw killed in the subsequent dream of six days later.

It will be interesting to examine the transits of the actual timing of the dream of the killing of Siegfried, and its predecessor of the night of December 12th. To take these dreams in order, Jung first dreamt that he saw the corpse of Siegfried in a deep hole within a cave, submerged in blood. Six nights later he had the dream of the actual deed.

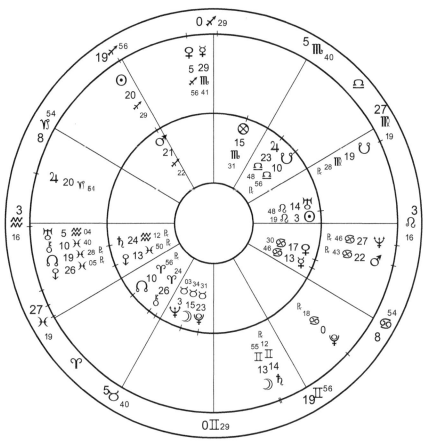

Fig. 8-3 Carl Gustav Jung, Transits for Saturday, December 13, 1913, 3:00 AM CET

The transits for late night December 12th are shown above. Note that the chart is chosen for 3:00 AM, although it could have been any time during the night, or even up to about 15 hours earlier, during the day, without substantially affecting these positions. The Moon would then be in early Gemini, and the Sun half a degree or so ahead. In these transits there are many chimes with the symbolism of emerging life purpose, and the desperate measures that might need to be invoked in order to achieve it. For one thing, transiting Saturn is in close applying square to natal Eris. Transiting

Neptune, associated with dream and fantasy imagery, also makes a sesqui-quadrate with natal Eris. Of course the semi-sextile of stationary transiting Eris to natal Chiron on this date represents a strong astrological factor as well, only a quarter of a degree from exact. The symbolism of Saturn with Eris connotes important life structure changes, based on a feeling of emerging mission in the world as different from the expectations of his peers. These changes were clearly coming on, more even than Jung realized at the time, with the advent of these dreams.

This period provided the gateway to all the inner fantasies that were to follow, so that this actual dream, and the one of six days hence, constituted nothing less than the beginning of the most important phase of Jung's life. As already related, in the following year he abandoned his responsibilities in the International Psychoanalytic Association and even his teaching position in order to concentrate on his clients and pursue his inner fantasies. The elucidation of these fantasies, dreams and waking visions, his process of "active imagination," would become the foundation of his life's work.

Pluto and Mars are also invoked by the transiting positions. Since this dream involved killing, the potentially violent and war-like nature of Mars and the death/rebirth symbolized by Pluto are important factors. Transiting Pluto is semi-square to natal Moon; the Sun is on his natal Mars, with transiting retrograde Mars also making an inconjunct to the position of natal Mars. Neptune is involved as well, as appropriate for dream and fantasy images. Transiting Neptune closely squares natal Chiron, and makes a quintile aspect to Jung's natal Moon, within one quarter of a degree of exact.

The key transits listed above are much closer on the subsequent night of December 18th. The following transits are given for midnight, because Jung relates in the journals that "It was a terrible night; I soon awoke." Of course it could have been earlier in the evening, or later, without much change.

Transiting Saturn is now a mere tenth of a degree (instead of one half) from the exact square to natal Eris. Transiting Neptune, Pluto and Eris have barely moved, especially since Eris has in the intervening six days gone through its station to direct motion. This station of Eris from retrograde into direct motion, in partile aspect to Jung's natal Chiron, I consider to be extremely significant and key to the formulation of *The Red Book*, Jung's self-analysis, and the launch of his life's work in the decoding of unconscious process.

In another chime, while the transiting Sun no longer conjuncts natal Mars it now trines natal Chiron within one tenth of a degree. Also, transiting Venus is now opposite transiting Saturn and squares natal Eris within half of a degree. All of these Eris aspects are extremely close.

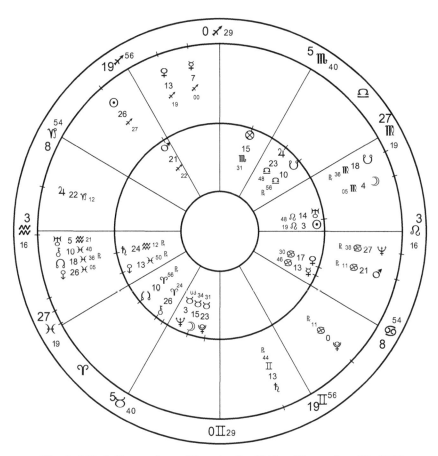

Fig. 8-4 Carl Gustav Jung, Transits for Friday, December 19, 1913,
00:00 AM CET

Following this period of the dream of the killing of Siegfried, as eventually published in *The Red Book*, the journals went on to the appearance of
Elijah and Salome, the wise old man and young erotic feminine. These two
archetypes are reflective of the transiting planets Saturn and Venus, opposite in the sky at this telling moment of the dream, both in square with
Jung's natal Eris. Elijah soon morphed into Philemon. This was the beloved
figure of the wise old man revered by Jung as an aspect of himself ever
after. In the tower at Bollingen where he spent private time throughout his
life, there was a secret inscription to Philemon, in Latin, "Philemon's sanc-
tuary, Faust's repentance." In time Jung would come to understand the figure of Salome as a representation of what he began to term the archetype
of the Anima.

The Events of December 1914

In November 1914, Jung began the actual writing of *The Red Book*. This was just preceding the station direct of Eris in exact aspect to natal Chiron. To the journal material describing his experiments in illuminating his own unconscious contents, Jung added many pages of commentary. Much later he transcribed the entire production in elaborate calligraphic script, accompanied by artistic drawings in vibrant colors.

His series of active imagination fantasies continued with the introduction of three new archetypal figures: Elijah, who would later become Philemon; the serpent, who also figures in many of his subsequent fantasies; and Salome, representative of his soul or as he came to term it, his Anima.

On the night when I considered the essence of the God, I became aware of an image: I lay in a dark depth. An old man stood before me. He looked like one of the old prophets. A black serpent lay at his feet. Some distance away I saw a house with columns. A beautiful maiden steps out of the door. She walks uncertainly and I see that she is blind. The old man waves to me, and I follow him to the house at the foot of a sheer wall of rock. The serpent creeps behind us. Darkness reigns inside the house. We are in a high hall with glittering walls. A bright stone the color of water lies in the background. As I look into its reflection, the images of Eve, the tree and the serpent appear to me. After this I catch sight of Odysseus an his journey on the high seas. Suddenly a door opens on the right, onto a garden full of bright sunshine. We step outside and the old man says to me, "Do you know where you are?"

I: "I am a stranger here and everything seems strange to me, anxious as in a dream. Who are you?"

E: "I am Elijah and this is my daughter, Salome"

I: "The daughter of Herod, the bloodthirsty woman?"

E: "Why do you judge so? You see that she is blind. She is my daughter, the daughter of the prophet."

I: "What miracle has united you?"

E: "It is no miracle, it was so from the beginning. My wisdom and my daughter are one."

I am shocked. I am incapable of grasping it...

S: "Do you love me?"

I: "How can I love you? How do you come to this question? I see only one thing, you are Salome, a tiger, your hands are stained with the blood of the holy one. How should I love you?"[17]

We can see the outlines of a deep archetype of implacable and even bloodthirsty will, represented as a feminine element, that he is slightly horrified by, but which he nonetheless feels holds the key to unlock an important part of unconscious process for him. His commentary on the journal material follows:

> Judgment must fall from you, even taste, but above all pride, even when it is based on merit. Utterly poor, miserable, unknowingly humiliated, go on through the gate. Turn your anger against yourself, since only you stop yourself from looking and from living.[18]

Here we see Jung reflecting on his solitary difficult and painful path – as indicated also by the quote that begins this chapter. We are reminded of the descent into the underworld common to many mythologies, one example being the Sumerian myth of Inanna, being forced to leave behind all that is pleasurable and ego-enhancing. This commentary, written in late 1914, just at the time of the closest approach of stationary transiting Eris in aspect to his natal Chiron, also shows that after painfully mulling over the necessity to kill one part of himself in order to allow the birth of another, that birth involved figures of archetypal significance and of deep process work; extremely appropriate to the symbolism of Eris and Chiron in combination.

Other Big Dreams and Visitations

A dream of Philemon with Kingfisher wings took place in the early weeks of February 1914, and Jung drew a picture of it in his journal. That same day he found a dead kingfisher in perfect condition on the lakeshore, an unusual occurrence. During this time, transiting Eris was semi-sextile to Jung's natal Chiron, while transiting Chiron was also conjunct his natal Eris.

There was a series of dreams, thrice repeated, that came in at the beginning and the end of June 1914 extending to the beginning of July. The third dream was different in that there were frost grapes that made a delicious juice that he then gave to a waiting multitude.

> Soon afterward, in the late spring and early summer of 1914, I had a thrice-repeated dream that in the middle of summer an arctic cold wave descended and froze the land to ice… In the third dream, frightful cold had again descended from out of the cosmos. This dream, however, had an unexpected end. There stood a leaf-bearing tree, but without fruit (my tree of life, I thought), whose leaves had been transformed by the effects of the frost into sweet grapes full of healing juices.[19]

The juicy grapes could refer to his subsequent works, which have indeed had a healing effect. The dream ends thus: "I plucked the grapes and gave them to a large waiting multitude."

It was only a month later that these visions truly came to pass, including the threatened delay on board ship, when he was caught in Aberdeen, Scotland, by the beginning of the Great War, and had to flee home by the fastest ship route possible. The northern sea was icy cold and the land frozen everywhere. In *The Red Book*, he describes these prophetic dreams, and goes on to say:

> In reality now, it was so. At the time when the great war broke out [August 1st, 1914] between the peoples of Europe, I found myself in Scotland, compelled by the war to choose the fastest ship and the shortest route home. I encountered the colossal cold that froze everything. I met up with the flood, the sea of blood [from earlier dream visions] and found my barren tree whose leaves the frost had transformed into a remedy. And I plucked my ripe fruit and gave it to you and I do not know what I poured out for you, what bitter-sweet intoxicating drink, which left on your tongues the after-taste of blood.[20]

From the vantage point of the intervening years, we are able to recognize that this time around the beginning of World War I was the formation of Jung's later and more mature psychoanalytic method that has indeed proven healing for the multitudes.

This series of the three prophetic visions corresponds well with the station retrograde of transiting Eris on June 24th; this was about a degree past the exact semi-sextile to natal Chiron. At the beginning of July, the time of the third prophetic dream, transiting Chiron was making several aspects to personal planets, being sesquiquadrate Jung's Sun degree within half a degree, square his Mars and trine his Venus. This shows the importance of the Chiron archetype, as well as the Eris archetype, during this time of the actual writing of *The Red Book*.

Beginning in the summer of 1916, when Jung had a profound psychic experience that resulted in his writing of *The Seven Sermons of the Dead*, his progressed Sun was opposed to his natal Eris within 1 degree. This aspect of progressed Sun in opposition to his natal Eris also pertained for the next year and a half, or the years of 1916-1917, and into 1918, which also saw the writing of the famous twin seminal descriptions of his approach to psychology, the Jungian school, published in his collected works as Vol. 7: *Two Essays in Analytical Psychology*.

Summary

In summation, these repeated transits to natal Eris, and transiting Eris in close aspect to natal Chiron, provide solid evidence for the strong presence of Eris in Jung's chart as fundamental to his process. Jung postulated an internal God consisting of both good and evil elements, and this dark concept makes sense as we come to better understand the Eris archetype.

Additionally, certain characteristics of the archetype can now be drawn more clearly. From Jung's work we can deduce that while there is a difficult and violent side to this energy, this is a natural response for a particular truth or activity to emerge. Certain egoic portions of Jung's psyche needed to be destroyed and surpassed, and this destruction was vitally necessary for his continued ability to function, as he felt called to, at the level of soul purpose.

There is thus a place at the table for dark process, called in some contexts "evil," and this archetypal idea can be linked with the implacable warrior energy of Eris, that yet has a higher positive goal in allowing impediments to be cleared in the important movement toward embracing one's destiny.

Notes

1. *Memories Dreams Reflections*, p. 222.
2. ibid p. 199.
3. ibid p. 179.
4. ibid p. 180.
5. *The Red Book*, pp. 240-241.
6. Jung was well-acquainted with this iconic work at the time of his writing of *The Red Book*. It is interesting to note that while with Nietzsche's chart we see far more clearly the Pluto than the Eris influence, the Eris influence is also there, Eris being trine the Sun, widely square the Moon, inconjunct Mars and bi-quintile to Mercury.
7. *Memories, Dreams, Reflections*, p. 330.
8. The mandala is reproduced on p. 364 of *The Red Book*.
9. *Memories, Dreams, Reflections*, p. 50.
10. ibid. See the footnote at the bottom of p. 50.
11. Jung to Burrow June 28, 1911. *Jung Papers*, Wissenschaftshistorische Sammlungen, ETH, Zurich, quoted in Shamdasani, *Jung and the Making of a Modern Psychology: The Dream of a Science*, p. 217.
12. Honegger's research with a patient under his and his mentor's supervision was pivotal for Jung. See Deirdre Bair's *Jung: A Biography*, pp. 171-190, her chapter entitled "The Solar Phallus Man."

13. *Letters*, pp. 23-24.
14. Kerr, p. 349.
15. *Memories Dreams Reflections*, pp. 171-2.
16. *The Red Book*, p. 237.
17. ibid pp. 245-246.
18. ibid p. 246.
19. *Memories, Dreams, Reflections*, p. 176.
20. *The Red Book*, p. 231.

9

The Goddess and the Warrior

Your inner self is an integral part of nature, bound to the laws of nature. Therefore to distrust this innermost self is unreasonable, for nature can be wholly trusted. If nature seems like an enemy to you, it is only because you do not understand its laws. The inner self, the real self, is nature; it is life; it is creation.

The Guide, channeled through Eva Pierrakos.[1]

Although I did not call her by that name then, my love for Wild Woman began when I was a little child. I was an aesthete rather than an athlete, and my only wish was to be an ecstatic wanderer. Rather than chairs and tables, I preferred the ground, trees, and caves, for in those places I felt I could lean against the cheek of God.

Clarissa Pinkola Estés[2]

In our continuing investigation of the astrology of Eris, this spiritual and feminine warrior that partakes of the wildness of nature and deep soul purpose, we come to other salient spokespersons: Eva Pierrakos and Clarissa Pinkola Estés. We will discuss Eva Pierrakos, who channeled the Pathwork material, resulting in the books *The Pathwork of Self-Transformation* and *Fear No Evil*, at the end of this chapter. It was Clarissa, in her book *Women Who Run With the Wolves*, published in 1992, that conjured up the "Wild Woman archetype," which made me immediately think of Eris. She is a Jungian analyst, and a story-teller, who felt called to expound, through describing and performing fairy tale, folk story and myth, the fundamental importance of a call to feminine wildness that she perceived was sorely needed by members of an overly civilized society that had stifled it. She became the hero of many people, men and women alike, who had been feeling disenfranchised by the attitude of the prevailing culture. Her subject matter has profound connections with the Eris archetype, but first let's explore the mythology of the woman warrior in a more universal context.

Another author of interest in this topic is Riane Eisler, who wrote *The Chalice and the Blade: Our History, Our Future* in 1987. In this study of early religious practice and of partnership versus dominator societies in prehistory, she proposed that a feminine goddess culture was the universal norm in what she termed, with archaeologist Maria Gimbutas, Old Europe – as it existed before 6,000 BC and the coming of the Bronze Age with its more advanced weaponry. According to this idea, the universal European Goddess culture encountered a masculine Warrior culture from the outlying areas and steppe regions of the European and Asian continents, which proceeded to overrun it and to dominate the feminine element in favor of a patriarchal society based on abilities of the stronger and fiercer sex.

This male-dominant society then engendered the classical Greek, Roman and Hebrew cultures and a clutch of religions that were based on an exclusively male deity rather than the Goddess. The story of the feminine and pagan elements that still survive in repressed form (in for example Christianity, with its dominant male father figure) makes for a fascinating thesis that has been taken as relevant as part of an outcry against masculine-oriented domination as the default mode of modern society. She proposes a partnership society as part of the nascent movement posing the alternative possibility of a return to feminist values and principles. Recent archaeological research has disproven much of the historical correctness of Gimbutas' theories, which have been shown to be true in part, or in particular locales, but are likely not accurate for the whole of Europe, as she claimed. Nevertheless Eisler's thesis has great value, in describing what could be possible were humankind to return to the ancient principles represented by a gynocentric society: connection, collaboration and partnership.

In pursuing the research for this book I realized that if 'Goddess' and 'Warrior' were two ways of being in the world, associated with predominantly feminine and masculine approaches, then the archetype of a Warrior Goddess was a synthesis of sorts, with the ability to be fierce and to fight as necessary, but with an overriding motivation for higher purpose, stemming from deep inside. This might also be considered vitally appropriate for an emerging Aquarian Age, with important values for unity, connection and the furtherance of social needs.

This led to considering in what other ways these two different approaches to life might combine, and Eisler gives us one answer; the warrior class might dominate the goddess culture and render it subservient, so that the feminine Goddess energy only exists underground and in secret as despised offshoots whose adherents might be persecuted or nearly forced out of existence, though still somehow surviving on the fringes of the mainstream culture. Such is one way to view the previous 2,000 years of First and Second World history. The feminist movement spoke of this in the Sixties in a rather clever word play as "his-story" rather than "her-story." In this case there an obvious need to redress the imbalance, as Eisler maintains.

When the goddess religion disappeared, it did not disappear entirely. The old goddess worship went underground, and there were various attempts to suppress it right through to the Middle Ages and the burning of witches. In making her case, Eisler states that the pregnant goddess figurines of Paleolithic pre-history, going back to the earliest traces of civilization in Europe, were echoed in the feminine-oriented religion of Neolithic times and even reflected in the medieval Christian period when goddess worship was is disrepute, by images that were yet still prevalent of the pregnant Virgin Mary and the Madonna with her Child.

In Eisler's view, a societal orientation based on a partnership model is long overdue wherein both sexes are equally honored, given scope for growth and awarded social recognition for substantial achievement. In fact this idea was prevalent in the suffragette movement from the turn of the century and also in the feminist movement of the Sixties and Seventies, forming one important basis for her work.

Her developmental model, which she calls "Cultural Transformation Theory", sees the split between Warrior and Goddess as fundamental, so that the choice seems forced on societies to decide on one or the other as sacred. In this Eisler neglects the possibility of a merger. Another potential way of combining these two concepts is represented by the idea of a Warrior Goddess, as exemplified in the Eris archetype, and there could be others as well.

The Warrior Goddess in Ancient Greece

Several instances of warrior goddess mythology can be discerned out of the classical period. Of course one example would be the early Greek goddess of our current subject matter, Eris, Goddess of Chaos and Discord, sister to Ares, God of War. Even though she was not a major goddess in classical mythology, there are powerful implications in her current resurgence as a new astrological archetype of this developing century.

Another extremely important Warrior Goddess is Pallas Athena, one of the primary goddesses of ancient Greece. She was widely worshipped, having many shrines in her honor, and known as protector not only of Athens but of many communities and of the union between man and woman as sanctified by marriage. She figured prominently in the Homeric epics *The Iliad* and *The Odyssey* and was of equal if not greater importance to the Sun God, Apollo.[3]

Athena's mythological birth is unique, and reveals a connection to the masculine as well as the feminine – she was born out of the head of Zeus. Because Zeus, the Ruler of the Gods, was suspicious of being overthrown by the offspring of Metis, Goddess of Wisdom, he decided to swallow his pregnant former partner. After this act, the God of the Forge, Hephaestus, wielded his axe and split open Zeus's head, from where sprang Athena, fully clothed and armed. She therefore, though feminine, represents a very father-oriented and patrilineal figure. She was virginal, but also presided over successful marriage, and most especially the resulting children. She is considered to figure in the philosophical support for a patriarchic descent and a reduction of the power of the female in her ability to give birth.[4]

A famous case of matrilineal descent versus patriarchy is immortalized in the Oresteia, the play by Aeschylus from the 5th century BC. Orestes stands accused of matricide, after avenging the death of his father, Agamemnon, by the hand of his mother, Clytemnestra. He murdered his mother and therefore stands accused by the Furies, representing the old spirit of feminine justice. Even though he offended against the feminine, Athena comes to his rescue and gives the crucial testimony, declaring that to avenge the father is only right. She offers herself as proof that, as she is born of no woman, the descent from the father is the more important. As Riane Eisler points out, this is more evidence for the suppression of the feminine, going back to the roots of Western European culture.[5]

Athena represents a goddess figure of many sides, war-like and protective, maternal and virginal, a general who wins many a battle but who takes sides in order to promote the protection of women, and of their progeny, rather than their subjugation. Reflecting her intelligence rather than her warrior might; she also was patron of the arts of weaving and of pottery, key industries as civilization evolved. She was known for thinking her way through the battle like an experienced general who knows when to apply pressure, and when to yield.

As such she might represent a transitional mythological symbol between traditional feminine values and the warrior culture that followed; thus not simply a matter of repression of the feminine but also having a quality of assimilation. Her roots go back to Egypt, and to Crete, where she represented the cult of the Goddess. Her creation myth was changed during the transition to classical period, when she was given the story of solo birth by the father.

In terms of astrological archetype, Athena has her own astrological emblem in the asteroid Pallas Athena, whose name is often shortened to Pallas. In her work on the Asteroid Goddesses, referring to the four major asteroids discovered in the early 19th century, Ceres, Pallas, Juno and Vesta, Demetra George has this to say:

Pallas, Athena, and Medusa as maiden, mother and crone, were the triple Moon goddess emanations of the Libyan snake goddess Neith. Originally, Athena was one and the same with Pallas and Medusa. However by the time she entered Greek culture, she had become a symbol of the new patriarchal order…'[6]

The myth of the slaying of Medusa probably arose from the loss of power of the goddess after her displacement by Mycenaean invaders and their establishment of a new patriarchal rule in the dynasty of King Perseus. The story that has come down through the ages has Perseus killing Medusa with the help of Athena, reinforcing her detachment from the old goddess worship. Another story out of the classical period has Athena as a girl accidentally killing her companion, Pallas. Note that Pallas in Greek represents a youthful maiden. In a potent reminder of her ancient association with goddess worship, Athena wears the Gorgon head on her shield, indicating her role in the death of the fearful snake-haired mortal. She is also frequently depicted with a serpent, another symbol from the time of the Goddess.[7]

In interpreting the astrological archetype, her wisdom and cleverness are emphasized, rather than her war-like character as a general. The astrological Pallas Athena is a female character whose womanly skills and cunning are made available to those who truly need them, in an acknowledged man's world, but on her own terms. Again, Demetra George:

> As the deity who stood closest to Jupiter/Zeus, Pallas Athena attained a high degree of prestige and status in Olympus. She was accepted as sister, colleague and equal in the world of men. In addition, Pallas Athena's virginity enabled her to cultivate many male friendships without the complication of sexual entanglement. [She] however paid a substantial price for this privileged position – the denial of her femininity and feminine origins. In her lament she cried "No mother gave me birth. Therefore, the father's claim and male supremacy in all things…"

This repudiation lies at the source of her pathology as the unconscious masculine side of a woman takes over and dominates the personality. Yes it was this very sacrifice that enabled [her] to enter the patriarchal world and provide a forum for harmonious communication between men and women. Thus, the ancient voice of the matriarchy was able to adapt and grow within the changing times rather than fade away into a past that was no more. However, there are those who perceive Pallas Athena as a symbol of a feminine goddess who sold out to the patriarchy.[8]

We might arrive at the conclusion that in this combination of Warrior and Goddess there is a distinct inherent hierarchal relationship of a feminine strength that has capitulated and assimilated with the victor warrior energies of the invading class.

Interestingly, of the 24 charts of feminists that I have researched, every one of whom had strong Eris in their charts, fully 21 had a strong Pallas as well, many with Eris in combination. Gloria Steinem has a close conjunction of Pallas and Eris, although out of sign, while Adrienne Rich has a conjunction of less than 2 degrees. Ti-Grace Atkinson, Catharine Mackinnon and Rebecca Walker have close squares between Pallas and Eris, while Kim Gandy has an inconjunct to within 1/10 of a degree. Mary Wollstonecraft has a trine of less than 2 degrees.

Another archetype of the mistrusted and rebellious feminine that is also related to the issue of patriarchy versus feminine power is the figure of Lilith from ancient Babylonian and Hebrew mythology. In Hebrew tradition, Lilith is the rejected first wife of Adam, who argued with him over issues of equality between the sexes. She was worshipped in ancient Babylonia as the handmaiden of Innana and also viewed with distrust as the archetype of wild and uncontrolled sexuality. She is associated with the withdrawal of the goddess in favor of the patriarchy, was at some point expunged from the bible, except for one reference in Isaiah, and was regarded as a rejected part of femininity that was wild and free, aligning herself with no man, choosing to obey neither Yahweh nor husband, instead consorting with demons and tempting men in their sleep to release their seed which she utilized to bear demon babies.

Lilith represents an important piece of the feminine that has been lost or even shunned in modern patriarchal society. She has thus come to represent the principle of equality between the sexes, being also associated with raw sexual power and its spiritual use as in Tantric practice. Just as Pallas Athena has come in modern times to represent the feminine archetype of warrior goddess living in uneasy truce within the patriarchal society, Lilith has been represented as the archetype that attaches to various forms of Dark Moon. There is also an asteroid that bears the name of Lilith. The one representation that has received most credence as the best representation to work with in modern Western Humanistic astrology is the one called Black Moon Lilith. This is actually a mystical point within the Moon's orbit, the empty of her two foci, rather than an actual astronomical body.[9]

Of the feminist charts that I examined, many had strong Black Moon Lilith as well. For example, Gloria Steinem has Lilith semi-square Chiron, square Mars, bi-quintile Saturn, and square Jupiter. Mary Wollstonecraft has Lilith trine Chiron, sesquiquadrate Mercury, inconjunct the Moon and square the nodal axis. Olympe de Gouges has Lilith semi-sextile Chiron, square Mars, bi-quintile Saturn and square Jupiter. Elizabeth Cady Stanton has Lilith semi-square Mars, trine Jupiter, and quintile Neptune. The rather rebellious Andrea Dworkin has Lilith square the Sun, conjunct the South Node, trine Pluto and opposed to Uranus.

Now let us turn to the examination of another example of Warrior Goddess archetype in the mythologies of the world.

Hindu Goddesses – Kali and Durga

Athena has ancient roots, going back to the African continent. Many other cultures have expressed warrior goddess figures; one of the most interesting being the Vedic culture of India. Amongst the plethora of gods and goddesses in the Hindu religion, two stand out as primary warrior goddesses: Kali and Durga.

In some classic Hindu iconography the Ten Mahavidyas are shown surrounding the image of the most powerful warrior goddess, Durga. The myth of the creation of Durga is of great consequence for this study of Eris. By most accounts, Durga was a special creation of the existing gods and goddesses to defeat a variety of demons, including the great demon Mahishasura. In the myth of her creation is revealed her purpose, namely to defeat those passions of the egoic state that are too intractable to be handled by softer means.

In order to banish demonic forces that were taking over the earthly environment the gods and goddesses got together and created a being of light. All their energy poured into her. She had to be strong to defeat the Buffalo demon called Mahishasura that was laying waste to the world, and that the male gods were powerless to injure. This represents the overweening power of the ego. When the battle was joined, it raged for days. Durga viciously attacked, and even though the demon shape-shifted many times, turning into different animals and warriors, she was always ready to strike the next blow with her ten arms holding her various weapons, until the demon lay dead.[10]

This symbolizes that Durga is created to be a fierce and totally unstoppable militant goddess, because it takes everything to slay the demon of ego lodged within the human personality. For a traditional Hindu picture of Durga, see the frontispiece of this book.

It is important to note that, like Eris, Durga has her light-filled and as well her darker side. The goddess Kali is considered to be one of the many manifestations of Durga, and she is dark indeed. When Durga is in dire need, Kali is said to leap from her forehead, black with rage.

Kali is known as the destroyer, emphasizing death and rebirth, and is depicted as black colored, nude, with a girdle of severed arms around her waist and a necklace of skulls. She stands on a corpse, and in one of her four arms brandishes a scimitar and in another a severed head. She multiplies ten-fold into the "Ten Mahavidyas" who are depicted in various settings, attributes, and mythologies, some quite similar to Kali, such as Tara, and others who are more mild. These multiple forms are often invoked in battles with demons, in support of Kali or of Durga, of whom they are conceived as offshoots or guises.[11]

Kali is terrible in aspect and fierce, and seems a feminine depiction of the third major stage in the Hindu worldview, which consists of principles of Creation (represented by the god Brahma), Maintenance (Vishnu) and Destruction (Shiva). She is associated with Shiva in the myths of her coming into being and, while she stands on a human corpse, she is also associated with Tantric sexuality, perhaps because she represents the ultimate destruction of illusion. In her is seen both the dissolution and as well the origin of life. From descriptions of her wrath and destructive power, it is easy to imagine associating her in Western astrological terms with the archetype of Pluto, who also mercilessly destroys what is no longer working in one's life or within the human psyche. Pluto represents the death that precedes the rebirth, and also the rebirth itself.

It is an extremely interesting thought that Kali and Durga, aspects of each other, dark destroyer and light-filled warrior for soul purpose, as they are represented in Hindu mythology, might be equivalent in Western terms to Pluto and Eris, identical planetary archetypes formed within the darkness of practically interstellar space, the farthest reaches of the solar system, and thus symbolizing the furthest depths of the psyche.

In considering the slayer of ego desires we are of course reminded of the Big Dream of C. G. Jung, in December of 1913, related in the previous chapter. In this dream he stalked and killed the great blond beast Siegfried, which he associated with his own ego desires; Jung thus began his dark night of the soul, and in so doing he found within himself dark as well as light-filled powers.

The Inner Demon

In his researches into his own unconscious as recorded in *The Red Book*, C. G. Jung found that when he looked deep inside himself, he found an evil presence, an element of darkness as well as of light. In one passage, quoted in the preceding chapter, he cried out against this darkness within him, and swore to wrestle with the demon he encountered there.

> I have evidently taken on a completely monstrous form in which I can no longer recognize myself. It seems to me that I have become a monstrous animal form for which I have exchanged my humanity. This way is surrounded by hellish magic, invisible nooses have been thrown over me and ensnare me.
>
> But the spirit of the depths approached me and said, "Climb down into your depths, sink!"
>
> …
>
> "Come close, I am ready. Ready, my soul, you who are a devil, to wrestle with you. You donned the mask of a God and I worshiped you. Now you don the mask of a devil, a frightful one, the mask of the banal, of eternal mediocrity! … the lust for battle burns in my limbs."[12]

There are profound implications here, as I have shown, for our current exploration of the dark gods within the depths of the human psyche, as symbolized by the astrological archetypes of Pluto, Chiron and now Eris. As a culture we are learning how to live with these darker places we encounter within ourselves, and this is one of the valuable contributions of both Eva Pierrakos and her Pathwork Foundation, and of Clarissa Pinkola Estés in *Women Who Run With the Wolves*.

The Wild Woman Archetype

In the compendium of tales and folk legends that comprise her well-known study, Clarissa Pinkola Estés brings forward some of these same archetypal ideas. I will give three examples from the stories that she here reveals, ones that shed the most light on the issues thus far elucidated. They are "Bluebeard" – the first major story in the book – "The Crescent Moon Bear," and "The Handless Maiden."

In "Bluebeard" a young princess gets married to a charismatic stranger, whose beard is so black as to seem almost blue. In the story that Estés relates he turns out to be a killer, which she identifies as a person she calls "the natural predator" that we find inside all of us, and that must somehow be contained and managed. She asks what we as a culture can do with "those inner beings who are quite mad ... who carry out destruction without a thought." In the story, the man that the youngest of three sisters marries seems harmless at first, although in the very beginning of the story he is identified as a "failed magician" and a "giant man with an eye for women" so that we have clues that everything is not completely safe. This story turns on an exaggerated type that is actually common, in milder form, throughout patriarchal Western culture, the male who preys on the more physically helpless female. There are various symbolic characters in the tale, in the form of the two older sisters, who represent the wisdom of mature womanhood, and also the three sisters' brothers, who represent the enlightened male energy that is available to rush to the defense of the central character. All the characters can also be thought of as representative of parts of the self, as Estés also notes.

After marrying, the youngest sister finds herself alone in the castle one day with an enormous key ring and invites her older sisters over to explore. These older and wiser ones discover a small door in the basement that only one small key will open – the key the magician has told her never to use. Inside the room lies a horror – the remains of all of Bluebeard's other wives in their gore. She hurriedly shuts the door only to find that the key is now bleeding too, and nothing that she can do will stop it. By the time the difficult husband returns she has stained all her gowns with blood. He guesses immediately what she has found and threatens to kill her, as well, but she begs for time. In the interval her older brothers arrive and slay the monster that she had married without knowing the depth of his evil.

It is important to recognize that while the story puts the locus of evil "out there" in the person of the predator, Bluebeard, and in one way can be seen as a cautionary tale that warns young girls not to be fooled, in another way the story is about the parts of every human psyche that have their dark and predator-like elements. Similar to the myth of Durga from Hindu legend, as referenced above, there has to be a valiant energy that rises up in response to an inner demon and takes forceful charge, as the brothers do in this story. The Eris archetype, representing a dark and possibly vengeful or difficult part of the psyche is at once both the problem and the solution. Eris can rise up to slay the egoic desire that has gotten out of hand, when manifesting from the highest principle of soul. This might require summoning up violent warrior instincts from within, symbolized by the brothers who come in the nick of time and hack the evil magus to pieces. This is in its essence a feminine warrior energy that is summoned, motivated not by blood lust but by deep and dire need.

She goes on to give a further example in another story. This involves the feminine psyche becoming skilled at how to work with various energies within her, including rage, or learning to be able to soothe the rage of others. All this is beautifully summed up in her analysis of the Japanese tale called "The Crescent Moon Bear."

The story concerns a young woman married to a man who returns from the war soul-weary and emotionally battered. He refuses her offers of food and sleeps out of the house as he is used to doing. In his rage he frightens her away as she attempts to succor him, and so she decides to seek assistance from the healer of the village. She asks the healer for a potion, but the healer tells her she lacks a key ingredient, and sends her up the mountain to the caves above the tree line, to pluck one white hair from the chest of the Crescent Moon Bear, who lives in this desolate place.

She has to climb a tall mountain and undergo many trials along the way. She eats little, because the food that she has with her is part of her plan. When she discovers the cave of the Crescent Moon Bear she puts the food out day after day, getting a little closer each time. Finally she stands right beside the food, so that this time, when the bear comes out of his cave to eat, he found her there, trembling but unafraid. "The bear turned its head sideways and roared so loud it made the bones in the woman's body hum… but she did not run away."[13]

The bear eventually decides that, because this woman has been good to him, he will give her one of the hairs from the crescent moon at his throat. She plucks it out. He growls and turns away. She comes down the mountain and back with her prize to the healer's cottage. The healer pronounces it a true hair from the chest of the Crescent Moon Bear, then suddenly turns and throws it into the fire. Of course the wife is surprised and hurt, but the healer explains that in going through her trials and in learning how to handle the bear, she has learned how to handle her husband as well.

In her analysis that follows, Ms. Estés makes clear that this in not really a story about how to deflect the rage lurking within the angry male psyche; the characters in this tale represent parts of the woman's own psyche. She refers to "woman's rage" and states that there is a way to master it, as in the story. And there is also a time to let it out as well. She says that repressing it will not work, that there is in actuality a place for "right rage," the time when violent action is necessary. In bringing in this element, she touches on a central theme of the Eris archetype, representing the feminine warrior that must take action, when action is necessary. Interestingly, Estés labels the parameters for rage-full action very carefully. "It has to be a serious offence; the offence has to be big, and against the soul or spirit. All other reasonable avenues for change have to be attempted first."[14]

145

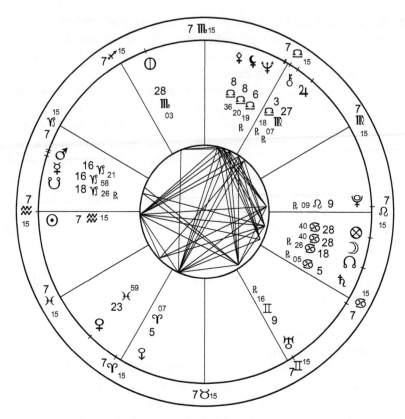

Fig. 9-1 Clarissa Pinkola Estés, January 27, 1945, Sunrise Chart,
Indianapolis, Indiana, USA 39N46 86W09

The relevance of the ideas that Ms Estés, in her Jungian fashion, brings forward to the Eris archetype is unmistakable, especially regarding deep process and the darker portions of the human psyche. I was convinced that she would prove to possess strong Eris. Her solar chart is shown above.

This chart is yet another example of suspecting strong Eris and then finding it. In showing it here, I have chosen to additionally display the major asteroid Pallas Athena, plus Lilith (this is Black Moon Lilith). Not only is Eris quite strong in this chart, but also it is opposite a quadruple conjunction of Chiron, Neptune, Lilith and Pallas.

We first of all note the T-square between Eris, Neptune and Saturn, focused on Saturn. It is also of great interest to see that Neptune is accompanied by a very close Pallas-Lilith conjunction. As referenced earlier, these are two archetypes of Western astrology that, like Eris, express both a dangerous side of feminine rage-full experience – encapsulated in the very nature of the Lilith archetype – and also the clever and assimilated warrior as symbolized by the goddess Athena and the asteroid Pallas.

The square between Eris and Saturn is particularly close, indicating one who absolutely cannot stand to silently witness iniquity without taking action of some kind as we find in many of the charts for women who feel compelled to fight for fairness and equality, most especially throughout the feminist movement of the nineteenth and twentieth centuries. Estés definitely represents one who in her work cries out against injustice. In her chart, Eris is also in a close sextile to the Sun, and trines Pluto and perhaps the Moon as well. This is appropriate symbolism for the shadow material that she brings forth directly from the unconscious (Moon and Pluto are both symbolic of unconscious process). The combination of Neptune and Saturn, here greatly emphasized by the presence of Eris, speaks of bringing the numinous realms beyond the purely physical down into concrete mani-festation, as indeed Ms. Estés has done.

With the Libra conjunction of Neptune and Pallas, an over-arching di-plomacy of spirit is indicated that enables negotiation with all kinds of energies, as this author demonstrates in her work with written and spoken word. Although the natal connection between Eris and Mercury is wide, it is quite interesting that the writing of this book was characterized by transiting Eris in close square with natal Mercury. The audio version was a best seller in 1989 before the date of print publication in 1992. She must have been in preparation for years. The first exact hit of transiting Eris to natal Mercury was a station in the summer of 1987. The entire date range summary of the Eris transit is as follows:

Transiting Eris in square with natal Mercury within 1 degree:
From May 24, 1984 to August 29, 1984
From April 30, 1985 to September 26, 1985
From April 7, 1986 to October 20, 1986
From March 18, 1987 to November 16, 1987:
    exact July 13, 1987 SR
From February 20, 1988 to June 9, 1992:
    exact May 31, 1988; August 24, 1988 R;
    exact May 5, 1989; September 22, 1989 R; April 13, 1990;
    exact October 16, 1990 R; March 23, 1991;
    exact November 11, 1991 R; February 27, 1992
From August 16, 1992 to May 12, 1993:
    exact December 21, 1992 R; January 17, 1993

No further exact hits; within 1 degree off and on until early 1997.

As you can see, this time period squares nicely with the writing, performing and publication of this classic work that represents so fully an articulation of the Eris archetype on the part of Ms Estés, and has come to define her ideas to the world as she developed in her own sense of her soul purpose.

The Handless Maiden

The final story that I would reference out of *Women Who Run With the Wolves* is the very last one in the book, called "The Handless Maiden." The story itself is a difficult one, and has similarities to the myth of Inanna – in which the goddess must descend to the underworld, losing everything, in order to come into the light of higher knowledge and the consciousness of her own power. It involves a maiden, encumbered by naiveté and a false father, traveling from girlhood to a life with her eventual husband. It is the story of the trials that she endured as she was forced to deal with the Devil himself.

The story begins with a miller, his wife and his beloved daughter. They had fallen on hard times and the miller had only the firewood left to depend on, that he gathered from the forest. One day while walking through the woods, carrying his axe, the miller came upon on old man, who stepped out from behind a tree and accosted him, saying "There's no need for you to torture yourself by cleaving wood. I shall dress you in riches if you will but give me what stands behind your mill."[15] Since behind the decrepit mill was only a flowering apple tree, the miller readily agreed. But he didn't know that he had just made a pact with the Devil. What he had forgotten was that his daughter, too, was behind the mill, sweeping.

When the Devil returns for the girl however, in some three years time, she has deceived him by placing herself, with clean hands and wearing a white dress, inside a magic circle drawn from chalk. The Devil cannot take her. He tells the miller that she must not bathe, and she does not, but the sweet rain of her tears cleanses her hands and the Devil, still, cannot take her. Finally he tells the miller that he must cut off his own daughter's hands, on pain of destruction of the entire village and its surroundings; the miller reluctantly agrees, sharpening his silver-tipped axe, and it is done. In the end, however, her tears again save her, washing clean the handless stubs of her arms. Now the Devil is defeated, but, her life in tatters, the girl leaves home to wander the world, as a beggar.

This is a story with tremendous symbolic resonance, a coming-of-age story with the elements of betrayal by the father, and of the remnants of the old goddess religion that are expressed in the chalk circle, the white garment and the silver-tipped axe that is utilized to maim her. The young woman realizes that she needs to leave everything behind and venture out into the world on her own. As she does so, she eventually comes upon a magic garden belonging to the King, where a tree grows that has sweet fruit. She helps herself to some of the fruit, with the aid of a spirit that graces her by its presence. When the King finds out about the theft he watches by night and spies upon her, and in the course of this he falls in love and marries her, and has silver hands made for her. But then he has to go away to fight a war.

So here is another in the stages of life's journey. After leaving home, and making her way, and finding a mate, a woman must yet deal with dependency. What if the man were gone? In fact she has a baby, and sends a message to the King, but the messenger falls asleep and a substitute message from the Devil tells the King bad news about the child. The messages continue to be scrambled, including a false one purportedly from the King that tells the servants to kill the Queen and her child. And so the young woman leaves, being forced to wander the world again, with her child, finally winding up in a wild forest. A woman in white bids her enter and cares for her and her child for seven long years, during which time her hands grow back again. Meanwhile the King, after returning home and finding her gone, has had to wander the world himself in search of her, in his lonely quest, until at last, after seven years, he comes to the same wild wood. When the King stumbles upon her he hardly recognizes her; but she has the silver hands locked away in a trunk, and so he realizes that it is she, and they are reunited.

This figure of seven years is an important number, the length of time it takes all the cells of the body to regenerate, they say, and the quarter period of Saturn, by conjunction, square and opposition, that great maturing influence. This was also the period of time documented by Gail Sheehy in her chronicle of struggle and change called *Passages*. In this regard it is interesting to note the extremely close square between Saturn and Eris in Clarissa Estés' chart.

In her analysis of this final story of her *Women Who Run With the Wolves* saga, Estés divides her analysis into seven parts as well; seven stages of the story. In her detailed descriptions of the symbolism contained within this tale, she refers to the archetypal wildness of the woman's spirit, which in the end is her salvation. When the Devil forces her to go unwashed and uncivilized, she is pushed closer to her fierce and wild nature, thus saving herself. Later in the story it is the woods that become her refuge. She also makes reference to the silver-tipped axe that cuts off the daughter's hands, as a symbol of the goddess worship of the olden times. This is a difficult part of the story, symbolizing a complete loss, the dark night of the soul, the nigredo, reminding us of the myth of Inanna – who lost everything in her descent into the underworld, a passage that permitted her to in time ascend stronger into the light of day. This also represents the dire beauty and the finality of the will encapsulated within the Eris archetype, the implacable destruction of whatever stands in the way of soul purpose.

When the King has had his own set of difficulties and is reunited with his queen, now healed, the story has its happy ending. Both have been strengthened by their time of trial. Estés makes the point that they have been made more whole by a touch of the wild spirit that all along lay deep within them.

In this modern retelling of the Warrior Goddess mythology by Estés, we have another excellent expression of the Eris archetype and a representation of the way of synthesis, in combining the concepts represented by Goddess and Warrior in their most fitting unity.

The Devil is a horrific figure in the story, forcing a father to cut off the hands of his own daughter in attempt to have her for himself. In one way, he is a character outside of the heroic feminine warrior represented by the maiden, and yet, in another he is merely a familiar part of the human psyche, as Jung has described. Recognizing that all these elements have psychic equivalents, we must thus conceive of the Devil character, as was also depicted in the Bluebeard tale, as some part of the human psyche that has energy for lust and destruction. This part of oneself equally might be able to be reclaimed from its outcast nature by the more conscious personality facing this energy and acknowledging its presence, flawed though it might be. And this is certainly one value of the story's retelling.

This work is similar to the astrological counseling work that can be done by utilizing the Chiron archetype of The Wounded Healer. Eris is now emerging as a Western archetype that reflects yet another aspect of depth psychology, not so much concerned with early wounding, but rather with soul intention that has been set aside, and which might exhibit dark tendencies, at least until more consciously acknowledged. The dark places within us result in what C. G. Jung, who had prominent Eris, called 'complexes' within the psyche. He felt that one task of the individuation process was to make these unconscious and disregarded parts of the psyche more consciously available, thus creating greater integration and wholeness. Facing these walled-off parts of ourselves then becomes a powerful road to healing.

Another important voice in this work of recognizing the dark places within us and bringing them into the light of consciousness is represented by Eva

Pierrakos. She was born in the early 20th century, and became a channel for an entity that came to be called The Guide. There were over 200 quite remarkable lectures that taught the examination of deep unconscious material and the acceptance of whatever is found in the hidden spaces within, dark or light. She eventually went on to create the Pathwork Foundation with her husband John C. Pierrakos.

The material that she brings forward in her many lectures reveal the darker side of the human psyche as a valuable component that is routinely overlooked or shunted aside by the more conscious personality. One of the books that came to be published is in fact called *Fear No Evil*, and quotes C. G. Jung on the point of acknowledging the darker material as well as the light-filled: "Human nature is capable of an infinite amount of evil. ... psychology must insist on the reality of evil and must reject any definition that regards it as insignificant or actually nonexistent."[16] The matching quote from the Pathwork lectures would be:

> You will see that by denying the evil in you, you do greater harm to the whole of your personality, to your manifest spirituality, than you realize. For by denying it, you inactivate an essential part of your energies and creative forces, so they stagnate... When evil is understood to be intrinsically a divine energy flow, momentarily distorted due to specific wrong ideas, concepts and perceptions, then it is no longer rejected in its essence.[17]

Because this material channeled by Eva Pierrakos makes such a close match with the treatment in the work of Jung and other Erisians of the concept of a dark as well as a light-filled god within the depths of the psyche, in close symbolic chime with the Eris archetype as we are coming to understand it, I was interested to see her birth map. Would her chart reveal a strong presence of Eris I wondered, or merely the signature of a clear channel for such material from the presence of the transcendent being beyond her?

We actually have a time of birth, provided by noted financial astrologer Bill Meridian. Her chart is given on the following page.

Indeed this Eris placement is remarkable, and speaks as well to the channeled nature of the material. We find Eris elevated in the chart, in a partile opposition to the Moon and a partile trine with Neptune, as is entirely appropriate for psychic communication beyond the bounds of the physical plane. This is quite a lovely statement of correspondence between her material and the Eris archetype. Additionally, this placement of Neptune is in partile conjunction with the stated rising degree of her chart. As if

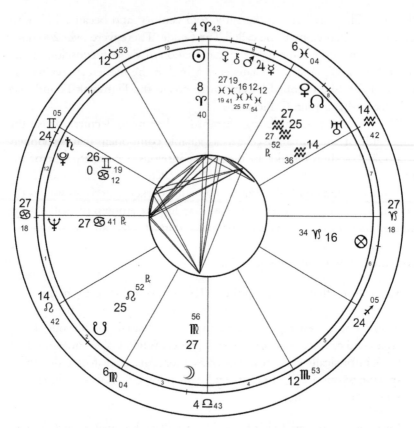

Fig. 9-2 Eva Pierrakos, March 30, 1915, 11:45 CET, Vienna, Austria

that were not enough, we could add that the Venus placement in her chart, conjunct her North Node, located in the eighth house of depth work, and ruling her eleventh house of group activities, is also in partile aspect with the Eris, Moon, Neptune and her Rising degree.

The chart of Eva Pierrakos therefore represents another neat statement of the symbolic chime between Eris and the recognition of a dark and potentially destructive energy within, as shown by the Pathwork Foundation's featured subject matter of depth work that includes a dark or even what might be considered an "evil" element, along with the light-filled side. This is similar to the famous formulation made by Blake, that "everything that lives is holy." In Eva Pierrakos, then, we have, as shown in her chart, and by her life-long dedication to this work, another iconic exemplar of the Eris archetype as spiritual warrior.

Notes

1. This excerpt from The Guide is quoted in *Fear No Evil*, p. 132, Eva Pierrakos and Donovan Thesenga.
2. *Women Who Run With the Wolves*, pp. 4-5.
3. Kerenyi, *Athena*, pp. 5-15.
4. Kerenyi, *Athena*, pp. 19-22.
5. *The Chalice And The Blade*, pp. 78-79.
6. *Asteroid Goddesses*, p. 84.
7. ibid pp. 84-85.
8. ibid pp. 90-92.
9. Perhaps the best reference work on the various forms of Lilith in modern Western Astrology is Kelly Hunter's *Living Lilith: Four Dimensions of the Cosmic Feminine*. Demetra George has also written a nice description of the mythology of Lilith in *Mysteries of the Dark Moon*. For commentary regarding specifically Black Moon Lilith I am indebted to Lynn Bell – personal communication.
10. http://www.esotericonline.net/profiles/blogs/archetypal-durga
11. *Tantric Visions of the Divine Feminine*, pp. 22-38.
12. *Red Book*, p. 241.
13. *Women Who Run With Wolves*, p. 349.
14. ibid p. 361.
15. ibid p. 390.
16. from *Aion*, quoted in *Psyche and Symbol*, edited by V. S. de Lazlo, Doubleday, New York, 1958, pp. 49-50.
17. Pathwork lecture #184, online:
http://pathwork.org/lectures/the-meaning-of-evil-and-its-transcendence/

10

Further and Deeper – More Examples

The Second World War presented a mirror to the human condition which blinded anyone who looked into it. For if tens of millions were killed in concentration camps out of the inexorable agonies and contractions of super-states founded upon the always insoluble contradictions of injustice, one was then obliged also to see that no matter how crippled and perverted an image of man was the society he had created, it was nonetheless his creation, his collective creation (at least his collective creation from the past) and if society was so murderous, then who could ignore the most hideous of questions about his own nature?

Norman Mailer[1]

Angelina Jolie

As our delineation of Eris continues, we come to a better vantage point to go further into some of the charts we have been examining. We begin with one that I have used many times in talks and discussions, and to which I have referred briefly in Chapter 2, namely the chart of Angelina Jolie.

As mentioned in the earlier chapter, the triple conjunction of Eris, Moon and Mars, located near the top of the chart (see following page), is exemplified in her career, and she has often played the female warrior on screen. (The tight triple conjunction is trine to Neptune, representing image and film.) Because the Aries stellium of five planets lies mostly in her ninth house, she is also a thoughtful person constantly seeking a higher perspective that will match her soul purpose desire for understanding. With her political activism, corresponding also to her eleventh house Sun, and her charity work in foreign lands, as befits that strong ninth house placement of nurturing Moon, she has many different sides to her nature, a complex personality.

Because we know that the Moon and its symbolism of mothering is emphasized by its elevated position and close conjunction with Eris, we would also surmise that this lady is involved in some potentially extreme manifestation of nurturing and motherhood, as is the case. In spite of her high-profile film and philanthropic career, Angelina Jolie is the mother of six, having adopted several children from the third world. The third world

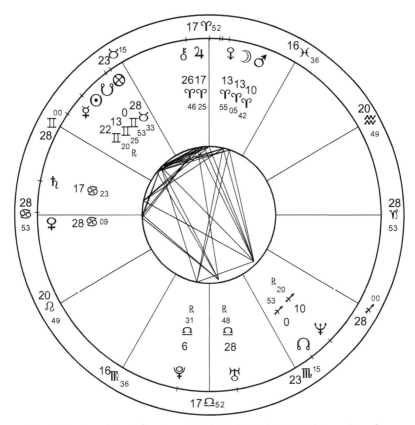

Fig. 10-1 Angelina Jolie, June 4, 1975, 9:09 AM PDT, Los Angeles,
California, USA 34N03 118W15

source of her three adoptive children is another refection of the ninth
house Moon-Eris conjunction.

In a symbol that represents the fierceness of the Eris archetype in combination with nurturing Moon, she wears a tattoo on her abdomen reading
"quod me nutrit me destruit" ('what nourishes me destroys me').

In describing Eris in this book thus far, I have often referred to the degree
of ruthlessness involved in this archetype; true Erisians will stop at nothing
for a cause to which they are, at soul-level, committed. We saw evidence of
this commitment regarding Ms. Jolie in May 2013, when she announced her
preventative double mastectomy that had been performed three months
earlier. She had this done because she felt she was likely to develop breast
cancer. She had discovered that she possessed the BRCA1 gene, which car-
ries the high-risk prognosis. Her stated reason was her motherhood; she did
not want to run the risk that her children would have to grow up without
a mother, as she herself had. She had lost her own mother to cancer. Her

open letter published in *The New York Times* on Mother's Day, May 14, 2013, said "My chances of developing breast cancer have dropped from 87 percent to under 5 percent. I can tell my children that they don't need to fear they will lose me to breast cancer." Since the Moon rules the breasts as well as motherhood, and since the Eris-Moon partile conjunction – symbolizing intense and implacable soul-purpose surrounding issues of motherhood – has also Mars, ruling surgery, nearby, her decision to undergo elective breast surgery for the cause of a higher purpose, namely to emotionally support her children, is a precise match for the archetypal combination.

On the day of the surgery, and in the months that followed leading up to the announcement on Mother's Day, transiting Pluto was at 10 or 11 degrees of Capricorn, squaring her Eris-Moon-Mars triple conjunction. Transiting Eris over the same time period was about 21½ degrees of Aries to 22½. This is a significant transit because her Jupiter and Chiron, 9 degrees from each other in the tenth house, have their midpoint at 22 Aries 05. The symbolism of this midpoint could be described as a radical philosophical stance that runs counter to prevailing beliefs, together with the pain of making choices that accord with this more particularized way of seeing things. Eris in transit to this midpoint would magnify this position and also reflect back on the natal position of Eris, so precisely symbolically resonant with the choice that she found the strength within herself to make for the sake of her vitally important role as mother.

The ninth house placement of Eris is particularly interesting for Jolie in view of the emphasis in her life on foreign travel, diplomacy, and education. She was early drawn to serious schooling, studying in her teens at the Lee Strasberg Theater Institute, and later attending New York University for filmmaking and writing. Her humanitarian accomplishments are well known, and she was named Goodwill Ambassador for the U.N. Refugee Agency in 2001, and received the Global Humanitarian Action Award for her activist stance for refugee rights. The movie that she wrote and directed, *In the Land of Blood and Honey*, is another example of both her interest in humanitarian causes and her fascination with a life or death struggle for survival with a foreign point of view, since it refers to the travails of the Muslim population of Serbia during the Bosnian war of the 1990s. This would come to be true as well for her next film as a director, *Unbroken*, released just as this book was going to press, about an athlete who, as a Japaneese prisoner during WWII, was able to stand up to torture in a foreign land. The plot of this second film that she has directed therefore has themes of inner strength of character and violence, as well as foreign culture, that also reflect her prominent ninth house Eris placement.

Woody Allen

Another famous American filmmaker, and an extremely prolific one as well, Woody Allen has been under siege recently because of his rather quirky personal life and his fascination with younger women. At 41 he was dating a seventeen year old, the inspiration for his film *Manhattan*, in which he starred along with Mariel Hemingway, and for which he was nominated for an Academy Award in 1978 for the screen play. It was his second such nomination of a total of fifteen for best original screenplay over the course of his lifetime thus far.

In 1991 he began an affair with Soon-yi Previn, whom he wound up marrying. She was about 19 at the time, the adoptive daughter of his then-girlfriend, the actor Mia Farrow. This landed him in considerable hot water; Mr. Allen insists however that his involvement was a simple story of falling in love. "The heart wants what it wants. You meet someone and you fall in love and that's that."[2] Mia Farrow was understandably upset and subsequently hurled accusations of child molestation involving their younger daughter, Dylan. Mr. Allen has steadily asserted that the purported molestation never took place, and indeed was never charged. A panel of experts concluded that the most likely explanation was coaching of the then-seven-year-old Dylan Farrow, their adoptive daughter, by a distraught and vengeful mother. As of the time of this writing, in early 2014, Woody Allen has been happily married to Soon-yi Previn for almost sixteen years, and they have two adoptive children of their own. The recent press has not been easy for him, as these allegations have resurfaced.

Mr. Allen has an eighth house Eris (see chart on following page), as befits someone for whom issues of sexuality and intimacy, as well as death, have been a fundamental part of his nature, and the nature of his art. Murder comes up in his movies with a fair degree of regularity. Many movies have also been made by him featuring beautiful women and in many cases with himself in the leading romantic role, even when he was far too old for a convincing portrayal. The youth factor might be indicated by his Mercury-Jupiter conjunction in Jupiter's own sign of Sagittarius, in a close trine with the Eris placement. Note that Mercury signifies youth, while Jupiter is co-ruler of both his seventh and eighth house cusps of partnership and intimate connection.

Mr. Allen has made a career out of portraying the classic nebbish, a worrier about everything, and for his amazing sense of humor. This latter is indicated by the Uranus-Mercury inconjunct, an aspect shored up by Eris in a nearly exact semi-sextile to Uranus and in trine with Mercury. As far as the worrier – rather than the warrior – archetype, he notably has Chiron at

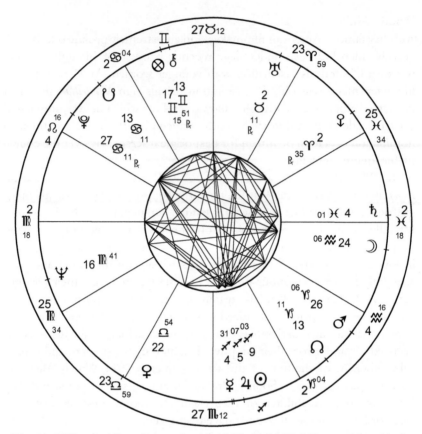

Fig. 10-2 Woody Allen, December 1, 1935, 10:55 PM, Bronx, New York, USA 40N51, 73W54

the top of his chart, in the tenth house of career, opposite his Sun degree and in quintile with Eris.

On January 13th, 1992, Woody Allen's relationship with Mia Farrow fell apart when she discovered via a collection of nude photographs on his mantle that he had been cheating on her with her 19-year-old adoptive daughter. Perhaps appropriately for a situation in which the true motivations are far from clear, transiting Neptune was exactly trine Woody Allen's natal Neptune – his seventh house ruler. Transiting Eris was also exactly inconjunct his Neptune, exact to within a few minutes of zodiacal longitude, indicating that a juncture of his life destiny had been reached. It is interesting to note that Neptune also rules photographic images.

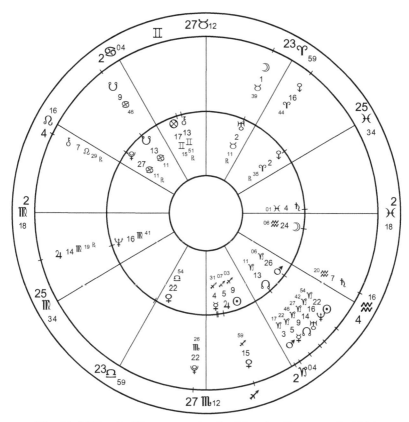

Fig. 10-3 Woody Allen - transits for Monday, January 13, 1992,
12:00 PM PST

The other more recent surfacing of the scandal took place on February 1st, 2014 in response to his being given a lifetime achievement award in the Golden Globe awards ceremony of January 12th. The transits for these two dates feature transiting Neptune in an almost exact conjunction with his natal Saturn, also his fifth house ruler.

The repeat accusations of molestation brought forward by his former adoptive daughter touched off a storm of commentary in the press; just as the Academy Awards were a little more than a month away, affecting his reputation. At the time of the re-emergence of the scandal, on February 1st, transiting Sun, Moon, Chiron, Jupiter, and Pluto in conjunction with a stationary Venus all closely aspected his natal Chiron in the tenth, hallmark of his career and also an indication of the pain that these recent allegations have caused him.

This day of allegations resurfacing in connection with his lifetime achievement award was an attack on him personally and his social standing and professional reputation. This is shown by the transit of Eris in close opposition, within one degree, to his natal Venus, which rules his tenth house of professional reputation. Transiting Mars was also in conjunction with his natal Venus that day, within one half degree, and parallel, triggering the longer lasting Eris transit.

In both sets of recent transits, for his Golden Globe award on January 12th, 2014, and for February 1st, Eris closely opposed his natal Venus, his Midheaven ruler, and was touched off on the awards ceremony evening by a fairly close square from transiting Sun (in conjunction with retrograde Venus) to transiting Eris and to his natal Venus, so hitting both endpoints of this important transit that signified this career-defining moment in his life. Especially considering the awards ceremony transit including retrograde Venus, this is an appropriate symbol for the retrospective award for his life's work, with the Eris piece an indication of how Woody Allen was following his sense of his own soul purpose in making the films that he made, in many cases defying the conventions of a conservative viewpoint, as with *Manhattan* and also *Annie Hall*. His nebbish character, similar to Chaplin's little tramp figure, has amused and bemused millions and become an iconographic character that constitutes a leitmotif running throughout his work.

Clint Eastwood

Another filmmaker of a different stripe, known for his lone warrior stance, as appropriate for the Eris archetype, would be Clint Eastwood. In a career that has spanned over five decades his early reputation for roles of tough masculinity has blossomed in his later years to the making of such acclaimed films as *Mystic River, Million Dollar Baby*, and 1992's *Unforgiven*, arguably one of the best Westerns ever made. He has portrayed the competent loner, spiritual and implacable warrior who takes no prisoners but always fights for ultimate justice, the man who can take care of anything. He demonstrated that character in real life in a recent case when, at 82, at the golf tournament he helps to run every year in Pebble Beach, California, he saved a man who could not breathe by repeated executions of the Heimlich maneuver.

We can see from his chart that Eris is located in the fifth house of artistic self-expression. As might be expected from a self-made personality, Eris is strong in this chart, connected to personal planets and to Chiron, and being the leader of the planetary pattern focused on Saturn. Eris is inconjunct Neptune, ruling filmmaking, at the top of his chart, square his Venus-Saturn opposition, and semi-square his Chiron, located on the descendant. As Chiron there would indicate, he is difficult to handle in relationship,

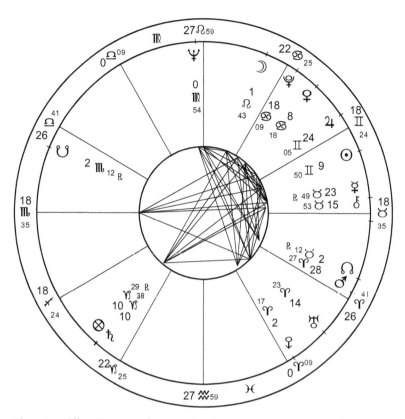

Fig. 10-4 Clint Eastwood, May 31, 1930, 5:35 PM PST, San Francisco, California, USA 37N46 122W25

being a serial monogamist into his eighties. Moreover, Eris makes a close trine aspect to his Moon, located in and ruler of the ninth or higher-mind sector of his chart, and also connects to his Mars, as his almost over-the-top masculine persona might lead us to expect, via the nearly exact semi-sextile to his North Node, which is conjunct Mars in the sixth house. As the strong Eris-Moon indicates, there is also more to him than meets the eye. Eastwood is an acclaimed composer, as well as a director and filmmaker. His acting too has its softer side. In *The Bridges of Madison County*, he portrayed a sensitive photographer to Meryl Streep's equally romantic turn as his muse. Fellow actor Justin Timberlake described what it was like working with him. "He's built an iconic leading-man persona out of that tough and gruff thing but he's really like a teddy bear... so disarming."[3]

Eastwood's musical talent is shown by his close Eris aspect with Neptune, and also with Mercury, which it closely septiles, thus bringing together a combination classically indicative of musical ability. Having won Academy

Awards for his scores, he was in later life an honoree Doctor of Music from the Berklee College of Music.

The Eris placement therefore gives us a more total picture of his character, which has a softness not ordinarily recognized. The masculine presence of his standard screen persona is shown by his Mars in conjunction with his North Node in the sixth house, in trine to Neptune and square the Moon. There is image as well as service orientation that is implied. He shows his masculine side in his work, which he definitely has strongly within him as one facet of his personality. This shows up over and over again throughout his career, particularly in the classic Western that he made, the movie *Unforgiven*, for which he won the Academy Award for best picture as well as for best director, an unmistakable stand-out moment in his career. The ultimate meaning of the Mars archetype in Eastwood's screen life is perhaps best revealed in the transits for the date of this Oscar night, March 29th, 1993.

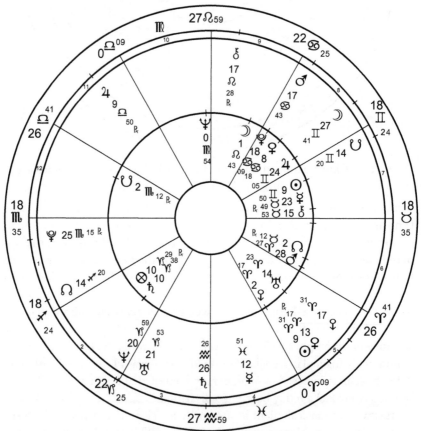

Fig. 10-5 Clint Eastwood, Transits for Monday, Mar 29, 1993,
9:00 PM PST

Transiting Eris is square to transiting Mars within a quarter of a degree, and transiting Mars conjuncts Eastwood's Pluto while Eris squares it. The Eris presence indicates soul purpose, and the stamina required in taking a project so near and dear to his heart to such a successful completion, portraying a gun-slinger from the old West, the role that he started with. The central character goes through much self-examination and deeply motivated changes in the course of the film, which essentially revolves around a plot element of upholding women's honor and the meting out of justice to those who would oppress them.

In this film, which Eastwood had been planning to make for years, there is the violent and masculine struggle to take down the bad guy, as well as violence and death. There is also a higher meaning that includes concepts of transformation and justice, which is indeed one theme of the movie. Noting that his Pluto is opposite his natal Saturn, this is appropriate to the symbolism implied by Eris transiting in square to his natal Pluto and inconjunct his ascendant. This aspect was within 2 degrees, from 1987 through at least 2004, so all through the period of the actual making of the film, and beyond. Transiting Neptune (symbolizing image and the film industry) was also square to transiting Eris during much of this period.

Eastwood has gone on to be nominated for best director honors for *Mystic River* and for *Million Dollar Baby*, as well as for *Letters from Iwo Jima*. These films definitely have their dark sides, are famous for their quality, for portraying moral ambiguity, and were conceived and executed during the time period that transiting Eris was within square of Eastwood's natal Pluto and inconjunct his ascendant.

Million Dollar Baby portrayed a woman warrior, in the person of a female boxer. We might expect an Eris involvement in this, especially since Eastwood went to huge lengths to make this film, putting up half the money. It went on to be acclaimed as a difficult but great American motion picture statement, winning four Oscars. The film was shot in June and July of 2004, when Saturn was transiting Eastwood's natal Pluto in the eighth house, and when Eris was at 20 degrees of Aries, still within two and a half degrees of its square to his natal Pluto and in close trine with both transiting Pluto at 20 degrees of Sagittarius and with Eastwood's progressed Sun at 20 degrees of Leo.

The Eris-Pluto connection is quite appropriately symbolic for the difficult and deeply challenging subject matter of this film, which is essentially an American feminist manifesto, featuring as it does an iconic female main character in her fierce battle for survival, who gives up everything for her quest.

Norman Mailer

We now turn to novelist and famously difficult personality Norman Mailer. A summary of his life:

> It could be said that Norman Mailer was a man and a writer half-way between fame and infamy and yet with little in the way of middle ground. He was, in varying combinations, a world-class drinker, feuder, provocateur, self-mythologizer and anti-feminist. He was a war protester, a mayoral candidate, a co-founder of The Village Voice, as well as a wife stabber, a serial husband (of six wives), and a father (of nine). He was a boxer, an actor, a filmmaker, a poet and a playwright. He was also a journalist and a novelist of enormous and singular narrative inventiveness and thrust, a two-time Pulitzer Prize winner, and one of the least boring and most tireless and tiresome public figures of the last half of the 20th century.[4]

The pugilistic stance with which Norman Mailer took on the world and the difficulty that everyone found in dealing with him, reminded me of the solitary stand of the confirmed and at times violent rebel, the signature of unresolved Eris. I was interested therefore in seeing his chart to verify this.

His documented birth certificate shows the time of birth as 9:05 am, although the Rodden rating for accuracy is given as "C" because his sixth and final wife declared in an interview that he was born at 7:04 am and he confirmed this to his editor stating the time had been altered. Considering his penchant for provocation and confrontation, it is possible that he was simply defending his wife's statement.

There is certainly evidence in his personality to confirm Eris rising (see chart on following page), so this is one case where an understanding of Eris can help in rectifying a chart. The earlier time would place Eris at the beginning of the second rather than the first house without substantially altering any of the aspects that Eris makes, chiefly the close trine to Mailer's Moon.

The trine between Eris and the Moon is evidenced by his close relationship with his mother, who had an extraordinarily powerful personality, and by his life-long fascination with women. He had a total of six wives, one of whom he stabbed in a late-night fight, although she refused to press charges. He also had nine children to whom he remained close.

His career was launched with what some would say was the definitive World War II novel, *The Naked and the Dead*, but his subsequent novels were not as well received. Although never far from the public eye, and a co-founder of the *Village Voice* newspaper, he did not strike literary gold again

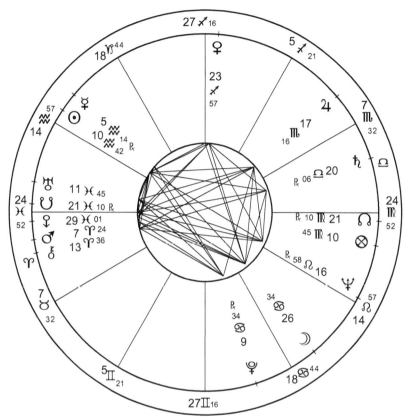

Fig. 10-6 Norman Mailer, January 31, 1923, 9:05 AM EST, Long Branch, New Jersey, USA 40N18 74W00

until his journalistic forays of the Sixties and Seventies, notably *The Armies of the Night* and *Miami and the Siege of Chicago*.

In a way *The Naked and the Dead* also had its journalistic side, reporting from an American soldier's perspective on events of the then-recent war in the South Pacific. Mailer also ran for Mayor of New York and was famous for spotting and reporting on trends before they happened, so that the placement of his Sun and Mercury in the eleventh house of social activism – as in the 9:05 AM birth certificate chart –makes total sense. His natal Eris is in wide orb of a sextile to his natal Mercury (7 degrees). As we have seen many times with prolific writers such as Mailer who deeply feel their purpose as warriors in the world, their expression of a deeply held perspective derives in part from their ability to write and to articulate. The sextile between Mercury and Mars, with Mars in the first and in wide conjunction with Eris rising, would also have the effect of strengthening the Eris-Mercury connection. His most famous writing featured either war or a military motif.

The pain that he described in writing of the events during the closing days of the war in the South Pacific against the Japanese is well symbolized by his Mars-Chiron conjunction in the first. Chiron with Mars indicates a wound to the self-esteem and to self-assertion, as does Chiron in the first. Two days after the publication of his first novel, with the onslaught of positive reviews and it being catapulted to the top of the best-seller list, he remarked, "I think the book may be better than I am."[5]

Regarding the wide Eris-Mars conjunction in his first house, he had a macho persona and loved to box. He was inducted into the army on March 27th, 1944, with transiting Sun and Eris conjunct his Mars. Since he would make his fame as a writer with the success of a war novel, this position of transiting Eris – magnifying the Eris-Mars natal conjunction – makes sense, not only in that he found himself in a military setting, but also in that his stated soul purpose was thereby satisfied. He had declared before his induction that his vision for his term of service was to write the great American war novel, which he then proceeded to accomplish. Note that Eris makes its closest aspect to Mailer's Moon, the ruler of his fifth house of artistic expression.

To see more combat, in order to glean the experience he felt necessary for crafting a war novel, Mailer deliberately volunteered for patrol duty on April 24th, 1945 – the date is recorded in the extensive recent biography of Mailer by J. Michael Lennon. On this date, transiting Mars is nearing the ascendant of the 9:05 AM chart, while transiting Moon in conjunction with transiting Chiron is opposing his natal Eris. The Moon opposition to natal Eris is exact at 2:15 PM his local time, in the Philippines, while the angular distance between transiting Chiron and natal Eris is little more than a degree, and transiting Mars is a degree and a half away from closing in on the ascendant, using the 9:05 AM time from his published birth certificate.

The actual writing for this project took place principally over the two summers that followed his discharge from the army, 1946 and 1947, as the conjunction between transiting Eris and his natal Mars became closer. He began writing in June of 1946. When Eris stationed retrograde a little more than half a degree from approaching his natal Mars, in the summer of 1946, he was getting into a stint of writing that by late August had produced the first 180 pages of his novel. The publisher Little Brown was interested but ultimately turned the novel down, in part because of the rampant obscenity throughout. Mailer eventually got Rinehart interested, after agreeing to reduce the profanity by twenty percent. The word "fug" was substituted for

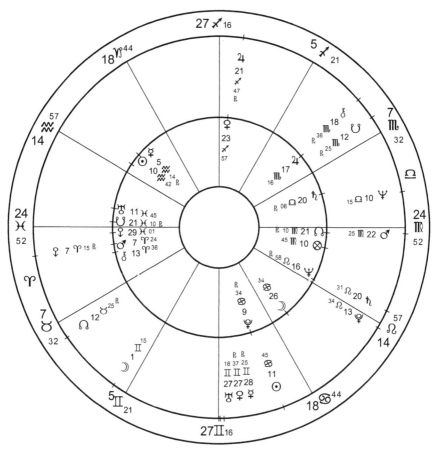

Fig. 10-7 Norman Mailer, Transits for Saturday, Jul 3, 1948,
09:00 PM CET

the more direct and vulgar term, which supposedly gave rise to the rock group called The Fugs many years later.

In the summer of 1947, as transiting Eris was once more closing in on his natal Mars, now well within half a degree, Mailer concentrated on finishing the novel to meet a September 30th deadline for a May 1948 publication date. He made it and then left for Europe. The Full Moon of September 30th was conjunct transiting Eris to within a few minutes of a degree with transiting Eris a degree away from his natal Mars.

When Eris next stationed retrograde, on July 3rd, 1948, within a few minutes of a degree of exactly conjunct Mailer's natal Mars, and with transiting Uranus in exact conjunction with transiting Mercury and Venus on his nadir, he was in Paris. His novel had just reached number one on the bestseller list and he was making plans to return to the States to celebrate.

A little more than three months later he would travel to Hollywood to see about getting a movie deal, followed by a temporary move to Vermont, just as Uranus crossed his nadir in retrograde. This was followed by a more permanent relocation to Hollywood six months later, in early June of 1949, with Uranus again in direct motion and still near his nadir. The transits of Uranus back and forth over his fourth house cusp during this time of frenetic travel accord well with the 9:05 AM chart. Uranus was also transiting in square with his natal Eris this entire period, as he made many moves to further his brightening career as a writer and a famous personality. Once he was recognized for his first novel, he never again lost touch with his public persona as a difficult and interesting commentator on his times. His next two novels more or less flopped but he never stopped writing, maintaining his reputation as a provocative author.

Branching out beyond the novel form, Mailer received great recognition for his essay, "The White Negro," a rebellious diatribe that appeared in the late summer of 1957 for the fall issue of *Dissent* magazine. Eris was still within two degrees of his Mars. The beginning of this essay reads like a manifesto for Eris:

> The Second World War presented a mirror to the human condition which blinded anyone who looked into it. For if tens of millions were killed in concentration camps out of the inexorable agonies and contractions of super-states founded upon the always insoluble contradictions of injustice, one was then obliged also to see that no matter how crippled and perverted an image of man was the society he had created, it was nonetheless his creation, his collective creation (at least his collective creation from the past) and if society was so murderous, then who could ignore the most hideous of questions about his own nature? …
>
> It is on this bleak scene that a phenomenon has appeared: the American existentialist—the hipster, the man who knows that if our collective condition is to live with instant death by atomic war, relatively quick death by the State… or with a slow death by conformity with every creative and rebellious instinct stifled (at what damage to the mind and the heart and the liver and the nerves no research foundation for cancer will discover in a hurry); if the fate of twentieth century man is to live with death from adolescence to premature senescence, why then the only life-giving answer is to accept the terms of death, to live with death as immediate danger, to divorce oneself from society, to exist without roots, to set out on that uncharted

journey into the rebellious imperatives of the self. In short, whether the life is criminal or not, the decision is to encourage the psychopath in oneself, to explore that domain of experience where security is boredom and therefore sickness, and one exists in the present, in that enormous present which is without past or future, memory or planned intention, the life where a man must go until he is beat, where he must gamble with his energies through all those small or large crises of courage and unforeseen situations which beset his day, where he must be with it or doomed not to swing. The unstated essence of Hip, its psychopathic brilliance, quivers with the knowledge that new kinds of victories increase one's power for new kinds of perception.[6]

Invoking World War II and the holocaust, as well as the atom bomb, also reminds us of Pluto, discovered in the early twentieth century and carrying within its dire archetype the seeds of such violence and destruction. As publication neared for Mailer's famous essay (above), with the retrograde station of Eris on July 5th, 1957, Eris was in exact square to his natal Pluto, to the minute, while transiting Pluto also formed an inconjunct with his natal Eris.

Since this essay served to open a new chapter in his literary life as a more journalistic writer, the Eris connection would seem to indicate that he was finding his writerly voice, a form of self-realization in accord with his sense of deeper soul purpose. Pluto, located natally in Mailer's fourth house of home and family concerns, would have the further meaning of fostering transformation in his own life. Indeed, his domestic life was in transition during this entire period of the late Fifties.

Alan Ginsberg, Jack Kerouac and their muse

Following on the heels of Norman Mailer's published rebellious diatribe from 1957 we turn to another memorable figure, an important member of the Beat Generation writers of the Fifties, poet Alan Ginsberg. The 'Beats' in general could be thought of as lonely spiritual warriors in search of a cause. They felt alienated from what they called "straight" society and were willing to go to any lengths to remove themselves from 'the rat race', which, to them, felt more like a rat *trap*.

These men also had some of the characteristics of the overly straight society that they were caught up in, namely that they were into alcohol as a major drug of choice, and were also male chauvinist and a bit homophobic. This is true even of Ginsberg, who had experimented with women as well as men partners, before at 28 years of age settling down to a relationship with a male soul mate, Peter Orlovsky, which lasted, although with ups and downs, for the rest of his life.

Ginsberg was writing of similar themes to those of Mailer in "The White Negro" for some years. It was in October 1955 that his breakthrough moment came with the public reading, at The Six Gallery in San Francisco, of the first part of his free verse poem *Howl*. The subsequent publication, followed by an obscenity trial, which in 1957 he won, established him as a literary figure of some standing.

When we take a look at Ginsberg's chart, for which we have a fairly accurate time, we find that Eris and Uranus, in conjunction, are rising within 7 degrees, in his first house, while Mars is just inside the twelfth house and also conjunct his ascendant.

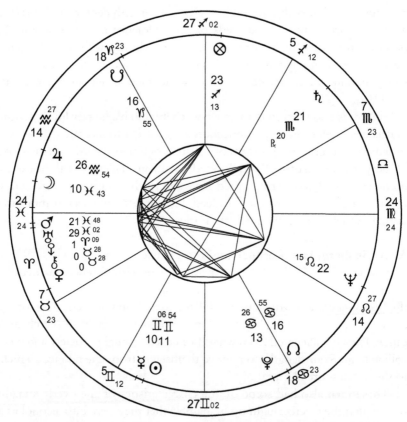

Fig. 10-8 Allen Ginsberg, June 3, 1926, 2:00 AM EDT, Newark, New Jersey, USA

This Eris position is similar to Norman Mailer's, but with Uranus in the mix, goes somewhat beyond it in extremity. True to this intense symbolism, Ginsberg lived a rather extreme life.

He began his departure from the normative behavior of his day when, in the early 1940s he pursued an intense life of sexual and other adventures as a closet homosexual. He was outside the bounds of academia even as he pursued his undergraduate degree from Columbia. Professors such as Lionel Trilling and Mark Van Doren encouraged him and despaired over his vagrant ways, although he eventually completed his degree. All the while he fooled around with young bebop personalities operating on the edge of society, whom he met during his freshman year and who were at various junctures banned from the school residence he lived in. These figures, including Jack Kerouac and Neal Cassady, and older personalities such as William Burroughs, the author of *Naked Lunch*, were aspiring writers and petty criminals, as well as being drug and alcohol addicts. He sampled these mind alterations along with them but never lost his ability to write. His mother was a huge influence; a strong personality, although certifiably insane, she passed in and out of horrible places like infamous Belleview in New York, which she barely survived, and eventually divorced his long-suffering father. She died in 1956.

After Ginsberg received his undergraduate degree in 1948, he stayed in New York for several years before leaving, in December 1953, for a sojourn in southern Mexico. In the late spring of 1954, he arrived in San Francisco, on the verge of national prominence for the raw and revealing poetical portrayal of life among the many outcasts of his close acquaintance and blood brother friendship. He wrote constantly, and his reporting of his lifestyle eventually resulted in the long free verse poem, "Howl". Here is the beginning of his epic work:

> I saw the best minds of my generation destroyed by madness, starving hysterical naked,
> dragging themselves through the negro streets at dawn looking for an angry fix,
> angelheaded hipsters burning for the ancient heavenly connection to the starry dynamo in the machinery of night,
> who poverty and tatters and hollow-eyed and high sat up smoking in the supernatural darkness of cold-water flats floating across the tops of cities contemplating jazz... [7]

In his chart, Mercury is closely conjunct the Sun, in the third house of writing, and these make a tight quintile aspect with Neptune, the signature of poetry, as well as a square with the Moon in illusive Pisces, located in the twelfth house. The Moon is trine to Pluto. Uranus on the ascendant is in exact quintile to Sun/Mercury, so that Uranus is bi-quintile Neptune within 1 degree, with Sun and Mercury at their midpoint. Eris also quintiles Sun/Mercury. The fact that Eris is closely semi-sextile his exact Venus-Chiron conjunction in the first house, at 0 Taurus 28, is also significant to his personality because his best work is so closely bound up with suffering, as the above lines clearly show.

Having moved to the West coast, he wrote the final phase of "Howl" in early August 1955. He gave the famous Six Gallery recital of Part I of his poem on October 7th, 1955 at that location in San Francisco, as one of a group of six poets presenting their work, with Kerouac supplying the wine. This led to the publication in 1956 of *Howl and Other Poems*. The reading and subsequent publication and obscenity trial catapulted him to fame and relative fortune. A look at the transits for this pivotal period, would, I was sure, be revealing, and because Ginsberg's soul purpose was evidently involved, likely bring Eris into the picture.

Sure enough, by that first summer of 1955, transiting Eris had moved to a point of sextile to his natal Mercury, within 1 degree when it stationed retrograde on July 5th. By the time of the poetry gathering, October 7th, 1955, it had backed off a bit, but was still only about a degree and a half away, and was augmented by the transiting Moon's position in square with transiting Eris that evening. Eris was also semi-sextile his natal Moon. Uranus transiting in square to his Venus-Chiron conjunction was closely trine his natal Eris, and getting ready to station a degree past the exact aspect that November. A stationing transiting Uranus on his Eris is quite an appropriate symbolism for thus abruptly shooting into national prominence, in alignment with what he conceived as his soul purpose, namely to chronicle the Beat Generation.

In the following summers Eris would station closer and closer to the exact sextile to his natal Mercury and in semi-sextile to his Moon, coming to exact with Mercury in the summer of 1959 and to the Moon in the summer of 1961.

After the publication of *Howl*, Ginsberg traveled to Europe and Tangiers to be with William Burroughs. There he had a good time, hanging out with his friends, sampling the local culture and various drugs, and helping with the manuscript for *Naked Lunch*. The publicity from the trial caused Viking to rush Kerouac's *On the Road* into print as well, so that the eventual result was extreme notoriety and even celebrity for the two authors, and to a lesser extent, all their friends. Ginsberg's and the book's vindication came

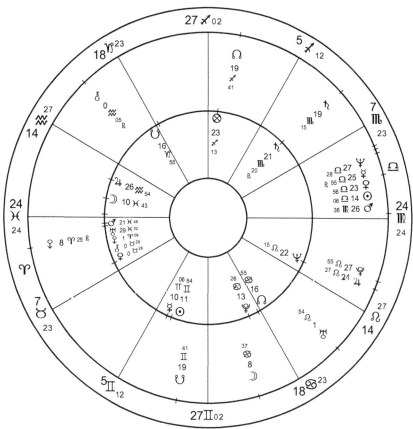

Fig. 10-9 Allen Ginsberg, Transits for Friday October 7, 1955,
8:00 PM PST

while he was abroad, on October 3rd, 1957, which was obviously a land-mark moment for him and for the Beats in general.

Indeed, the transits for October 3rd, 1957, in New York are striking (chart not shown). Transiting Eris had moved closer to the sextile with his natal Mercury, a degree off, and was making a close grand trine in the sky that day with Saturn in Sagittarius and Uranus in Leo. This was at about 10 degrees of the various fire signs, with Eris a degree behind at almost 9 degrees. His writerly Mercury at 10 plus Gemini and his Moon, symbolizing the public, at 10 plus Pisces, were thus implicated, with transiting Uranus inconjuncting natal Moon within a few minutes. Jupiter and the Sun were conjunct that day at 10 and 11 degrees of Libra, opposed to transiting Eris and trine his natal Mercury-Sun, completing the happy and fortunate picture.

173

I was also fascinated to further investigate the subsequent few years of Ginsberg's life, because after the publication of *Howl and Other Poems* in 1956, followed by the national furor raised by the obscenity trial that was only resolved in late 1957 in the book's favor, transiting Eris actually got even closer to making an exact aspect to his natal Mercury, and to his Moon. I was curious to see if further literary output would be thus implied, and indeed there followed the creation of his most famous poem, which was in fact an homage to his mother.

After touring Europe extensively, Ginsberg returned to the United States and composed what is considered his best poem, "Kaddish for Naomi Ginsberg", for his mother, recently deceased. The transit of Eris to his natal Mercury, and in semi-sextile to his natal Moon, representing mother, grew closer through these intervening years, becoming exact to natal Mercury for the first time in the summer of 1959 when he was putting the finishing touches on this work, and to his Moon in the summers of 1961 and 1962, when it stationed within a few minutes of a degree of exact. *Kaddish and Other Poems* was finally published in February 1962.

While Ginsberg was developing as a writer, his friend Jack Kerouac, four years older, and having already written several of his unpublished classics, was slowly burning out. Jack's dependence on alcoholism was difficult to shake, and that and his reclusive nature kept him running from the limelight that the more outrageous younger writer seemed to adore. Like Ginsberg, Kerouac was closely involved with his mother, and lived with her off and on, all his life.

Kerouac had coined the term Beat Generation when searching for a title for his novel *On the Road*, written in 1949, and eventually receiving worldwide recognition in 1957 when it was published by Viking Press. This was synchronous with the publicity generated by the Six Gallery poetry reading and the publication and obscenity trial of *Howl and Other Poems*. Kerouac was present at the San Francisco reading and remained friends with Allen Ginsberg and Neal Cassady for the remainder of his too-short life.

The story he wrote about the American underground had come to him after many "gone adventures" with his friends, most notably Neal Cassady, as he traveled the highways and byways of the country, writing in his journal while Cassady was rapidly talking and fast-driving and never missing a beat. Neal had been raised on the streets of Denver by his hobo father after his mother had passed away when he was ten, and was reputed to have stolen over 500 cars before he was 21. When he came to New York in late 1946, at age 20, with his 16-year-old wife, LuAnn Henderson, he met Ginsberg, who was then a Columbia University undergraduate, and Kerouac, who had been released from his football scholarship and was still hanging around Columbia. He also met several others who would remain friends for life, including William Burroughs.

All were pretty far out there in terms of lifestyle, but Cassady was unique in his stamina and his appetite for alcohol, drugs or sex. He was legendary for multiple partners of either sex and for the sheer quantity of his daily orgasms. The openly gay Allen Ginsberg, and Jack Kerouac, who struggled with his sexuality life-long, exhibiting homosexual tendencies but remaining closeted and in serial partnership with women, were two of Cassady's many sexual partners.

Neal Cassady is immortalized in Kerouac's *On the Road*, as Dean Moriarty, and was in many ways the inspiration for the book. He is also referenced in Ginsberg's *Howl* as "N.C., secret hero of these poems." In another of Kerouac's many novels, *Visions of Cody*, Neal Cassady appears as Cody Pomeroy, and many years later Cassady was the inspiration for the main character in Ken Kesey's *One Flew Over the Cuckoo's Nest*. *On the Road* owes even more to Neal Cassady than the activities of Cassady and Kerouac as traveling companions. A letter from Cassady, over 13,000 words long, called "the Joan Anderson letter," was received by Kerouac in December 1950, and was the inspiration for its breathless stream of consciousness style.[8]

The "scroll" version of Kerouac's work, its nearly final form, was produced in four months of straight typing during April to August, 1951.

Although many other poets and authors were eventually involved, these three form an essential triumvirate of writers who strove to escape the mind-numbing stultification they found in 1940s' and 50s' society. They were in this way the precursors of the hippie generation of the Sixties. A quote from a Kerouac biographer is telling: "To be beat is to be yourself, at whatever cost."[9] This echoes the quest for soul purpose to be found in the Eris archetype.

Naturally I was interested to see the Eris position in all three of their charts. I theorized that the overly masculine Neal Cassady would have the next most prominent Eris placement to Ginsberg, and that he would also possess a strong Uranus, and perhaps Pluto, as well. His chart is given in Fig. 10-10.

The most striking Eris aspect is the near-exact square to Mars, fitting well with Cassady's intense masculine self-image, even though bi-sexual in his practices. Uranus is also implicated, as was predictable, by its conjunction with Eris and square to Mars, and by the close inconjunct to Neptune and trine to his prominent angular Saturn. The discipline of that Saturn rising helped in creating a family man who could hold down a job, for stretches at least, until the call of the road once more claimed him.

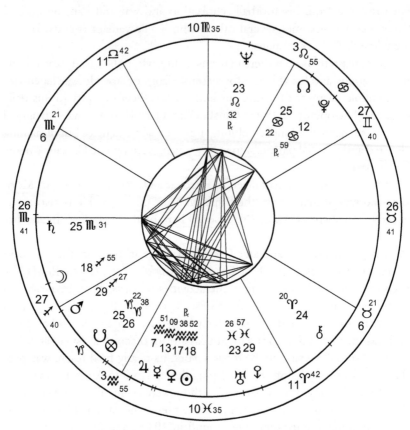

Fig. 10-10 Neal Cassady, February 8, 1926, 2:05 AM MST,
Salt Lake City, Utah, USA

These outer planet combinations are associated with non-institutional religious leanings, the intention of the Beats to forge a new spiritual path that would transcend the rampant materialism of the culture in which they were raised. This is expressed over and over in the surviving literature, as they articulated their dissatisfaction with the empty rules of society, which were to be victoriously trumped by activations of holy poverty, Buddhism and the sacred beyond, including drugs, and the endless quest for "kicks." In Cassady's chart Chiron plays a huge role in this patterning, being closely inconjunct Saturn, trine Neptune, and semi-sextile to Uranus. The tight Aquarius stellium including Jupiter, Mercury and Venus, plus the Sun, speaks to his fun-loving enthusiasm and quest for a better vision of society itself.

Ginsberg's Mars square Saturn and Mars trine Neptune echo these same themes, while Cassady's Eris is in almost exact conjunction, within 8 minutes of a degree, to the midpoint of Ginsberg's 2-degree Uranus-Eris conjunction, rising.

We turn now to Jack Kerouac, seeking a link with the themes of the other two charts in this grouping, and in particular an Eris connection.

Kerouac has Venus in close conjunction with Eris in the seventh house of relationships, indicating his sense of appreciation for the wild and crazy warrior lifestyle of his beloved friend Neal, and, although they frequently quarreled, of Allen Ginsberg also. His Eris matched Ginsberg's, and was closer to an exact square with Cassady's Mars. When I saw this Venus-Eris connection it reminded me of Anais Nin, born twenty years earlier with a similar close conjunction of Venus and Eris, who was among the first to express appreciation for the writing of that noted Erisian, D. H. Lawrence.

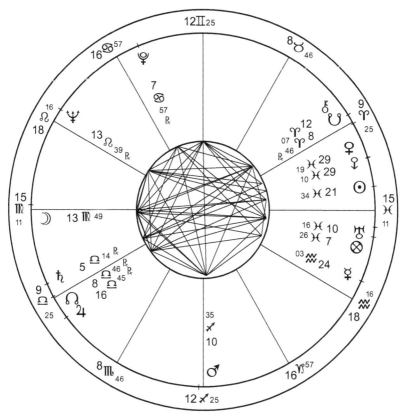

Fig. 10-11 Jack Kerouac, March 12, 1922, 5:10 PM EST, Lowell, Massachusetts, USA 42N38 71W19

It seems to make sense that Jack Kerouac, born with the Venus-Eris conjunction, would be attracted at soul level to Cassady, born with the strong square between Eris and Mars. When Jack went out west to live with Neal and his wife, Carolyn Cassady, eventually entering into a ménage a trois with them in the spring of 1952, she claimed it was always Neal that he loved best. A reflection of Carolyn's outlines the differences in their temperaments along the lines of these personal planets, Neal's Mars contrasted with Kerouac's Venus:

> [Jack] was shy and introverted but his upbringing had trained him to be macho. He was sensitive, tender and compassionate but these were qualities that he had been taught not to show so he put on a macho bluff much of the time. Neal, however, was spontaneously male macho without any effort. Jack wished he had Neal's prowess with women and loved watching him do it.[10]

In Kerouac's own words:

> Neal is more like Dostoyevsky that anybody else I know. He looks like Dostoyevsky, he gambled like Dostoyevsky, he regards sex like Dostoyevsky, he writes like Dostoyevsky. I got my rhythm from Neal, my Okie rhythm... that's the way he talks. Neal was a great Midwest poolroom saint. Neal Cassady and I love each other greatly.[11]

The chart for Carolyn Cassady is also quite revealing in this regard, because of her own Eris placement. Born a year later than Kerouac, she has also a close conjunction between Venus and Eris.

Thus, the two best-known lovers of Neal Cassady, who were both utterly fascinated by him, had this similar placement of Eris and Venus in conjunction.

In Kerouac's angular Mars, square to the Moon, which is rising, and to Uranus, also participating in the grand trine in fire signs between Mars, Chiron and Neptune, we see many of the same themes as in the charts of the other two Beat writers we are examining.

When Cassady and Kerouac met, in late 1946, there were several important outer planet transits with Eris involved. The date is not precisely known, although was likely in mid to late December.

In late December, Eris stationed less than half a degree from exactly opposed to Kerouac's natal Saturn, ruler of his fifth house of artistic creativity. Transiting Pluto conjuncted Keruouc's Neptune in Leo, while opposing Cassady's Mercury in the same degees of Aquarius. Transiting Eris also aspected Cassady's Jupiter, another strong factor in their synastry, and

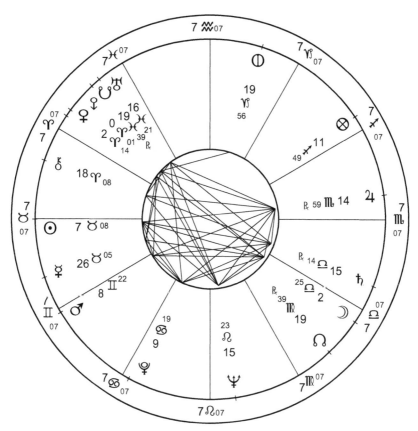

Fig. 10-12 Carolyn Cassady, Apr 28, 1923, Sunrise Chart CST, Lansing, Michigan, USA 42N44 84W33

was in partile sextile to their Composite Sun degree. Transiting Chiron at the same degree of Scorpio triggered the Eris transit for this particular late December period, while transiting Venus and Jupiter in conjunction made a semi-square aspect to Kerouac's Saturn.

Their meeting united his sense of soul purpose with the core of his artistic output. The effect of Cassady on Kerouac was to focalize his inchoate sense of himself as an artist. It is interesting to note in this regard that Neal Cassady himself had Saturn rising in square with Kerouac's Mercury in the 25th degree of Aquarius.

Another transit of note in the life of this interesting, charismatic and flawed American author is April 2nd, 1951, when Kerouac began typing the final draft of *On the Road*, utilizing a 120 foot roll of taped up tracing paper that he had made for the occasion, so that he would not have to re-insert the paper as he typed. In this feat, resulting in the "sausage roll manuscript" that was recently on view at the British Museum, he managed the 86,000 words in 20 days, on Benzedrine, barely pausing for pea soup and coffee.

These transits, for the birth of the near-final version of *On the Road*, are equally fascinating. Saturn, Kerouac's fifth house ruler, is again involved, with Eris still opposed, and with transiting Saturn opposing his natal Eris-Venus, again indicating the connection with his art (fifth house) and with Cassady, and the tremendous focus indicated by this effort. This transit was quite active from November 1950 on through the summer of 1951, and there is evidence that the new stream-of-consciousness style that he pioneered in the scroll document was a greater conscious choice for him since mid-December.

Transiting Eris was almost exactly square to Kerouac's natal Pluto that day, with transiting Uranus conjunct, while the Sun conjuncted his natal Chiron, as transiting Chiron squared his natal Eris and Venus. The dark gods within him were coming out as he transcribed his notes into the breathless

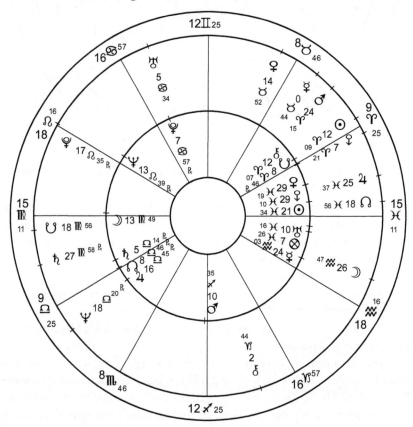

Fig. 10-13 Jack Kerouac, Transits for Monday, April 2, 1951, 12:00 PM EST

prose that became the record of his painful wanderings through an American society on the verge of massive transformation.

In the months subsequent to the creation of this storied draft version, Kerouac was showing it to friends and potential publishers, notably Viking. They eventually published *On the Road,* although not until 1957 when the Beats were suddenly big news. When it came out, an instant best seller, Kerouac was shot into unwanted notoriety. When Kerouac and a friend crept down to the newsstand for the early edition of the NY Times on the morning of September 5, 1957, to see what would be said, they found a rave review for the newly published novel, so that "Jack Kerouac" became a household name. His ultimate reaction was to continue drinking to escape. This was another dramatic turning point in his life. The transits for this date need to be looked at (sec Fig. 10-14 below).

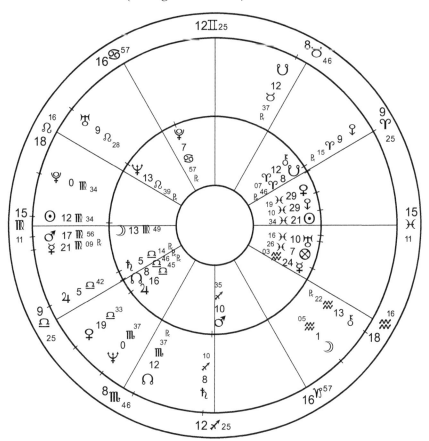

Fig. 10-14 Jack Kerouac, Transits for Thursday September 5, 1957, 6:00 AM EDT

This was the same year as the obscenity trial for *Howl and Other Poems* that, along with *On the Road*, really put the Beats on the map. We find that transiting Eris, in precise trine with transiting Uranus, was then in close semi-sextile with Kerouac's natal Uranus degree – with transiting Uranus inconjunct – making the same aspects to Ginsberg's natal Moon, which is one factor in the synastry of these two quintessential beat writers. These aspects to Kerouac's natal Uranus make a nice chime with the suddenness of his fame as he, in pursuit of soul purpose, produced the novel for which he is still best known. Transiting Mars had also just crossed his Ascendant, and retrograde Mercury opposed his Sun, while Jupiter was in close conjunction with Saturn, his fifth house ruler, prominent in telling moments as discussed above.

Transiting Eris, a degree past its square with his natal Pluto and a degree away from semi-sextile to his natal Uranus, serves to unite the themes of revolutionary transformation present in his natal chart, with transiting Eris on this date just a few minutes of a degree away from semi-sextile the exact degree and minute of the Uranus/Pluto midpoint at 9 Taurus 08. These two outer planets characterized the tumultuous decade of the Sixties that was about to be born, and of which Kerouac and the publication of *On the Road* was one important precursor.

Robert Anton Wilson

We now turn to another writer, and well-known Erisian, founder of a movement that he referred to as Discordia – with the slogan "Hail Eris" as part of its framework. From this indication, and from the nature of his stance as an iconoclastic investigator and truth-sayer, no matter what the occasion, we would suspect a strong Eris. His actual chart has been somewhat shrouded in mystery because the 6.00 AM time that he gave out is suspect as he also stated that, before he lost it, an astrologer had looked at his birth certificate and told him he was "Leo rising". It must therefore have been a PM chart, a fact brought out in the following reference:

> I happened to be going through some old papers, and came across a letter Robert Anton Wilson wrote me in the late 70s in response to a fan letter I had sent him. I must have asked him about his birth data, because he obligingly gave me this information: "I lost my birth certificate recently. Was born Jan. 18, 1932, around 6 in the AM. (Leo rising, according to an astrologer who looked at the birth certificate before I lost it) in Brooklyn, New York." The problem is that Leo was not rising at 6 AM. How-

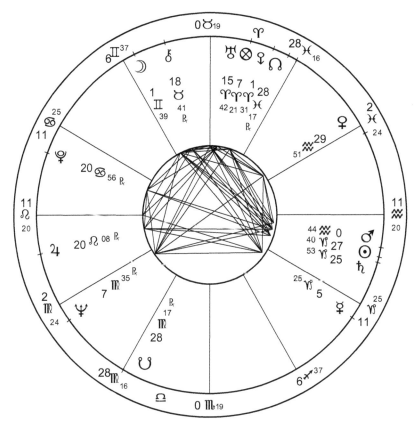

Fig. 10-15 Robert Anton Wilson, January 18, 1932, 6:00 PM, Brooklyn, Kings, New York, USA 40N38 73W56

ever, Leo (Tropical) was rising at 6 PM. It's not a stretch to suppose RAW remembered 6 o'clock but got AM and PM mixed up.

A web search turned up charts for 6 AM (but no indication of data source). So here I present the pm chart.[12]

Another comment reads

the data for the death of his daughter, Luna? That was apparently the most emotionally shredding event of his life. Ah, just found it. October 2, 1976. IIRC he was living in San Francisco. The 6:00 PM chart you've given has a progressed Moon-Saturn conjunction exact within 11'! (This was within a degree of natal Mars, and about half a degree from trine natal Moon.) This gives very strong credence to the chart. Add the backdrop of the emotional upheaval of progressed Mars opposite progressed Neptune within 29'.

For the same event, the 6:00 AM has no such pattern. In fact, it shows the opposite. Progressed Ascendant was conjunct natal Venus within 13'. That would have made this one of the happiest times of his life, full of love.[13]

Using the chart for 6 PM for Robert Anton Wilson also gives a far better placement of Eris, and one indicating that investigation of new territories and love of higher learning were key elements of his life, because Eris winds up in his ninth house, which makes sense in view of his many mystical writings and explorations of higher mind.

The corrected chart for 6 PM is given on the previous page as Fig. 10-15.

Eris is square to his Mercury, an aspect that often symbolizes a prolific writer, and Robert Anton Wilson certainly was one, with a total of 35 books to his credit. He defined himself first and foremost as a writer, even referring to himself in the third person as The Author.

Eris is also semi-sextile Venus, sextile Mars and the Sun, and in extremely close sextile with his Moon, and as well contra-parallel. The Moon is elevated and located in his tenth house of career. Because the Moon is also the ruler of his Pluto, and of his mystical twelfth house, this Eris emphasis thus makes another important chime with his life and work. The fifth house ruler, Jupiter, would also be placed in his first, and we know that parenting was important to him, in part because of his close relationship with his daughter Luna. Her very name indicates the importance of the Moon, and of the Moon-Eris sextile, in his chart.

The tragic circumstances of his daughter Luna's death, at the age of 15, during a store robbery in Berkeley, California, where she was working at the time, is referenced in the Internet comment alluded to earlier. The transit bi-wheel to his chart for this date is given as Fig. 10-16.

The time for this chart is somewhat arbitrary, as the robbery of the store where Luna was working took place late at night. Her body was found the next morning. As a father, it was as though he was facing his own death. His later comment, published in *Cosmic Trigger*: "this was of a different order of hellishness than other griefs: losing parents or brothers or friends just does not compare with losing a child you have adored since infancy. I am going to suffer as I have never suffered before, I thought, almost in awe."[14]

As was indicated in the Internet comment, the secondary progressed positions for his Saturn and his Moon on this date are 0 Aqu 52 and 1 Aqu 04, in close conjunction with each other and in extremely close conjunction with his natal Mars, and in close aspect also to his natal Moon and Eris positions.. There are many close transits on this date as well, and we can tease out the meaning of some of them.

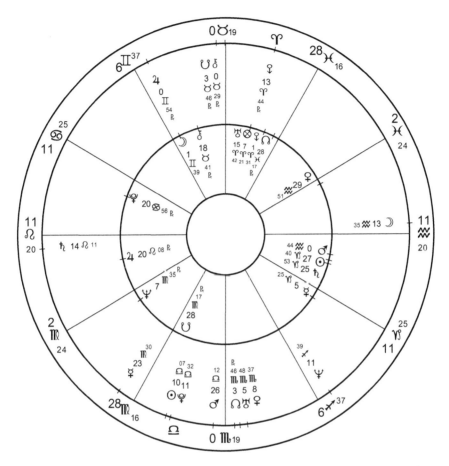

Fig. 10-16 Robert Anton Wilson, Transits, Oct 2, 1976, 10:00 PM PDT

Transiting Eris conjuncted his natal Uranus, an indication of the suddenness of this event, so fundamental in his life, and stood near the midpoint of his natal Moon-Venus square. Transiting Jupiter, in the first degree of Gemini, closely semi-sextile to transiting Chiron, conjoined the Moon, sextiled Eris, squared Venus, and trined Mars, bringing his natal Jupiter, the ruler of his fifth house of children, quite dramatically into the picture. In an indication of the suffering involved, transiting Chiron, directly on his MC, squared Mars and conjuncted his Moon/Eris midpoint.

Transiting Mars at 26 Libra was closely square his Sun-Saturn conjunction, while transiting Saturn on his Ascendant was conjunct his secondary progressed Jupiter at 14 Leo 30, while they both were in trine to his Uranus and quintile his Moon, within one degree. The striking thing about this set of transits is that Jupiter, Mars, Saturn, Chiron and Eris are all implicated, as is appropriate for the impact that such a sudden and dramatic event would have had on a devoted father. You might say that he himself aged more rapidly during this time of his tremendous grief, which is the province of Saturn. The Mars and Saturn transits would speak to the violence and the loss occasioned by this event, and also reflect back on his natal Sun-Saturn-Mars triple conjunction.

Eris being so fully implicated in these transits clues us in as well to how severely this terrible act of violence shaped him, forming the person that he afterward became. We can understand this searing moment as being deeply connected to the theme of the evolution of his soul.

Another interesting transit chart for Robert Anton Wilson is the one for his death, for which we have an accurate date and time (see Fig. 10-17).

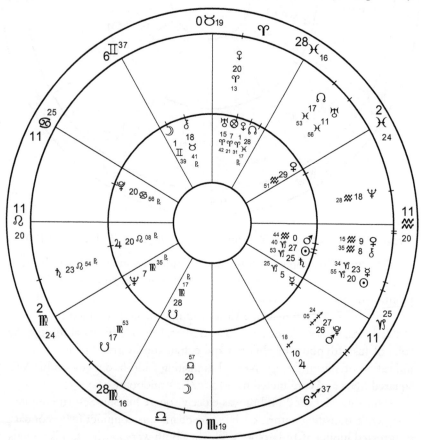

Fig. 10-17 Robert Anton Wilson, Transits for Thursday,
Jan 11, 2007, 4:50 AM PST

It was on January 11th, 2007, at 4:50 AM PST that Robert Anton Wilson passed from this world to some other, and America lost one of its most cosmically attuned and irreverent voices. The transits for this are remarkable, and bring Eris into the picture once again.

The Last Quarter Moon at the time of his death was exact, at 20 degrees and 55 minutes of Capricorn and Libra, and made a T-square with his natal Pluto, to the minute. The other planet transiting in square to this same degree was Eris, completing a partile grand cross to this significant point in his natal chart. The precision of this alignment at the time of his death is quite remarkable, weaving together his natal Pluto (death), the transiting Sun and Moon, and transiting Eris. It is certainly interesting that Robert Anton Wilson, who wrote as cogently about death as he did about any other esoteric subject matter, and who identified himself throughout his life with Eris, would go out in so manifest a demonstration of the synchronicity of the spheres.

Ursula Le Guin

Another mid-twentieth century writer with a strong Eris, Ursula Le Guin is a science fiction author known for the highly literary quality of her novels and short stories. Her work initially fascinated me because it is like no other writer's in its scope and emotional detail of her characters, in a science fiction setting. She is by a matter of convenience a science fiction author, and prefers not to be pigeon-holed in this way. She states she only incidentally created new worlds and societies for her characters to inhabit in order to free herself from any kind of conventional approach. She is nevertheless considered a master of this form and has won many awards for it. A review of her work in *Newsweek* had this to say:

> She wields her pen with a moral and psychological sophistication rarely seen... and while science fiction techniques often buttress her stories they rarely take them over. What she really does is write fables: splendidly intricate and hugely imaginative tales about such mundane concerns as life, death, love, and sex.[15]

In creating imaginary societies she had the advantage of being the daughter of the anthropologist Alfred Kroeber, and of having had Native Americans for family friends while growing up. This gave a jump-start to her powerful imagination and her ability to create different cultural settings. For imagination, and the creation of new worlds far beyond the bounds of conventional thinking, we would immediately think of Neptune and Uranus being prominent in her chart. Her chart also displays a strong Eris, as would be indicated in her life by the strong stand she has consistently made for herself and her art. She has a compelling way of seeing things, and a determination to make her mark with a powerfully expressed viewpoint that is uniquely her own.

We have an accurate birth time for her chart. As credential for the amazing imaginative reach demonstrated in her fiction, she has the close opposition from Uranus to Mercury, with also a close contra-parallel between them. There is also an extremely close contra-parallel between Neptune and the Sun, while Neptune is in sesquiquadrate her Midheaven, trine her Ascendant, semi-sextile Venus, her chart ruler. Uranus and Neptune are in bi-quintile aspect within half a degree, and Eris aspects them both as well, emphasizing these two outer planet archetypes that figure in her artistry. Eris is closely inconjunct Neptune and conjunct Uranus. Chiron, represent-

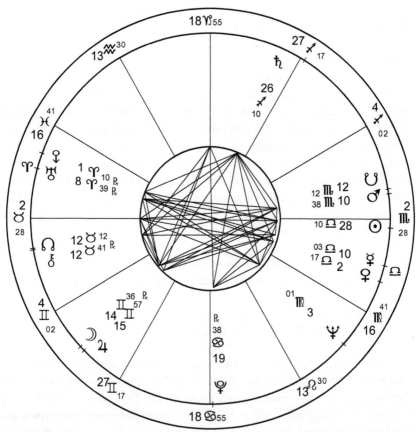

Fig. 10-18 Ursula Le Guin, October 21, 1929, 5:31 PM PST, Berkeley, California, USA 37N52 122W16

ing the Wounded Healer, is conjunct the North Node in her first house. This makes sense owing to the emotional depth of her characters and also their wounding.

Her tendency to find her own way through life by means of rebellion as necessary, is shown by her strong Eris placement. Eris is opposite Venus within about a degree, and is square Saturn and inconjunct the Sun, as well as quintile her Moon-Jupiter conjunction in the second house. In addition to being conjunct Uranus, Eris is also the focus of a Yod from Neptune and the Sun, closely opposed to their midpoint.

With South Node conjunct an angular Mars, she is comfortable in a male role, especially as regards her writing, which in the science fiction genre is, or at least was, a man's game. Female science fiction authors of the 1950s often chose pseudonyms to disguise their feminine origin. It is also interesting to note that only in 1967 did Le Guinn begin to explore the feminine role in her characters, by creating an androgynous race on a distant planet that alternated phases as male and female. In her own words:

> The book had a woman in it, but I didn't know how to write about women. I blundered around awhile and then found some guidance in feminist theory. I got excited when I discovered feminist literary criticism was something I could read and actually enjoy. I read *The Norton Book of Literature by Women* from cover to cover. It was a bible for me. It taught me that I didn't have to write like an honorary man anymore, that I could write like a woman and feel liberated in doing so.[16]

She always knew that she wanted to be a writer, and was trying to get published from 1953, when at the age of 23 she asked her famous father to allow her to contact his friend, the publisher Alfred Knopf, who rejected her first novel. It was never published, and by her own admission was not very good.[17]

Finally after "years of rejections," her next effort, the first of her Hainish series novels was published in 1964. It was called *Rocannon's World*.

Her writing from the late 50s on would have been sparked by the opposition of transiting Eris to her natal Mercury, which peaked between 1959 and 1964. Her awards came later, in 1971 and 1974, for her fourth and fifth novels, *The Left Hand of Darkness* (begun in 1967) and *The Dispossessed*.

When I first saw these dates and compared them to the dates of the opposition from transiting Eris to her natal Mercury, that was years earlier, I conjectured that the initial impulse and early writing must have been years earlier as well, and this was confirmed. She has an unusual style and is a perfectionist about completions, and public acceptance was also slow. Each of the first four novels took years to execute and be published. The first of the series was conceived in the late 50s and only published in 1964. In a 1994 interview, she has this to say about her perfectionism, which could also be regarded as a sense of mission, in keeping with her strong Eris:

> Artists pursue a sacred call, although some would buck and rear at having their work labeled like this. Artists are lucky to have a form in which to express themselves; there is sacredness about that, and a terrific sense of responsibility. We've got to do it right. Why do we have to do it right? Because that's the whole point: either it's right or it's all wrong.[18]

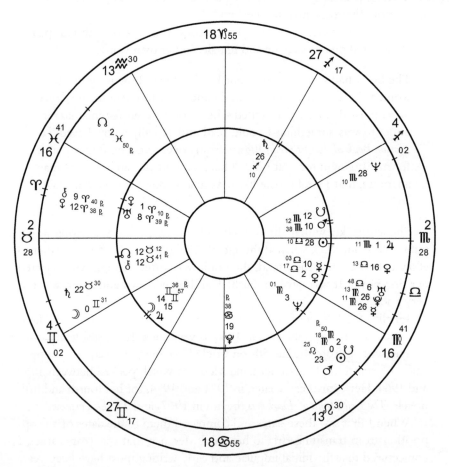

Fig. 10-19 Le Guin, Transits for August 23, 1970, 10:00 PM CET

It is of interest to see the transits for her Hugo award for *The Left Hand of Darkness*, the novel in which she portrays androgynous characters of an alien world far out in the depths of space being visited by a human emissary from the Galactic culture. Her native characters go through alternate seasons as male and female, so that every member of this humanoid race is able to conceive a child during their periods of feminine ascendancy. The date for this prestigious award, the equivalent of an Oscar for science fiction writing and crowning her early career, was August 23rd, 1970, in Heidelberg, Germany. The transit chart is given in Fig. 10-19.

The transits for this moment are quite dramatic. Mercury was conjoined transiting Pluto that evening, squaring her natal Saturn, ruler of her tenth house of career. The transiting Sun and South Node were conjunct her fifth-house Neptune and in sextile to transiting Jupiter, making a Yod to her natal Eris, for Jupiter within one minute of a degree. The Moon was chiming in as it entered Gemini, square her Neptune and closely sextile her Eris. Simultaneously transiting Eris was closely semi-sextile her prominent Chiron and sextile her Moon. The strong presence of Eris in these transits for the timing of her greatest honor indicates the spiritual connection between Le Guin's soul-level intention and the pursuit of her chosen craft.

Hayao Miyazaki

Finally, we have the chart of major animated-filmmaker Hayao Miyazaki. His work features feminine heroes who grow through their experience as they display a clever and graceful combination of charm, innocence and martial arts forcefulness. This has been true in all his best-known work, beginning with *Nausicaä of the Valley of the Wind* in 1984, *Princess Mononoke* in 1997, *Spirited Away* in 2001, and *Howl's Moving Castle* in 2004/2006.

He also has a strong Eris, which is in a triple conjunction with the Moon and the South Node, and participates in a grand trine with Pluto and Mars. As well, Eris is opposite Neptune, as befits a filmmaker, in square to Mercury and closely parallel both Sun and Venus; the latter being the ruler of the fifth house of artistic creativity in his solar chart.

Since Venus is invoked with Eris, along with Mars, it is not surprising that there are both masculine and feminine heroes in the stories that he brings to the screen. Almost always, a young female and decidedly spiritual figure plays the role of the central character. His heroines are usually accompanied by a strong male figure, who is vital to their survival, so that these characters possess a female as well as a warrior quality.

Pluto is quite closely trined by Eris in Miyazaki's chart, and themes of death, rebirth and transformation are important in his films. For example,

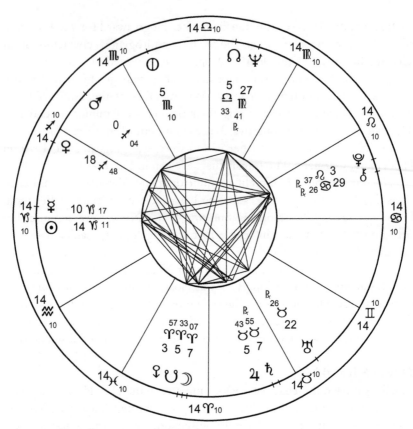

Fig. 10-20 Hayao Miyazaki, January 5, 1941, Sunrise Chart JST, Tokyo, Japan 35N42 139E46

in *Spirited Away*, the young wizard Haku – who changes into a dragon at will – becomes deathly ill and only a magic potion that has been given to Chihiro, the young female central character, will be the antidote. The compassion she displays, and her timely magic, restores him to health. The parable that Miyazaki presents through richly luminous animation is essentially holistic, and yet also takes into account the potential for difficult as well as heroic behavior on the part of its characters. Although she is in many ways a normal 'tween' with all the insecurities associated with this delicate age, Chihiro grows before our very eyes, and is able to rise above, exhibiting a fierce ability to confront and face down her enemy when the situation demands that she do so. She therefore exemplifies the higher manifestation of the Eris archetype.

A more recent film, *Howl's Moving Castle*, has many similar elements, including the transformation of the young heroine at the beginning of the movie into an old woman. In this guise she meets up with the young wizard of the title, befriending him and helping him in a similar fashion to the plot of *Spirited Away*. After several plot twists that include Howl's changing into a war-bird, along with bombing airplanes, near-death and destruction, and further acts of magic, she gradually becomes youthful again.

Miyazaki has stated that his plot adaptation for this movie was based in part on his pacifist reaction to the Iraq invasion of 2003. Horrible scenes of violence become eventually resolved into a happy ending.[19]

His breakthrough came in 1984, when Eris was squaring his Sun degree, with *Nausicaä of the Valley of the Wind*, a film based on Ursula Le Guin's Earthsea series, and featuring a female protagonist. He achieved international recognition eleven years later, when transiting Eris was trine his natal Venus, in his solar chart the ruler of the fifth house of artistic expression.

The dates for the exact hits of Eris in trine with natal Venus, are:

July 15, 1995 SR,
May 26, 1996,
September 3, 1996 R,
May 2, 1997,
September 30, 1997 R,
April 11, 1998,
October 24, 1998 R,
March 21, 1999,
November 19, 1999 R,
February 24, 2000,
January 5, 2001 SD.

The first exact hit was a retrograde station in July of 1995, and marks the start of international fame with the development of his classic, *Princess Mononoke*, released in the summer of 1997 and receiving the Japan Academy Prize in March of 1998, the first animation film ever to do so.

The transits for the evening when Mr. Miyazaki won the Japan Academy Prize for best picture, in his native land, are given in Fig. 10-21. Transiting Eris was in nearly exact conjunction with transiting Saturn, in extremely close trine to his fifth house ruler, Venus. The significance of the moment is also shown by transiting Mars, ruler of transiting Eris and Saturn, conjunct his natal Eris. Saturn is Miyazaki's Sun ruler, and therefore another symbol for his life commitment. The powerful presence of Eris in these transits for his principle awards for his life's work indicates its transformative and ultimately healing nature, and the soul purpose with which he has developed as an artist.

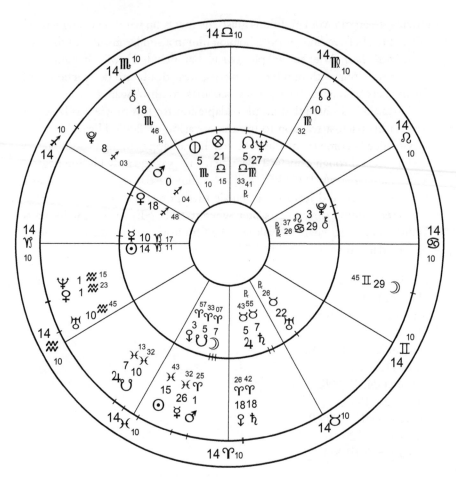

Fig. 10-21 Hayao Miyazaki, Transits for Friday, Mar 6, 1998, 9:00 PM JST

The final exact hit of transiting Eris in trine with his natal Venus, a station direct in January of 2001, and coincident with his birthday, signals the release of his most important film, *Spirited Away*, winner of the U.S. Academy Award for the English language version and the highest grossing film of any category in Japanese history.

When he received the Academy Award for *Spirited Away*, on March 23rd, 2003, transiting Eris, in exact trine to transiting Pluto to within a few minutes of a degree, was still in trine to his natal Venus by less than a degree, as transiting Pluto conjuncted it. The Sun also closely conjoined his natal Eris. Transiting Pluto on that day was also opposed to the degree of Mars in the U. S. chart, with transiting Eris sextile; and the date of the awards ceremony was in fact just four days after the U. S. invasion of Iraq on March 19th. His pacifist reaction to the Iraq war was Miyazaki's stated purpose behind his involvement in his next film, *Howl's Moving Castle*, as indicated above. Thus it is an interesting synchronicity that as the U.S. Mars, signifying its military, was being transited by this outer planet pairing, his natal pacifist and artistic Venus, being aspected at this same time by transiting Pluto, and by transiting Eris, was simultaneously stimulated.

As Mr. Miyazaki's chart and life experiences indicate, and many more examples besides, both from client work and from investigating other notable charts, there is a powerful archetype operating here that can be characterized as Eris – spiritual warrior energy in support of soul purpose.

In the following two chapters I give interpretations on this basis for Eris in the twelve houses, and in combination with natal planets.

Notes
1. 'The White Negro', *Dissent* magazine, Fall 1957.
2. *Time* magazine, August 31st, 1992, reported in Walter Isaacson's biography.
3. Interview http://metro.co.uk/2012/11/29/justin-timberlake-clint-eastwood-is-tough-but-hes-really-like-a-teddy-bear-3078105/
4. *New York Times* Book Review of *Normal Mailer: A Double Life*, by Graydon Carter, October 17th, 2013.
5. *A Double Life*, p. 5.
6. Excerpt from "The White Negro," published in the Fall issue of *Dissent* Magazine.
7. "Howl" *Collected Poems, 1947-1980*.
8. This letter, lost for almost sixty years, recently surfaced in West Hollywood and saw the light of public scrutiny for the first time since the 1950s, when videographed on Monday, December 1st, 2014, in San Francisco, in preparation for an intended sale at auction later that month that did not in fact take place, due to competing claims of ownership from both the Cassady and the Kerouac estates. Remarkably, the transits to Neal Cassady's chart for this date show a strong Eris influence, because transiting Eris, at 22 degrees of Aries, was exactly trine to transiting Jupiter, to the degree, and these are trine and conjunct Cassady's natal Neptune located at 23 degrees of Leo in the ninth house of publishing, and his natal Chiron at 24 degrees of Aries, in his fifth house of artistic creativity. See Fig. 10-10 for Cassady's chart.
9. Amburn, *Subterranean Kerouac*, p. 96.

10. Carolyn Cassady, quoted in Barry Miles *The King of the Beats*, p. 227.

11. *New York Post* interview reported by Barry Miles in *Jack Kerouac – King of the Beats*, pp. 227-228.

12. Posted on Solunars.net on March 9th, 2008 by by gmugmble.

13. Posted on Solunars.net on March 10th, 2008 by Jim Eshelman – URL http://solunars.net/viewtopic.php?f=21&t=154.

14. Wilson, Robert Anton. *Cosmic Trigger*, New Falcon Publications, Tempe, AZ, 1977, p. 232.

15. *Newsweek* quote – referenced in http://www.ursulakleguin.com/BiographicalSketch.html

16. Interview by Jonathon White, 1994 – published in swarthmore.edu.

17. Interview appearing in *The Paris Review*, © 2014.

18. Interview by Jonathon White, 1994 – published in swarthmore.edu.

19. Devin Gordon "A Positive Pessimist" – retrieved 2008. Quoted in the Wikipedia article for *Howl's Moving Castle*.

An Eris Cookbook

Interpretations for Eris in the natal houses, and in aspect.

11

Eris in the Natal Houses

The proof of the pudding is in the eating.
English Proverb

Eris by sign results in Aries for every person born after 1927 – so that it might take a few more years of research to become clearer and more certain regarding the delineation of Eris in the signs themselves. In the houses, Eris seems to give strength to the house of her placement wherever she is found in the natal chart, and in particular with issues relating to soul purpose. The areas symbolized by this house are emphasized and even obsessed over, with better results as the person's evolutionary purpose becomes clearer to himself or herself. This set of interpretations would also apply to Eris in natal aspect to the house ruler, and could be considered for the solar chart house position or the Whole Sign house position as well.

For Eris in combination with the natal planets themselves see the next chapter.

Eris in the First House
You are a strong stand for yourself, and for what you believe. You must believe utterly in what you are doing in order to be effective, and when you do, look out! Whatever you truly set your mind upon, it will happen. You can sometimes be a difficult person to handle, especially when you feel shortchanged or otherwise thwarted in what you are trying to accomplish. When you are in pursuit of your deeply felt quest, you let nothing get in your way, including others around you who might have different ideas. At other times, you can be deceptively mild. With run-of-the-mill situations that do not stir you deeply, you could represent the more ordinary mix of decisiveness combined with indecision, but when something comes up that really touches your soul, then you are a dynamo of activity. Your fundamental needs and desires are very important to you, and you must also recognize that it could be a lifetime task to fully identify what it is that you feel that you absolutely stand for, that you cannot choose not to be, and that condi-

tions what you feel the need to accomplish above all else. Because you have such a strong personality there is a trap inherent in this placement of Eris, one that you might originally stumble into, namely the ego idealization of the little self. You will, over the course of time, come to better understand yourself at deeper levels, and the soul purpose that truly motivates you. When you do, you also feel into a greater role of purposeful connection with others around you. Moving beyond your initial starting point in this way could become one of the most important goals that your life has to offer.

Eris in the Second House

You are a strong advocate for yourself in finding your personal sense of security, your place to stand, in your individual way and on your own timing. Your life has been devoted, to some extent, to discovering what it is that you truly need to feel safe and complete in yourself. You seek grounding in a resourced place corresponding to your inner compass of what feels right for you, independent of other voices or attitudes. Once you have found such direction, you will never lose that feeling of what it is that makes sense for you, but will build upon it. Like nothing else can do, this sense of personal values allows you to move out into the world beyond your start-ing point with a feeling of true confidence and verve. In finding your own way forward, you might be tempted to seek monetary comfort as a cure-all, finally moving beyond that idea into one that is more universal, and spiritu-ally motivated, or else continue to refine your understanding of what, to you, financial security truly means. You could discover in the material realm a pathway rather than an end-point, a means to a more complex destination that includes the life path of others into the picture. You are then utilizing your skill with the material world as a means to higher purpose.

Eris in the Third House

You are the possessor of a brilliant and very practical mind and what is more, you know how best to use it for higher purpose. You find within yourself an extreme focus on communicating your ideas to others around you, via your spoken word, writing or teaching. The soul-level plan you have embedded deep within you might also involve the ability to eventually use your gift to further a wider set of objectives. This sense of mission is of necessity a work in progress. You are in essence on a life-long journey of taking your ideas forward into the service of the greater good, both on your own behalf and for others around you as well. This is actually a gift that keeps on benefiting you, although only as long as you can continue to give it away. On starting out, your talent might be relatively unformed, and you may find that you cannot rest until you have explored every facet of what you have to offer. As you further refine what it is that you have to say, you find that it is your individual point of view that begins to come through, based on your own experience with the world around you and what you make of it. You are gradually evolving your own way of seeing and your unique voice to express that sensibility. Once you do, you have the makings of one who can transform society itself.

Eris in the Fourth House
You are someone who values your depths more greatly than the surface layers of your personality; although it might take you a long period of study in order to fully recognize this as your underlying goal. In the meantime, through many false starts, you could live a problematic existence on the outside of your true nature. More than most, it would seem to be your task to integrate the unconscious material that you find deep inside yourself, in a way that makes sense to you going forward. You are thus fundamentally concerned with discovering who and what you really are. Similar to the Jungian life-long task of individuation, yours is essentially a process of integration and renewal. The notion of Selfhood that you develop in this way is independent of early conditioning, or wounding, and as well of the nullities of consensus thinking that might apply to others in general but not to the specifics of your own situation. Once you have come to a better understanding of yourself, with your depths more fully included into the picture of how you see your true personhood, you are able to embody an idea of soul purpose that you have perhaps always known and yet been unable to actualize. You will also be more available for the ordinary tasks of life, as exemplified in home and family concerns, coming at these with a better sense of who you really are.

Eris in the Fifth House
Personal creativity is an area of life that is fundamental to your well being. You are someone who is always engendering new worlds within and outside of yourself to express yourself in. You are thus following your own path and constantly producing artistic output in your own individual way. As you follow your inspiration, whatever that might be, if you are not being yourself at all costs you feel the lack and it drives you slightly insane. You might in this instance, in desperation to find the proper channel for your energies, seek recognition from the world around you in ways that are less than fully constructive. As you mature, you could also find that you are fascinated by

the analogs to self-expression, such as children – your own or those of others – stage acting, even in real life, and artistry of all kinds: music, painting, poetry, dance. In these fields of endeavor, your creative self-actualization is at stake, and it is therefore vitally important that you understand yourself fully, as you progress through life, in order that you give your creative output from the actual center of your being, as a vivid emanation of who you at base really are. Once you arrive at even the glimmer of an understanding of your true Self, the purity of your motivation is never in question.

Eris in the Sixth House
You have a real love of service to others, and for the purity of your purpose and the eventual product of your efforts. To give of yourself to the surrounding collective is something of a soul level mission for you. You might be engaged in a lifelong quest to find how best to put your shoulder to the wheel of need in a meaningful way. In this you aspire to shine your own rather intense light onto issues that you feel are necessary for society to progress or for individual members of it, that have come into your purview, to uncover their best and highest path. You thus have a strong desire to be helpful, and could even have the habit at times of offering your assistance whether or not it is immediately evident that your aid is being sought. This is a charming trait at times but can obviously be overdone. In your early years you might need to beware of giving too much of yourself away or seeking a false premise for your self-worth through the attitude of others outside your own determination and judgment. Once you have fully grasped how valuable you are as a human being, and have developed your ego, it becomes a great joy to transcend it. As you arrive at a better sense of your own proclivities and talents, you become in a better position to go on to explore and more fully come to understand what you can do to be of true service to the needs of others around you and of society itself.

Eris in the Seventh House
You are an incredibly strong stand for partnership in your life, and a great believer in its efficacy in solving problems too complex for you to be able to handle entirely on your own. You might be someone who truly subscribes to the phrase that "two heads are better than one," and you might even possess a strong yen for partnering up no matter what. Even though you enjoy cooperating in this way with others, and are dedicated to the concept of partnership, you could also be engaged in a life long process of feeling into yourself more fully as an individual. You could find that you have a tendency to give your power away; you may not always own it. You therefore seek

to find in another the strength of character that you desire to exemplify in yourself, and when you do, you celebrate that part of a close partner's makeup and are willing to go far in supporting them in what they do. As you mature and obtain a more informed sense of yourself, a qualitative change can occur in which you value yourself and your contribution more highly. When you do, you are still available for others but in a new way that more fully honors your own end of the arrangement. This better understanding of yourself and of the ways that you operate in the world around you makes of you an even more willing partner and allows the relationships that you undertake to take on renewed life as an experience that is geared toward shared success, stemming from your own sense of deep purpose.

Eris in the Eighth House

You are someone who has a zeal for life – as well as for better understanding the end of life – and who loves deeply and passionately although perhaps not steadily. Your ardor could sometimes in fact get the best of you, creating problems for existing relationships. You might feel a sense of ownership for special partners, so that this could also prove to be a challenge to these relationships, something to be working through. You could find within yourself an obsession regarding areas such as intimacy and the exploration of the wild territory of your private interior world. On the other hand, your inner intensity could be so strong that you feel that you have to tone it down for the consumption of others, therefore making a habit of hiding out. You are on a vitally important mission to establish intimacy and deep connection with other humans that you encounter, and, in the final analysis, with yourself. You have a strong need to plumb the depths of whatever emotional realities lie within you, that you can attune to, and to leave no psychic stone unturned in your quest for wholeness. Once you have more fully connected with yourself and entered into the exploration of your motivations and of who, at soul level, you really are, you can forge a deeper and more caring bond with those you choose as partners. This naturally leads to a more conscious act of sharing. At this point of self-knowledge, it is the care and ownership of the relationship itself that moves you deeply and that allows your continued growth, along with, as well, that of the intimate partners in your life.

Eris in the Ninth House

You are extremely focused on areas of study that lead you into further self-knowledge, as informed by a sincere philosophy of life. There is an unstoppable drive in you to get at a better understanding of a more deeply informed worldview, one that is independently motivated by your own soul level characteristics. This could lead to academic excellence along the way, but the book learning of the academy is not your actual goal. You will wind up picking and choosing those aspects of knowledge that make sense to your own unique way of seeing things. Also, this quest of yours is not knowledge for the sake of knowledge, although this superficial goal might indeed represent one of the traps of this placement. Your mission is serious, at least to you, and might be an almost holy pilgrimage, one that lets nothing whatsoever stand in its way. It is not necessarily practical in the eyes of the world, although exceedingly so from the standpoint of getting into better alignment with your higher Self. Your searching therefore becomes more and more refined as you mature, and become better acquainted with who you really are, on the inside. The things that interest you might be classified as whatever takes you beyond the boundaries of consensus thought and the physical nuts and bolts of daily living into a more pure exploration of other dimensions of reality. It is not contemplation alone that drives you, but rather the urge to penetrate the barriers of ordinary understanding and to make of this exploration something that is uniquely your own.

Eris in the Tenth House

This placement is the hallmark of a powerful personality, especially in regard to achievement. You are compelled by an urge for success that can take you far, and that to attain it can lead you into moving mountains. Once you have conquered in one field, though, you could find yourself ready for another, for it is an internal quest for perfection of purpose that truly dives you, in alignment with more complete self-knowledge. You are characterized by what might seem like a driving ambition to obtain the accolades of the world around you, and which yet eventually morphs into a subtle and more personal mission for specialized progress of a manner that only you, of all the humans on the planet, can provide. While in your early years you could strive for recognition as the measure of success, and seem ruthless in achieving your goals, in your more mature phase it is strictly by means of your own internal guidelines that you arrive at what you can actually consider triumph, by finding important cosmic resonance with what you are really all about, on the inside. These inner requirements, as you come to know them, then become the compass by which you steer, and might actually turn out to be a means for discovering more clues to your true Self. The inner exploration in which you are thus dynamically engaged derives from an in-depth process similar to the Jungian psychological concept of individuation. Looking back to the time that you first set foot upon this path, versus your later set of developments and concerns, enables you to see results far beyond what you originally thought you were attempting. These accomplishments could in fact come to constitute your true life's work, as part of a rich process of continued soul level evolution.

Eris in the Eleventh House

You are fascinated by society, but from a definite remove. You have an un-stoppable drive to find a better social setup for you to fit yourself into, even though what currently exists seems to never entirely fill the bill. What really counts for you is your individually unique idea of a future that you can re-ally live with, and that you feel could also support the best intentions of the people to whom you are drawn. You have your own way of seeing things, and follow the beat of that distant drummer, a siren song that moves you greatly and that derives from a voice inside you that is distinctly your own. Even though your concept is formed on the basis of what you glean from your surroundings, the current social system is not your target because your vision tends to be several steps ahead of it. When you are ready to reveal your mature concept, you might find it a better match for what has to come next, in terms of social progress, than ever you would have imagined. As you get closer to knowing your truth that you feel the great and abiding need to share with your fellow humans, you come to better know yourself at deep levels also. The slow cooker of your process has really followed nothing else all along other than the promptings of your own inner com-pass. And yet this work eventually becomes, to your great surprise, at least one part of a comprehensive road map for the world at large. You could thus turn out to have a tremendous impact on the society that you have run up against during the entire course of your years of development.

Eris in the Twelfth House

You operate at something of a remove from the natural everyday reality that surrounds you. There lies within your depths a rich world, psychically distant from these everyday realms, and it is one that you are almost com-pulsively drawn to further explore. You choose not to obey this inner calling to your peril for outside of that path, your tracks might take you away from yourself, into rampant escapism of one form or another, which is poten-tially self-destructive. Your only viable alternative would seem to be that you give yourself up to your fate and resolve to follow this voyage of inner discovery wherever it may lead. It might feel like a sense of secret mission, a world apart that only you inhabit and yet which is actually all the reality that you need as long as you are left alone to pursue it entirely on your own terms. This speaks to a feeling that is difficult to grasp within the more ordinary logic of causes and effects, perhaps a desire to turn the world around you inside out and see what its never-before-seen hidden dimension has to offer. This inner path might have the rich flavor of myth or fantasy, dream symbolism that brings otherworldly dimensions closer to the material plane and the rest of humankind. As you further explore along these lines you awaken to a better understanding of what lies beyond the physical and also of yourself at these deeper and less obvious layers of your being. You might therefore come to see yourself as a natural conduit between the natural mode of earthly existence and these realms of the imagination and the deep unconscious worlds that lie within.

12

Eris in Aspect with Natal Planets

If you follow nature you will not be able to vanquish the tragic to any real degree in your art… Let us recognize the fact once and for all: the natural appearance, natural form, natural color, natural rhythm, natural relations most often express the tragic . . . We must free ourselves from our attachment to the external, for only then do we transcend the tragic, and are enabled consciously to contemplate the repose which is within all things.
(Piet Mondrian, Sun-Mercury-Eris triple conjunction, 1920)

Eris With the Personal Planets

When Eris is in contact with any of the personal planets, Sun, Moon, Mercury, Venus or Mars, there is a great intensification of that planet's basic modality in the life of the native, and in connection with the person's evolving sense of soul purpose. This would be especially so in the case of the major dynamic aspects of conjunction, square and opposition, but equally true in more muted fashion for trines, sextiles and the minor aspects as well. I have for example found the quintile, within close orb of 1 to 2 degrees, to definitely be significant, as well as the sesquiquadrate, semi-square and semi-sextile. The inconjunct may give a quirky personality. The flowing aspects of trine, sextile and quintile, while on the whole easier to integrate, appear to be no less potent.

Eris in aspect with the Sun

With Eris in aspect to your natal Sun, there is a pronounced iconoclastic streak to your nature. You are a born innovator, someone who has to go your own way, be yourself at all costs. Although you might find it a difficulty to swim against the current, surprisingly that never stops you for a minute. When the odds are against you, why those are the odds that you thrive on, and that is just the way you like it. Regarding a cause, if you are not sure why you are in it, you have trouble carrying on. Conventional ideas and run of the mill reasons for making an effort are not for you, and you will wonder why you are in the battle. You are the toughest competitor of all whenever you feel that you are totally behind a cause that you are striving for. You do not hesitate to pull out all the stops, even anger if it serves your purpose, or a glowering demeanor; whatever it takes to make sure things go your way. When you have soul-level alignment with what you are committing to is the time when you are absolutely at your best; then, literally nothing can stop you. You are therefore on a life-long mission to truly know yourself, at deep levels, so that the battles that you choose are only those that are fully worth it. When you can feel yourself to be correct in your choices, from a knowing and centered place, you are unbeatable, for you understand that your struggle is one that helps advance the cause of society itself.

Eris in aspect with the Moon

With Eris in aspect to your natal Moon, you are possessed of a natural grace and joy of life, with a sweet disposition, and a confidence rooted in your acceptance by others for your affable and encouraging personality. You are strong in your emotional presence and nurturing toward others around you, perhaps even mothering them at times. Because you enjoy life you enjoy people, and feel connected with all of mankind. You have a strong soul-purpose intention to foster peace and harmony wherever possible, although you will never sacrifice your principles in order to do so. You are in your most characteristic moments quite simple and happy, with a poised spirituality that has no nonsense about it, and no need of intellectual backing. Because you feel a certain kinship with everyone you meet, and are in general contented in yourself, when you are at your best you have no need to fear anyone, or to worry that anything bad can ever happen to you. You are likely to value partnership and have an inclination to marry for life. In a man's chart, there is a strong emotional presence that is relatively rare in a masculine personality, so that you have a good sense of your female side. This is true of a woman's chart as well, although in this case it is less remarked upon. For either a man or a woman with this placement, children are extremely important, so that there is a strong urge to have them and to care for them. There is also a powerful desire to know yourself and your path of service to others. When you become clearer regarding this sense of mission in your life, you feel more at home in the world around you. Your creative endeavors are also in some sense your children, and you feel affectionate toward them as well.

Eris in aspect with Mercury

With Eris in aspect to your natal Mercury, you are possessed of a powerful intellectual bent, that can take the form of spoken or written communication, or the detective work necessary to probe mentally the philosophical depths of the world around you. You may be an articulate spokesperson for a particular point of view that is uniquely your own. You live to put this gift into the service of the collective that surrounds you, although you do so in your own particular way. What you thereby express has little to do with conventional thinking and attitudes. The better you know yourself at the deepest levels of your being, the better you can exercise your gift of intelligence to express these deeper levels to others; it is in getting at the very essence of what moves you deeply that you truly shine. You could be a novelist or non-fiction writer, with also the potential for the more modern expressions of word play: blogging or creating song lyrics. You could also explore avenues of comedic speaking and writing, especially if Uranus is involved. All the intellectual roads that you traverse have the power to bring you into closer connection with yourself. It is a life-long study to discover who you really are, on the inside, and once you do, you find that you are in a far better position to express your unique attitudes to the world around you.

Eris in aspect with Venus

With Eris in aspect with your natal Venus you have a refined and cultured way of seeing the world around you and yet with an aesthetic vision and a set of ethical judgments that is uniquely your own. You have an artistic bent, and perhaps one that is productive. You are likely to be a little wild yourself, and you definitely appreciate strength of character in others, even to the point of an extra level of intensity that can get them into trouble with the more establishment orientation that, in their quest to find their distinctive voice, they inevitably run up against. Relationship matters to you, greatly, and yet you will not be content with anyone that is in any way ordinary or routine. You are a sensual being who loves to play the edge between enjoying comfortable surroundings, even luxury, and going beyond your comfort zone in search of that sense of extreme experience that is the very breath of life to you. You are affable and diplomatic by nature, and yet in a way that is uniquely yours. Whether you are a man or a woman, you possess a strong feminine side, and a sophisticated and peace-loving viewpoint. Strength of character is always available to you, especially when it really matters. Your search for your own individual values becomes extremely important to you as you mature, and can take on the form of a serious quest, until such time as you feel you have settled into the groove that truly matches your innermost soul.

Eris in aspect with Mars

With Eris in aspect with your natal Mars, you have a strong intentionality to your makeup, along with what could be termed a lust for competition and success, and as well a take-no-prisoners attitude that immediately cuts to the chase and gets the job done. This would be true in a slightly different sense, in either a man's or a woman's chart. You are full of machismo energy, perhaps athletic and certainly at least quite interested in sexual activity, and have a knack for getting what you want when you decide to really go for it. The object of your quest could change as you mature, and yet what you ultimately stand for is always what comes out of the very core of you, in a totally uncompromising fashion. It seems like you are always hungry for more, whether success, sexual conquest, or accolades, as long as whatever it is that motivates you is a product of your own deep center. You thus have your own set of unique values that drive you, and have trouble accepting the standards of others as any kind of guide for your own behavior. If it makes sense to you, deep down inside yourself, then you will adhere to the rules, but not otherwise. Because this is so, it is extremely important for you to attempt to discern your inner realities in great depth of understanding. Without this understanding you might be somewhat lost, and misdirect your considerable energies. With, however, the advantage of the knowledge of your deep soul purpose, you will thrive.

Eris in Aspect With Jupiter and Saturn

Eris with either or both of these planets makes for greater understanding of social perspectives, a feeling of being part of the story of society. These persons are often drawn to practice law or politics, community oriented or of wider scope, and have the desire to influence the public in its almost hidden quest to find a more significant role for spirituality in modern life.

Eris in aspect with Jupiter

With Eris in aspect with your natal Jupiter, you project an air of friendly optimism and self-assurance, which could perhaps turn aggressive or dogmatic at times. You are likely to be well liked, because although often intense with regard to your own contribution, you are inclined to accept people for who they are. There is an attitude of acceptance for the good that you expect to discover in others and also in yourself. You are terrific at self-promotion, public relations, and politics, and are able to promote others as well, as long as you feel in alignment with where the work is coming from. You do see the humorous side of life and will go to great lengths for a laugh. You sometimes just go for it, in spite of what others might consider to be the rules. You have an almost over-the-top sense of self-esteem that takes you far, as long as you feel a chime with what you know to be true for your own self, deep inside; however, if on the other hand your outer presentation and your inner knowing become incongruent in any way, there is trouble brewing until you can reconcile your actions with your underlying values. It is therefore quite important for you, as you go through life, to determine what it is that you absolutely believe without qualification, emanating from your soul center. This self-understanding then allows you to really become a strong stand for yourself and for what you believe in, that to which you can give your most earnest support.

Eris in aspect with Saturn

With Eris in aspect with your natal Saturn, you are industrious, bringing a sense of dedication and of duty, or just plain hard work, to pretty much everything that you do. You are also something of a loner and might feel as though you must solve any tasks by yourself. You are likely very good at handling details. There is a touch of formality about you, as well as respect for others and sincere regard for their welfare, so that you fit in well with social settings. There might be an important feeling of authority that permeates your life; you give it willingly when socially indicated, and in the right circumstances feel entitled to it yourself. You highly value concepts of justice, and might be inclined to root for an underdog or go out of your way to make sure that arrangements are fair to all parties. It is virtually impossible for you to witness an injustice without taking some action to attempt to correct it, forcefully at times, and always with total sincerity. You are very practical, and act for the good of the collective as much as seems right for you to do so. You could feel separated from the surrounding social system until such time as you find the correct formula for involvement in a way that makes complete sense to you, stemming from a deep place inside. For this reason it is vitally important for you to know yourself well at these deeper levels of your being, so that you feel that you truly understand where you are coming from. Then, by acting from your soul center at all times, everything else in your life falls into place.

Eris in Aspect With Uranus, Neptune, Pluto and Chiron

With Eris in aspect with outer planets and Chiron, these powerful features of the person's natal chart are emphasized but they are of a generational rather than a personal nature. It is when the outer planets make aspects to the personal planets that these factors are enhanced and made more directly the focus of deep work and soul purpose activity.

Eris in aspect with Uranus

With Eris in aspect with your natal Uranus, freedom is your lifeblood, the air you breathe. You are therefore a bit of a rebel, with a sense of mischievousness riding along with you like a second skin. You have the need to constantly explore what it means to be uniquely you, and to give yourself the space to do that. You have a terrific sense of humor, slightly offbeat and naturally funny. Because you are so definitely invested in your own way of seeing things, you do not have an easy time following the rules laid out for society in general, or in behaving in a way that corresponds to the dictates of consensus thinking. You must develop your understanding of what you have deep inside yourself for your life to really begin to make sense to you. When you get your psychic bearings, you are incredibly intuitive, and benefit from the awareness you receive by tapping into the information that is always, somehow, available to you when you reach inside for it. You are tuned to the hidden aspects of the cosmos, as only becomes clearer with reflection, and with the passage of time. Synchronicity is your guide. As you proceed through life, things may sometimes take you by surprise, and then you discover that these unexpected events have something important to convey to you regarding your soul purpose. As you mature in your understanding of who you really are, down inside, you get better at making the vital connection with your inner universe, allowing your life path to come into better focus.

Eris in aspect with Neptune
With Eris in aspect with your natal Neptune, part of you may be quite ethereal, with only one foot at most planted firmly in considerations of the here and now. There is a mystical air about you and an appreciation for musical and poetic excursions beyond the material plane. Something within you is purely idealized, and you could at times dwell in illusion, potentially confusion, or picture yourself a victim of circumstance. You have it within you to imagine other worlds and realities beyond this present one. You can feel isolated by the power of your private images until such time as you can learn to channel this gift and to ground it practicality. You are also extremely sensitive to energy and the psychic space of others, and may struggle to find self-definition independently unless and until you learn to trust your own instinctual sense of yourself that emanates from your deepest center. It is therefore vital that, as you mature, you devote effort to this task of interior exploration. One perfect outlet for your imagination might be through poetry, or the visual arts, music and dance The spiritual world bursts through to this one in these media expressions that can allow your soul to sail beyond physical boundaries while staying grounded in the performance. It is entirely possible for you to maintain a graceful connection to everyday life, especially when you can expand your viewpoint to a larger perspective than

day-to-day getting and spending. You benefit when you seek within yourself a reason to make the transition to a more inclusive view of your life springing from your own deep inner vision.

Eris in aspect with Pluto

With Eris in aspect to your natal Pluto, you have an intensity of intention that can take you far once you learn how best to employ it. You are a hard worker, and possess enormous reservoirs of stamina. When you are focused on an objective you will not let anything at all stand in your way. You will take whatever action seems likely to succeed, and might bend or even break the rules that society lives by – or use people around you – in order to achieve your ends. You can in this way be something of a handful, especially when aroused to anger or passion, becoming forceful to the extreme. You have within you an evolutionary call and a profound desire to take your life to the next plateau of meaning, and you may go through many changes along the way to achieving that which you unconsciously and perhaps compulsively desire. You could make many false starts and travel misdirected aims that are mere masquerade for the real truth that you seek inside. Sexual obsession is potentially one symptom of these misplaced objectives, or a dogmatic urge to be right or the craving for absolute control over social situations. You in actuality possess a drive for self-mastery and for the ultimate transformation of those traits from your past that you feel the profound need to eliminate, and which could be the result of many lifetimes. The heartfelt exploration of your interior world is vitally important for you. The inner work that is required is profound and lifelong, and will ultimately transform you. Life becomes sweeter and more meaningful top to bottom, once you have placed yourself into closer alignment with your soul direction.

Eris in aspect with Chiron

With Eris in aspect to your natal Chiron, you have a relationship to suffering, your own and that of others, that is at times problematic but always connected to deeper purpose. You have a habit of telling the truth, no matter how difficult that might be, and to take on issues of injustice that you witness, or that you can come to understand philosophically, vowing to take a leadership role in fighting these endemic social evils. You are extremely sensitive to others' pain, perhaps because you yourself have gone through some degree of trauma growing up. You might have been hurt in your early experiences with parental figures, and by taking on and attempting to alleviate the suffering that you see in the world around you, discover the means to work through some of the pain you have internalized. You have a strong intention to transform the hurt that lies within you, creating a service-oriented orientation. You might feel trapped in situations, or see the society itself as narrow and stultifying. At some point you might feel that you have taken all that you can of such limiting circumstances, and feel compelled to break out. As you do, it is important that you remain as true as you can to your own deep center, that unique inner place corresponding to your soul purpose and belonging to no one else. Once you have more fully explored your own inner world, you are better able to see the truth of where you are in fact coming from, and are better equipped to fight the battles that you feel are truly necessary. You do better therefore, once you can come into alignment with what you hold to be your own uniquely valid principles, that are well worth the fight.

Appendices

Appendix A
List of Charts and Sources

In the following list of chart data and sources, the abbreviation "ADB" refers to AstroDataBank online as the source. Accuracy is given as the standard Rodden rating values and abbreviated "RR." For an explanation of the Rodden rating system see http://www.astro.com/astro-databank/Help:RR. Additionally, the abbreviation "Wiki" refers to the source being Wikipedia (with therefore no actual time of birth).

Fig. 1-1 Angela Davis: January 26, 1944, 12:30 PM CWT, Birmingham, Alabama, USA (ADB – RR: AA)

Fig. 1-2 Jane Fonda: December 21, 1937, 9:14 AM EST, New York, New York, USA (ADB – RR: AA)

Fig. 2-1 Angelina Jolie: June 4, 1975, 9:09 AM PDT, Los Angeles, California, USA (ADB – RR: AA)

Fig. 2-2 Zhang Ziyi: Feb 9, 1979, Sunrise Chart, Beijing, China (Wiki – RR: X)

Fig. 2-3 Michelle Yeoh: Aug 6, 1962, Sunrise Chart, Ipoh, Malaysia (Wiki – RR: X)

Fig. 2-4 Peter O'Toole: Aug 2, 1932, 12:15 AM GDT, Wicklow, Ireland (ADB – RR: A)

Fig. 2-5 Doug Liman: Jul 24, 1965, Sunrise Chart, New York, New York, USA (Wiki – RR: X)

Fig. 2-6 Ang Lee: Oct 23, 1954, Sunrise Chart, P'ing-tung, Taiwan (Wiki RR:X)

Fig. 2-7 Peter Jackson: Oct 31, 1961, 6:45 PM NZT, Wellington, New Zealand (ADB – RR: B)

Fig. 2-8 Luc Besson: Mar 18, 1959, 1:45 PM CET, Paris, France (ADB – RR: AA)

Fig. 2-9 David Lynch: Jan 20, 1946, 3:00 AM MST, Missoula, Montana, USA (ADB – RR: AA)

Fig. 2-10 Quentin Tarantino: Mar 27, 1963, Sunrise Chart, Knoxville, Tennessee, USA (Wiki – RR: X)

Fig. 2-11 Uma Thurman: Apr 29, 1970, 1:51 PM EDT, Boston, Massachusetts, USA (ADB – RR: AA)

Fig. 2-12 Andy Wachowski: Dec 29, 1967, Sunrise Chart, Chicago, Illinois, USA (Wiki – RR: X)

Fig. 2-13 Lana Wachowski: Jun 21, 1965, Sunrise Chart, Chicago, Illinois, USA (Wiki – RR: X)

Fig. 2-14 Andrea Dworkin: Sep 26, 1946, 5:03 PM EDT, Camden, New Jersey, USA (ADB – RR: AA)

Fig. 2-15 Gloria Steinem: Mar 25, 1934, 10:00 PM EST, Toledo, Ohio, USA (ADB – RR: AA)

Fig. 2-16 Betty Friedan: Feb 4, 1921, 4:00 AM CST, Peoria, Illinois, USA (ADB – RR: AA)

Fig. 2-17 Susan B. Anthony: Feb 15, 1820, Sunrise Chart, Adams, Massachusetts, USA (ADB – RR: X)

Fig. 2-18 Lucy Stone: Aug 13, 1818, Sunrise Chart, West Brookfield, Massachusetts, USA (Wiki – RR: X)

Fig. 2-19 Elizabeth Cady Stanton: Nov 12, 1815, Sunrise Chart, Johnstown, New York, USA (ADB – RR: X)

Fig. 2-20 Bruce Cockburn: May 27, 1945, 8:50 AM EWT (Rectified) Ottawa, Canada (Wiki – RR: C)

Fig. 2-21 Ani DiFranco: Sep 23, 1970, Sunrise Chart, Buffalo, New York, USA (Wiki – RR: X)

Fig. 2-22 Amy Ray: Apr 12, 1964, Sunrise Chart, Decatur, Georgia, USA (Wiki – RR: X)

Fig. 2-23 Emily Saliers: Jul 22, 1963, Sunrise Chart, New Haven, Connecticut, USA (Wiki – RR: X)

Fig. 2-24 Tori Amos: Aug 22, 1963, 1:10 PM EST, Newton, North Carolina, USA (ADB – RR: AA)

Fig. 3-1 Mary Wollstonecraft: Apr 27, 1759, Sunrise Chart, London, England (ADB – RR: X)

Fig. 3-3 Albert Einstein: Mar 14, 1879, 11:30 AM LMT, Ulm, Germany (ADB – RR: AA)

Fig. 4-1 Herman Melville: Aug 1, 1819, 11:30 PM LMT, New York, New York, USA (ADB – RR: AA)

Fig. 5-1 D. H. Lawrence: Sep 11, 1885, 9:45 AM GMT, Eastwood, Nottinghamshire, England (ADB – RR: A)

Fig. 6-1 William Blake: Nov 28, 1757, 7:45 PM LMT, London, England (ADB – RR: A)

Fig. 7-1 James Hillman: Apr 12, 1926, 9:08 AM EST, Atlantic City, New Jersey, USA (ADB – RR: A)

Fig. 7-2 Sigmund Freud: May 6, 1856, 6:30 PM -.96, Príbor, Czech Republic (ADB – RR: AA)

Fig. 7-3 USA: Jul 4, 1776, 5:13:55 PM (Rectified) LMT, Philadelphia, Pennsylvania, USA. (The time is based on the Sibly 5:10 PM chart as rectified by Dane Rudhyar and presented in his book *The Astrology of America's Destiny* RR: C)

Fig. 7-5 Eris Discovery: Jan 5, 2005, 11:20 AM PST, Pasadena, California, USA (ADB – RR: A)

Fig. 8-1 Carl Gustav Jung: Jul 26, 1875, 7:37 PM LMT, Kesswil, Switzerland (ADB – RR: C "As the sun was setting")

Fig. 8-2 Toni Wolff: Sep 18, 1888, 2:30 AM -.50 Zurich, Switzerland (ADB – RR: AA)

Fig. 9-1 Clarissa Pinkola Estés: Jan 27, 1945, Sunrise Chart, Indianapolis, Indianna, USA (Wiki – RR: X)

Fig. 9-2 Eva Pierrakos: Mar 30, 1915, 11:45 AM CET, Vienna, Austria (ADB – RR: A)

Fig. 10-2 Woody Allen: Dec 1, 1935, 10:55 PM EST, Bronx, New York, USA (ADB – RR: AA)

Fig. 10-4 Clint Eastwood: May 31, 1930, 5:35 PM PST, San Francisco, California, USA (ADB – RR: AA)

Fig. 10-6 Norman Mailer: Jan 31, 1923, 9:05 AM EST, Long Branch, New Jersey, USA (ADB – RR: C)

Fig. 10-8 Allen Ginsberg: Jun 3, 1926, 2:00 AM EDT, Newark, New Jersey, USA (ADB – RR: A)

Fig. 10-10 Neal Cassady: Feb 8, 1926, 2:05 AM MST, Salt Lake City, Utah, USA (ADB – RR: A)

Fig. 10-11 Jack Kerouac: Mar 12, 1922, 5:10 PM EST, Lowell, Massachusetts, USA (ADB – RR: A)

Fig. 10-12 Carolyn Cassady: Apr 28, 1923, Sunrise Chart, Lansing, Michigan, USA (Wiki – RR: X)

Fig. 10-15 Robert Anton Wilson: Jan 18, 1932, 6:00 PM EST, Brooklyn, Kings, New York (ADB with time corrected to 6 PM from Internet information– see Chapter 10. RR: C)

Fig. 10-18 Ursula Le Guin: Oct 21, 1929, 5:31 PM PST, Berkeley, California, USA (ADB – RR: AA)

Fig. 10-20 Hayao Miyazaki: Jan 5, 1941, Sunrise Chart, Tokyo, Japan (Wiki RR: X)

These charts were created with Henry's TimePassages astrology software, which provides standard Western techniques and interpretations, with some unique features. One optional treatment is to relocate a planet conjunct the next house cusp, within 3 degrees, into the next house for a more accurate placement. This is based on the idea that a planet conjunct the MC or Rising is best understood as a tenth house or as a first house planet, applied by extension to all the house cusps in the chart. An example is the chart of Angelina Jolie, Fig. 2-1 on page 11, where Jupiter is displayed as a tenth house factor.

Appendix B

Charts of Feminists

These are the data for the charts of all the major feminists that I have been able to concretely locate as leading figures in the movement. I was struck by the fact that every chart that I researched in this way had a strong Eris placement. In what follows, the abbreviation "ADB" refers to AstroData-Bank online and if unattributed, the source is Wikipedia.

Olympe de Gouges, playwright and feminist activist, abolitionist in pre-revolutionary France. In her *Declaration of the Rights of Woman and the Female Citizen* (1791) she challenged the 18th century societal bias of inequality for women versus men; born May 7th, 1748, Montauban, France (Rodden Rating: X). She has Eris closely opposite Mars and inconjunct Venus, her Sun ruler. Eris is also quintile a prominent Jupiter and sextile/trine the nodal axis of her solar chart. As befits a writer, Eris makes a close bi-quintile to Mercury.

Mary Wollstonecraft, author *The Vindication of the Rights of Women*; born April 27th, 1759, London, birth time unknown (Rodden Rating: X). Her chart is described in detail in Chapter 3.

Lucretia Mott, American leader of the early Feminist movement; born January 3rd, 1793, in Nantucket, Massachusetts, USA (Rodden Rating: X). In Lucretia Mott's solar chart, Eris is in aspect with the Sun, being widely conjunct. Eris also participates in her Uranus-Pluto opposition, being exactly inconjunct Uranus, as befits a revolutionary figure, and semi-sextile to Pluto. Eris in close sextile with Jupiter in her eleventh solar house reveals her advocacy for a better society, while her Eris closely square Saturn and opposed to Chiron shows her compassionate stance for justice.

Elizabeth Cady Stanton, advocate for women's rights and co-founder of the 1848 Seneca Falls Convention, advancing for the first time the cause of female suffrage; born November 12th, 1815, Johnstown, New York, USA (ADB, Rodden Rating: X). Her chart is given in Chapter 2, Fig. 2-19.

Lucy Stone, prominent orator, abolitionist and suffragette, was a powerful and outspoken advocate for women's rights; born August 13th, 1818, West Brookfield, Massachusetts, USA (Rodden Rating: X). Her chart is given in Chapter 2, Fig. 2-18.

Susan B. Anthony, American social reformer and suffragette; born February 15th, 1820, Adams MA, USA (ADB, Rodden Rating: X). Her chart is given in Chapter 2, Fig. 2-17.

Mary Edwards Walker, American feminist, abolitionist, alleged spy, prisoner of war and surgeon. As a Civil War doctor, she was captured behind enemy lines and became the only woman to ever have received the Medal of Honor. She was a suffragette in the post-war years through the late teens of the 20th century; born Nov 26th, 1832, Oswego, New York, USA (Rodden Rating: X). She has Eris closely sextile to Mercury, in close bi-quintile aspect to Saturn, and square her Mars/Chiron conjunction in the sixth solar house of service to others.

Victoria Woodhull, suffragette, early leader of the American voting rights movement, in 1872 the first female candidate for U.S. President. She was also the first woman to start a weekly newspaper; born September 23rd, 1838, 5:45 AM, Homer, Ohio, USA (ADB, Rodden Rating: C). She has an exact Sun-Jupiter conjunction on her Ascendant, square to Chiron at the Midheaven, and Eris emphasizes both these points by making a bi-quintile to the Sun/Jupiter and a trine to Chiron. Eris is also closely square Saturn, inconjunct Mercury and additionally aspects Pluto and the Moon.

Emma Goldman, revolutionary, anarchist and advocate for women's rights, and potentially violent and controversial character who was born in Eastern Europe and became famous in turn-of-the-century New York; birth data: June 27th, 1869, at 3 PM, in Kaunas, Lithuania (ADB, Rodden Rating: DD). She has Eris trine the Sun and almost exactly square Saturn. With her Uranus-Venus conjunction in Cancer; Venus could well be her chart ruler by some of the speculative times for her chart (2:15 PM LMT). Eris is also in trine to this conjunction, and sextile to Pluto and Jupiter. Eris trines the Sun/Uranus midpoint within arc-minutes.

Margaret Sanger, founder of Planned Parenthood; born September 14th, 1879, at 2:30 AM, Corning New York, USA (ADB, Rodden Rating: C). Eris is in the eighth house in Pisces, opposition Sun, sextile Chiron-Neptune at the top of the chart; quintile her close Pluto-Mars conjunction in the tenth house; closely semi-sextile Saturn.

Simone de Beauvoir, revolutionary writer, philosopher, political activist and feminist, author of *The Second Sex*, was born on January 9th, 1908, 4:30 AM, -.20, Paris, France (ADB, Rodden Rating: AA). She also has strong Eris, which takes part in her Saturn-Eris-Mars-Moon stellium on the Nadir, covering 7 degrees of late Pisces. Eris in addition closely squares Pluto and quintiles Uranus, both less than one degree, and makes aspects to Jupiter and the Sun.

Betty Friedan, who wrote *The Feminine Mystique*, was a very well-known advocate for women's rights, credited with initiating a so-called "second-wave" of American feminism in the Sixties. She founded the National Organization for Women; born February 4th, 1921, 4:00 AM, Peoria, Illinois, USA (ADB, Rodden Rating: AA). Her chart is given in Chapter 2, Fig. 2-16.

Adrienne Rich, well-known and widely read lesbian poet and advocate for women's rights; born May 16th, 1929, 3:10 PM, Baltimore, Maryland, USA (ADB, Rodden Rating: AA). She has Eris closely trine Mars, square Saturn, sextile the Sun and septile Jupiter. She would be expected to possess a Mercury-Eris connection because of the importance for her of writing. While she has no longitudinal aspect between Eris and Mercury, she does have a close contraparallel.

Gloria Steinem, activist, feminist and journalist, co-founder of *Ms Magazine*; born March 25th, 1934, 10:00 PM, Toledo, Ohio, USA (ADB, Rodden Rating: AA). Her chart is given in Chapter 2, Fig. 2-15.

Susan Brownmiller, feminist journalist, author and civil rights activist, she famously wrote Against *Our Will, Men, Women and Rape*; born February 15th, 1935, Brooklyn, Kings, New York, USA (Rodden Rating: X). She has Eris semi-sextile Saturn, sextile the North Node, in close sextile with Chiron and in trine and contraparallel with Pluto. This is telling symbolism since Pluto and Chiron are astrological archetypes associated with her most well known subject matter.

Carol Gilligan, feminist, psychologist, ethics theorist, university professor; born November 28th, 1936, New York, USA (Rodden Rating: X). She has Eris trine the Sun and Pluto, opposite Mars and square Jupiter. She also has an exact parallel between Eris and Mercury, as well as Eris in close parallel with Jupiter. The strong Eris-Jupiter combination is symbolically appropriate for her philosophical work and life-long teaching career.

Ti-Grace Atkinson, American feminist and author, joined NOW in the Sixties and was an influential author and advocate for women's rights; born November 9th, 1938, Baton Rouge, Louisiana, USA (Rodden Rating: X). She has Mercury and Venus in close conjunction with Eris in nearly exact trine. Eris is sesquiquadrate the Sun, trine Pluto forming a close grand trine in Fire signs, and square Chiron. Like Carol Gilligan and as befits a feminist writer, she has Eris in close parallel with Mercury.

Erica Jong, writer and teacher, and author of *Fear of Flying*, an influence on so-called second wave feminism, was born March 26th, 1942, 10:25 AM, Manhattan, New York, USA (ADB, Rodden Rating: AA). Her Eris is conjunct the Sun within half a degree and closely trine Pluto. Eris aspects Jupiter, Saturn and Uranus, and is opposed to Neptune. Eris is also semi-square Venus within 40 arc-minutes, corresponding to relationships – the characteristic subject matter of her writing.

Angela Davis, radical feminist and civil rights activist, professor, scholar and author. She has spoken out against racism in America and has been involved in prison reform; born January 26th, 1944, 12:30 PM, Birmingham, Alabama, USA (ADB, Rodden Rating: AA). Her chart is presented in Chapter 1; see Fig. 1-1.

Rita Mae Brown, writer, feminist, advocate for lesbian and civil rights, sportsperson; born November 28th, 1944, 4:45 AM, Hanover, Pennsylvania, USA (ADB, Rodden Rating: A). She has Eris trine the Sun and Mars, square Saturn, sextile Uranus, exactly opposite Neptune and opposite Chiron. Eris is also in close parallel with the Sun, also parallel to Mars and contraparallel to Uranus. She holds a degree from NYU in cinematography, reflecting the close aspect to Neptune.

Jo Freeman, feminist, political scientist, writer, attorney, community organizer and civil rights activist; was born August 26th, 1945, Atlanta Georgia, USA (Rodden Rating: X). She has Eris closely opposed to a triple conjunction in early Libra of Jupiter, Neptune and Chiron. Eris also squares the nodal axis in her solar chart. She has many other Eris aspects with Eris inconjunct the Sun, sesquiquadrate Mercury, contraparallel Venus and Saturn, quintile Uranus and trine Pluto.

Andrea Dworkin, activist, feminist and advocate for lesbian rights. Critical of pornography; born September 26th, 1946, 5:03 PM, Camden, New Jersey, USA (ADB, Rodden Rating: AA). Her chart is presented in Chapters 1 and 2; see Fig. 2-14.

Hillary Rodham Clinton, feminist, politician, former First Lady and now favored for the U.S. presidency; born October 26th, 1947, 8:02 AM, Chicago, Illinois, USA (ADB, Rodden Rating: DD). She has Eris in combination with many planets in her chart, inconjunct the Sun, trine and parallel Jupiter, bi-quintile Chiron, parallel and sesquiquadrate to Mercury. Her passion for equality and justice is reflected in a close sesquiquadrate from Eris to Saturn as well as to Mercury, forming a very tight sesqui-yod to Eris, within mere minutes of a degree for all three aspects.

Kim Gandy, American feminist and mathematician, served in the National Organization for Women for over 20 years, the last 8 years as president before being termed out in 2009; born January 25th, 1954, Bossier City, Louisiana, USA (Rodden Rating: X). She has Eris sextile and parallel the Sun and Mercury, sextile Venus, inconjunct Saturn, and quintile Chiron in Capricorn. Eris is as well sesquiquadrate Mars and also Pluto, forming a sesqui-yod. Her mathematical and organizational bent is reflected in the very close parallel between Eris, the Sun and Mercury.

Rebecca Walker, feminist, activist, author and contributor to many magazines such as *Ms Magazine*, *Harper's* and *Mademoiselle*. The daughter of Alice Walker, she was for many years a contributing editor to Ms, after writing an influential article while still in college mobilizing a new generation of feminist voices called "Becoming the Third Wave." After graduating cum laude from Yale she has been involved in political activism and a non-profit organization she co-founded called the *Third Wave Foundation*; born November 17th, 1969, Chicago, Illinois, USA (Rodden Rating: X). She has Eris in close sesquiquadrate with a tight triple conjunction of the Sun, Mercury and Neptune, in Scorpio. The closest aspect is to Mercury and to the Sun/Neptune midpoint. She also has Eris inconjunct Venus, sextile Mars, opposite Uranus and contraparallel to Pluto. Her idealism, as reflected in her activities is echoed her solar chart by the symbolism of Eris with the Sun and Neptune.

Appendix C

Charts of Paradigm Shifters

The thesis presented in collecting these charts is that all of these personages, mostly male, are possessed with strong Eris, by the very fact that they are known for standing their era's existing established science on its head, the most famous example being the heliocentric theory of Copernicus. Like the charts of feminist leaders collected as Appendix B, this list was compiled by considering the most prominent of these individuals and examining their charts. The examples are not chosen for the strength of their Eris, but rather for their place in the record books They partake of the rarefied air of those who strove to birth new scientific concepts into being. There are a few anti-scientific ones as well, since social activist paradigm challengers are also included. In what follows, the abbreviation "ADB" refers to AstroDataBank online and if unattributed, the source is Wikipedia.

Nicolaus Copernicus, paradigm shifter extraordinaire, was born on February 28th, 1473 (Gregorian) at 17:13 LMT, Torun, Poland (ADB, Adjusted for LMT from 5 PM – based on "astrologers present at his birth" Rodden Rating: AA). He seems to have been the first modern Western astronomer to recognize that the Sun was the center of the Earth-Sun system, as a better and simpler explanation for observable planetary motion. He had a spiritual motivation as well as a mathematical one, because he felt that the Circle was predominant in a God-created universe and that the Earthly sphere would therefore logically move in a circle around the Sun.[1] Well aware of the stir this notion would bring about, the ridicule it would suffer and the potential persecution that its adherents would face, he published his heliocentric theory – that it was the Earth that revolved around the Sun – late in life, so that in fact the first copy was presented to him on his deathbed. His natal chart does contain ample evidence of strong Eris, making close aspects to many of the other planets in his chart, being sextile Mars, closely sextile both Saturn and Chiron, residing near the midpoint of their trine, sesquiquadrate his Jupiter-Moon conjunction, and also inconjunct both Pluto and Neptune, forming a yod to Eris. There is a close contra-parallel between Eris and Mercury, his chart ruler. It is also interesting to note that Coperni-

225

cus' Saturn-Neptune partile inconjunct is a perfect chime for someone who would take a spiritual approach to existing structures, and dream new ones into being. This aspect is greatly emphasized by the partile Eris connection to these two planets, with Saturn, Neptune and Eris all at 18 degrees of their respective signs. I have often found it to be so that the Eris connection to natal planets emphasizes these planets for the individual in ways that correspond to deeper issues of the soul or the personality.

Galileo Galilei, who followed Copernicus by nearly a century, was born on February 26th, 1564 (Gregorian) at 3:41 PM, Pisa, Italy (ADB, the time based on charts that he himself drew up, Rodden Rating: A). He was inspired by the heliocentric theory and was able to provide proof for some of its predictions after he invented a more powerful telescope and was able to show a doubting public the phases of Venus, and the moons of Jupiter. In his chart, Eris is in Taurus, elevated in the tenth house of career, and closely aspects his personal planets. Eris makes a square to his probable ascendant, and is closely sextile his Venus-Pluto conjunction in Pisces, and also inconjunct his probable Moon position and quintile his Sun. Eris is also trine Chiron. This latter aspect makes sense in his biography, since Galileo famously suffered for his radical belief in the heliocentric theory of the solar system. Having been declared a heretic by the Church for these beliefs, he was forced to recant, and remained under house arrest for the rest of his life.

Johannes Kepler, a contemporary of Galileo, was born on January 6th, 1572 (Gregorian) at 14:37 LMT, Weil der Stadt, Germany (ADB, based on his own biographical details, and might have been up to two hours earlier, Rodden Rating: B). He was a supporter of the heliocentric theory and provided crucial refinements to Copernicus' original vision when he stated in his laws of planetary motion that the planets, in their elliptical (rather than circular) orbits around the Sun, sweep out equal areas in equal time, no matter where in their orbit they are found. Kepler's Eris, at the powerful sixteenth degree of Taurus, makes a partile trine with his Sun, and is also trine Venus, bi-quintile Mars, in close opposition to Saturn, sextile Jupiter and trine Uranus. His Jupiter, at 18+ degrees of Pisces, sextile Venus and the Sun, supports by square and trine the Saturn-Neptune partile inconjunct in the chart of Nicolaus Copernicus, being at the same degree of Pisces. This is fascinating considering that he became the closest subsequent link to the original heliocentric model, until Newton's work was made known nearly eight decades after Kepler's work was published.

Isaac Newton, who came along in the following century, and supported the Copernican model, as well as almost totally revolutionizing the then-extant theory of light, was born on January 4th, 1663 (Gregorian) at about 1:38 LMT, Wolsthorpe Manor, England (ADB, "one or two hours after midnight", Rodden Rating: C). He was the one who fully confirmed the heliocentric model by his famous inverse-square law describing gravity, finally providing a scientific explanation for the movements of the planets, as well as falling bodies in the terrestrial context. His work was radical at the time of its publication, and eventually came to define physics and mathematics for subsequent ages. He has Eris elevated and in partile conjunction with his Moon, widely opposed to the Sun, sextile Mars and trine Venus. All three outer planet archetypes are also activated, since Eris is closely sesquiquadrate Uranus, inconjunct Neptune and semi-sextile to Pluto. The combination of Eris with Pluto and with Uranus suggests a revolutionary; indeed, in intellectual disciplines, Newton was this. Additionally, his Jupiter-Saturn conjunction, five and a half degrees apart, creates a great deal of focus within his personality because it is located in his fifth house of creative self-expression. When the Royal Society first published his inverse-square law of gravity in relation to the movements of the planets, called (in Latin) "On the Motion of Bodies in Orbit," there was a Full Moon that night that was conjunct Newton's Eris within little more than a degree, while transiting Eris and Saturn, in partile conjunction, were simultaneously in partile opposition to his Jupiter-Saturn midpoint in the fifth house.

Antoine Lavoisier, another paradigm shifter who reinvented the science of chemistry in pre-revolutionary France, giving Oxygen its name, was born on August 26th, 1743, at 9:30 AM LMT, Paris, France (ADB, based on a vague reference to morning, Rodden Rating: C). His chart also shows strong Eris, residing at 2 Sagittarius, in partile square with his Virgo Sun. Eris also squares Saturn and Mercury, which are in triple conjunction with his Sun, is closely semi-square Venus, and is quintile Jupiter and septile Uranus, both within 1 degree.

James Clerk Maxwell, who formulated the science of electromagnetic radiation, bringing together for the first time electricity, magnetism, and light, as manifestations of the same phenomenon, was born on June 13th, 1831, time unknown, Edinburgh, Scotland (ADB, Rodden Rating: X). Even without knowing the time, he too has strong Eris, being in partile conjunction with Jupiter and trine the Sun, also opposed Saturn, widely conjunct Uranus, semi-sextile Neptune and semi-square Pluto.

Nikola Tesla, a rebel scientist who invented the concept of the electric motor as well as Alternating Current or AC, for better transmission of electricity, was born on July 10th, 1856 (Gregorian) at midnight, Smiljan, Croatia (ADB, Rodden Rating: B). He has Eris in a very close partile trine to Saturn, in Water signs, and also in close partile sextile to Pluto, so that Pluto resides on the Eris/Saturn midpoint. Eris is also semi-sextile Chiron, and sesquiquadrate to Mars.

Max Planck, who has been compared to Einstein in his importance for modern physics, originated the quantum theory at the turn of the 20th century. He was born on April 23rd, 1858, time unknown, Kiel, Germany (ADB, Rodden Rating: X). He has Eris sextile Sun, closely sextile Pluto, quintile Venus, square Mars and closely sesquiquadrate Saturn.

Albert Einstein, who was of course another paradigm shifter par excellence, single-handedly changing the face of modern physics with his theory of relativity and the conservation of mass and energy, was born on March 14th 1879, and has Eris in Pisces at the top of his chart, nearly coincident with his Midheaven. His chart is given in Appendix A and described in detail in the second half of Chapter 3.

Max Born, a physicist and mathematician who was instrumental in the development of quantum mechanics, worked closely with Werner Heisenberg. He was born on December 11th, 1882, birth time unknown, Breslau, Poland (ADB, Rodden Rating: X). His chart shows many Eris aspects, among them a relatively close square to the Sun, as well as Mars and Venus, and a square within half a degree to Mercury, all in Sagittarius. Eris is also sextile Saturn and Neptune, quintile Pluto and also in close square to the Sun/Venus midpoint.

Wolfgang Pauli, another of the pioneers of the quantum theory, who was known for inventing the "Pauli exclusion principle," and for postulating the existence of a particle that became known as the neutrino, was born on April 25, 1900, at approximately 1:43 PM, Vienna, Austria (ADB, as rectified by Noel Tyl based on details regarding a horoscope that Pauli once had drawn up, Rodden Rating: C). Pauli has Eris in wide semi-square to the Sun, and square Pluto. He also has in his chart an opposition between a Venus-Neptune conjunction, located at 20 and 24 degrees of Gemini, and Chiron at 24 degrees of Sagittarius. Eris at the 22-degree mark of Pisces is therefore the apex of a very precise T-square from these planets. The particular planets involved in this Eris configuration are quite interesting because, in the 1930s, Pauli had a breakdown and, living near Zurich, went to C. G. Jung for therapy. The two men subsequently became friends who collaborated philosophically with each other. In the late 1940s Jung corresponded with and received a great deal of support from Pauli regarding the formulation of his *Principle of Synchronicity*, which was published some years later.[2] Pauli's Neptune conjunction with Venus, his second house ruler, opposite Chiron, as emphasized by Eris, makes for a symbolic chime with these events. This is because Neptune has symbolism in common with the numinous and magical (essentially anti-logical and, as Jung terms it, acausal) concept of their investigation together of the principle of synchronicity, formed as an important part of their relationship (Venus) based on spiritual principles (Neptune) and derived from an experience of healing (Chiron). Interestingly, their synastry reveals quite a few Eris aspects as well. Although 25 years apart from each other, Jung's Eris is strongly connected to Pauli's Uranus, Pluto and Mars, while Pauli's Eris is sextile Jung's Pluto, square his Mars and inconjunct his Jupiter; all extremely close aspects.

Werner Heisenberg, who was responsible for greatly clarifying the understanding and the mathematics of the quantum theory, was born on December 5th, 1901 at 4:45 PM, Würzburg, Germany (ADB, Rodden Rating: AA). He also has strong Eris, being widely square his Sun-Uranus conjunction in Sagittarius, trine Mercury, septile Venus, and quintile Mars. Between June and July of 1925, he formulated a reinterpretation of the quantum theory and, in September 1925, published an important paper calling for its acceptance. By 1926, he had published his new mathematical equations. In 1927 came his famous "Uncertainty Principle." In late September 1925, when the first paper was published, Heisenberg's natal Eris was transited by Uranus, while the Sun entering into Libra opposed the position of transiting Eris at 0 degrees Aries. Transiting Eris therefore made a partile square to his natal Neptune at 0 degrees of Cancer and a partile sextile to his Venus at 0 degrees of Aquarius. Right in the middle of his time of inspiration, Eris was stationary, having stationed retrograde in 1925 on June 27th. It is interesting to note that Neptune, transited by Eris in square, is the ruler of his eleventh house of group participation. He was working in concert with several of his colleagues as he formulated the mathematics of quantum theory during this period, so that some of the papers bear three names.

Alan Turing, who was a brilliant British mathematician responsible for cracking the code of the Nazi's Enigma machine during the years of World

War II, is also credited for inventing the first computer. The mathematical structure that underlies all of theoretical computational science is referred to as a "Turing Machine." He was born on June 23rd, 1912 at 2:15 AM, London, England (ADB, Rodden Rating: A) and has Eris in square with a triple conjunction of Venus, Pluto and the Sun. The square with the leading planet, Venus, is within half of degree. He also has Eris closely sextile Saturn, trine Neptune and sesquiquadrate Mars.

Dane Rudhyar, astrologer, philosopher, musician, and paradigm shifter in his major field, created in the 1930s a new branch of Western astrology that came to be known as Humanistic Astrology that was sensitive to recent advances in psychology, for example the Jungian school. He was born on March 23rd, 1895, at 0:42 AM, Paris, France (ADB, according to his own rectified birth time, Rodden Rating: C). He has Eris at 20 Pisces 47, in close conjunction with his North Node within 1 degree, also in close sesquiquadrate to Saturn, closely trine Uranus (associated with astrology), and also in a very close square to the Jupiter/Neptune midpoint at 20 Gemini 32 – highlighting the triple conjunction of Pluto, Mars, and Neptune in that sign. The inclusion of the Jupiter/Neptune midpoint in this Eris configuration pulls these planets even closer together in his chart. This is fitting symbolism for one who took the spiritual side of both music and astrology to a new high-water mark with his many, philosophically oriented, books and articles.

Marc Edmund Jones, another pioneer of modern humanistic Western astrology who invented and helped to channel the Sabian Symbols for each degree of the zodiac, was born on October 1st, 1888, at 8:37 AM, St Louis, Missouri, USA (ADB, Rodden Rating: A). Like Rudhyar, his Eris also closely aspects Uranus in Libra – in this case, by an inconjunct within 1 degree. Eris is also inconjunct his tight Moon-Saturn conjunction in Leo, forming a yod to Eris, and is square Mars in Sagittarius, quintile Neptune in Gemini, and precisely sesquiquadrate Mercury in early Scorpio, also sesquiquadrate Venus (in conjunction with Mercury). So this is another example of undeniably strong Eris, and in combination with planets (Saturn and Uranus) that define his powerful leadership impact on the field of astrology.

Thomas Kuhn, the historian of science, who invented the term "paradigm," and revolutionized his field, is also possessed of strong Eris. He was born on July 18th, 1922, time unknown, Cincinnati, Ohio, USA (Rodden Rating: X). He has Eris at 0 degrees of Aries, conjunct the South Node and opposite Saturn within 2½ degrees. His Eris trines his Sun, is inconjunct Venus, parallel Mars, square Mercury and in exact sesquiquadrate with Neptune. His Eris thus pulls more closely together his natal Mercury-Saturn square, a very good thing for an historian. In 1961 and 1962, when his landmark book *The Structure of Scientific Revolutions* was published, transiting Eris was at 9-10 degrees of Aries, thus squaring his natal Pluto, opposing natal Jupiter, and trining natal Mars – all exact or within one degree.

Masaru Emoto, the recently deceased disruptive scientist of Water, has shifted the way that we think about matter. He famously demonstrated that the structure of the crystals that are formed from a water sample as it freezes depends on the quality of positive attention that has been paid to the sample. Classical music helps, as does a positive word written on paper – defamatory words having the opposite effect. He was born on July 22nd, 1943, at 4:50 PM, Yokohama, Japan (ADB, from his older sister to Vaughn Paul Manley, writing in *The Mountain Astrologer*, Feb./March 2006, Rodden Rating: A). He has a partile Moon-Eris conjunction. Eris is in a close trine to his triple conjunction of Mercury, Jupiter, and Pluto, making a partile trine to the Jupiter/Pluto midpoint. Eris is also sextile Uranus within less than 2 degrees, opposite Neptune, and closely bi-quintile Chiron. Incidentally, a number of these scientists have close Eris-Moon aspects – as did Einstein (a partile square).

Henry David Thoreau, who, although not a scientist, was a cultural iconoclast and helped to shift the thinking of his times on the issue of living close to nature, was born on July 12th, 1817, time unknown, Concord, Massachusetts, USA (ADB, Rodden Rating: X). He has Eris at 13 degrees Aquarius aspecting other outer planets in Sagittarius: quintile Jupiter, sextile Uranus, and septile Neptune, all within about a degree. His Eris is also semi-square Pluto in Pisces and sesquiquadrate his Mercury in the first degree of Cancer. The back-to-nature movement that he more or less founded was an idea that was made far more popular by the Hippie movement of the tumultuous 1960s, and Thoreau's Sagittarius planets have an interesting connection to the Uranus-Pluto conjunction, first at 17 and then at 16 degrees of Virgo, that defined this era, his Uranus/Neptune midpoint being in almost perfect square at 17¼ degrees. When Thoreau began his two-year escape from modern civilization at Walden Pond, on July 4th, 1845, in the process writing his classic *Walden*, transiting Eris at 0 degree Pisces was in a tight trine to his natal Mercury at 1 degree Cancer, with transiting Uranus in Aries sextile his natal Eris. Pluto, also in Aries, made a close quintile (only 6 arc minutes from exact) to his natal Eris, while the transiting Cancer New Moon of that same day was in partile (to the degree) inconjunct to his natal Eris. Nine years later, in 1854, when Eris stationed less than a degree away from his Saturn in Pisces, the work was finally published.

Barbara Marx Hubbard, another paradigm shifter in terms of social science, considers herself a futurist and would like to see things change. She is a dynamic spokesperson for the coming of the Aquarian Age, an innovator among feminist voices and one who is a champion of an onrushing cultural paradigm shift; a changing of the guard in Western social evolution. She has been, in 1984, a candidate for vice-president of the United States. She created the term: "The birthing of humanity." She was born on December 22nd, 1929, time unknown, near New York, NY, USA (Rodden Rating: X). She has Eris at 0 degrees of Aries, in partile square to her Sun degree. Additionally, her Saturn-Uranus natal square, which characterizes her Aquarian lack of sympathy for an outmoded status quo, is greatly emphasized by the presence of Eris conjunct Uranus and in a very close square to Saturn. Eris is inconjunct Neptune, and also parallel to Mercury, the signature of a prolific speaker and writer, as indeed she is. The Amazon website has this to say: "A world-renowned visionary futurist, evolutionary educator and inspiring speaker, Barbara is the author of six acclaimed books that communicate the new worldview of conscious evolution. She is the co-founder and chair of the Foundation for Conscious Evolution, and additionally co-founded many progressive organizations, including The Association for Global New Thought, as well as The World Future Society." Her own commentary includes the following gem from 2012: "It has become obvious that a creative minority of humanity is undergoing a profound inner mutation or transformation. Evolutionary ideas are not only serving to make sense of this change, but also acting to catalyze the potential within us to transform."[3]

Notes
1. *Copernicus and the Aristotelian Tradition*, p.351.
2. *Pauli and Jung: The Meeting of Two Great Minds*, pp.99-109.
3. Quoted in the description of an event called Conscious Evolutionaries Chicago,http://www.meetup.com/Chicago-Cross-Cultural-Meetup-Group/events/76679082/

APPENDIX D

Historical Survey

No discussion of Eris as a new outer planet archetype would be complete without at least an outline of the historical periods when Eris was in axial and square alignment with the other outer planets. Astrologer Richard Tarnas, in *Cosmos and Psyche*, provides an exhaustive study of certain planetary combinations that shows the power of analyzing such periods of history. In his book, Tarnas defined a method whereby he recommends 15 degree orbs on either side of the exact conjunction or opposition, with 10 degrees for the intervening squares. Although the 15 degree orb that Tarnas uses is large, he makes a good case for it in his already classic work. These define periods when the archetypal themes of the outer planet archetypes of Saturn, Uranus, Neptune and Pluto are thus combined, without reference to whether the period is one of conjunction or opposition. For example the French Revolution of 1789-1799 was almost exactly coincident with a Uranus-Pluto opposition, and the subsequent 1960s' rebellious period saw very similar themes, upon a much later conjunction. The period that he gives for this latter combination, using the 15 degree orb, is 1960-1972, which fits nicely with the volatile 60s. He also cites Jupiter with Uranus as periods of scientific and intellectual invention. In this Appendix, I give, in outline form, some indication of the combinations of Eris with the outermost traditional Western planets, Uranus, Neptune and Pluto.

This is merely the beginning of such a study, which further research will more thoroughly flesh out. An updated version of this document appears on my website at http://www.astrograph.com/Eris-Info

Uranus-Eris

The hallmark of these periods would be the cry for freedom inherent in the Uranus archetype, and the no-holds-barred struggle to achieve it that typifies the Eris archetype, therefore characterizing these periods when they combine as times of proto-revolutionary activity that attempts to throw off the chains of prejudice or persecution. One such period would logically then be the founding of the freer Western society of the New World, especially in North America, to which many originally emigrated in order to flee religious oppression in Europe. Looking back into still earlier periods, it's interesting that the Magna Carta (1215), that epic pronouncement that in England limited the absolute power of kings, was signed under a Uranus–Eris square.

1377–1385 Opposition (15˚)

In 1378, in Florence, the *tulmulto dei Ciompi* – the revolt of the wool carders – brought workers into power; a moratorium was declared on debts and interest rates were reduced. The business class was, however, soon returned to power. Feudalism was more common in 14th century England, and during the same period of time, in 1381, a significant rebellion was fomented on the part of serfs who sought the end of the feudal system, and for a brief moment achieved it. They had been greatly oppressed for many years. This was termed "The Peasant's Revolt" or "The Great Uprising," and has been much studied by historians, and was once considered a defining moment in English history. The rebels demanded the end to feudalism, and this was briefly granted by the young King Richard II, when he met with them outside the City of London. After the rebellion became violent, killing many of the aristocracy and also foreigners living in London, it was dispersed, its leaders executed and the feudal system reinstated.

Also in 1378, a quirky and very unusual (Uranus) Papal Schism resulted in two Popes, one in Avignon, France, and one in Rome. This was actually the continuation of a ploy for power on the part of France. One fomenting rationale was an attempt by the new Pope in Rome, in 1378, to curb corruption. This moment also contributed to religious freedom in that some of the groundwork was laid for the Protestant Reformation, 150 years later.

In England, the teachings of John Wycliffe grew to a point of active conflict when he was expelled from Oxford in 1381. The lay mysticism he preached was another precursor to the Reformation, so that the theme of greater religious freedom was again invoked by this act. Wycliffe's translation of the Bible appeared in 1382 – and was the inspiration and chief cause of the Lollard movement, a pre-Reformation movement that rejected many of the distinctive teachings of the then-extant Church, inspiring subsequent rebellious movements within an increasingly fractured Christendom.

1422–1431 Conjunction (15˚)

The very beginning of this period marked the death of Henry V of England and the ascension of his infant son, Henry VI, ruling for 15 years through his regents, which changed the rulership of England and the characteristics of the long standing war between England and France. A new element of uncertainty arose.

This period also saw the ascension of Joan of Arc in 1429, the defeat of the English invading army, and her subsequent martyr's death by burning (1431). This was considered an important turning point of the Hundred Years War, and resulted in the crowning of the Dauphin as an actual native-born King, leading to the eventual return of France to the French some two decades later. Joan of Arc was ultimately sainted by the Catholic Church, becoming one of the principal patron saints of France. As befits a violently battling religious figure, she herself was born under the preceding Neptune-Eris square of 1407-1418, probably in 1412, when the square was within a few degrees of exactitude.

1465–1473 Opposition (15°)
The printing and popularization of many classic manuscripts in Renaissance Italy made for a new kind of intellectual freedom. The "Dark Ages" were beginning to recede. Many manuscripts from the Classic era now found their way into publication as science and humanism was reborn. It was in many ways an early precursor to the Age of Enlightenment.

This followed the remarkable decade of the 1450s – with Eris and Neptune in axial alignment – when Gutenberg published his Bible and when the fall of Constantinople in 1453 brought Byzantine scholars and their precious preserved manuscripts to the safety of the European continent.

In Italy, the Florentine Renaissance was in relative disarray, between the death of Cosimo de Medici in 1464 and the secure takeover by his grandson, Lorenzo, who acceded to power in 1469 at the early age of 21 and did not stabilize his reign until the mid-1470s. Soon he would come to be called Lorenzo the Magnificent, in the era of Botticelli and Verrocchio. A decade later, Leonardo da Vinci and Pico della Mirandola were in their prime. Thus these years from the mid-1460s onward were the chaos before the birth of the golden age of the Florentine Renaissance.

In England this was also a time of violent uncertainty and rebellion, as the Wars of the Roses raged, dominating England from 1461-1471. During this time period the country's ruler switched several times from the House of Lancaster (Henry VI) to the House of York (Edward IV) and then back again. Edward VI was restored to the throne in 1470, but was deposed in May of 1471 when Edward IV was reinstated.

1512–1520   Conjunction (15°)

This period was an age of innovation, in keeping with the symbolism of the Uranian archetype, simultaneously stimulated by both Jupiter and by Eris over the first two years. These years of the culmination of the Italian High Renaissance saw the rise of Humanism as a new kind of art flourished, with the completion of Michelangelo's Sistine Chapel, and of Raphael's series of paintings for Pope Julius II, including some of his most famous works like *The School of Athens* and *Mount Parnassus*. Titian was at the height of his early period, *The Assumption of the Virgin* being completed in 1516. In Nuremberg, Albrecht Dürer was engraving and painting his greatest works, such as *Adam and Eve*.

These were also the years of Luther's rebellion against the papacy – initiated by his railing attack against corrupt Church practices. In 1517, the 95 *Theses of Protest* were written, and over the next two years were translated from Latin into German and widely circulated. He questioned whether the Christian laity could not read for themselves the Bible in the vernacular, tolerating no intermediary between themselves and God. This began the Protestant Reformation and established new vistas of religious freedom.

Also, in global exploration, this period saw new developments that greatly expanded the consciousness of Western minds regarding the dimensions and true characteristics of the earth. Balboa first sighted the Pacific in 1513. In this same year, Ponce de Leon became the first European to set foot in Florida, which he named. Ferdinand Magellan led the first expedition to sail into, and name, the Pacific Ocean, rounding the tip of South America in October 1520.

It is interesting to note that the equally important first voyages of Amerigo Vespucci were somewhat earlier, when Eris and Uranus were also in combination, although not in dynamic aspect. His explorations of 1499-1500 were the first to observe the size of the South American land mass and he was first to correctly assert that it was in actually a new continent that had been discovered. Eris and Uranus were closely sextile, within 4 degrees for almost the entirety of these two years.

1555–1562   Opposition (15°)

Another blow for religious freedom was struck in September 1555, when the Peace of Augsburg was signed between Charles V, Holy Roman Emperor and the Lutheran Schmalkaldic League, establishing the principle that rulers within the Empire could choose the religion of their realms. It was the triumph of the Reformation.

In England, the ascension of Queen Elizabeth I in 1558 represented a move toward the re-establishment of Protestantism, while Catholic worship in secret was also tolerated.

1603–1612 Conjunction (15˚)
This was the time of revolutionary science in the persons of Kepler and Galileo, who separately in 1610 were each able to provide proof in different ways of Copernicus' heliocentric theory of the Solar System.

In England, the beginning of this period coincided with the end of the long-standing reign of Queen Elizabeth and the coronation of King James I. This changing of the guard in the English monarchy resulted in greater persecution of Catholics, and inspired their reaction in one of the most famous revolutionary acts in English history: the Gunpowder Plot of 1605. This was intended to assassinate the King and destroy the entire House of Lords in session. The plot was foiled when Guy Fawkes was discovered guarding the gunpowder in the cellars on November 5th, 1605, which has been commemorated ever since as Guy Fawkes Night and celebrated with bonfires. The Guy Fawkes mask has become a symbol for revolutionary activity.

The *King James Bible*, published in 1611, encouraged the principle that every person was free to read the Word of God for him or herself, another factor in the burgeoning power of the common man, enabling greater religious freedom from centralized authority.

This period also saw the establishment of the first permanent colony in the New World, at Jamestown, in 1607. The symbolism associated with Uranus includes revolutionary new beginnings and this certainly was one. The determination of the colonists to establish themselves in new territory makes for a nice fit with the Eris symbolism of survival at any cost. The hardship of this event could be summarized in the loss of 80% of the population due to disease and starvation from 1609-1610 and a vicious war with the local indigenous population. These natives had originally helped the colonists but were subsequently drawn into warfare resulting by 1610 in their being wiped out.[1] This settlement paved the way for the colonial period of American history that in turn led to the American Revolution of 1776 to 1781 (see 1780-1790).

1653–1670 Opposition (15°)

In England, this was the period of the Restoration of the Monarchy, beginning in 1660. It was the pendulum swing back to the status quo before the English Civil War of 1642-1651 that had put the Parliamentarians in power under the puritanical Oliver Cromwell. In keeping with the surge of Uranian energy, the Restoration signaled greater religious freedom and was far more tolerant to British Catholicism.

During this period also, John Milton wrote *Paradise Lost*, dictated from 1658 to 1664, and published in 1667. The poem presents Protestant themes of separation from religious dogma and the freedom to choose for oneself. Blake averred that Milton had a great deal of sympathy for the opposition to organized religion in presenting his story of the rebellion in Heaven and the subsequent Fall from Eden, calling him, in praise, "one of the Devil's party."

Interestingly, this followed directly upon the Uranus-Neptune conjunction of 1643-1658, marking a period of time from the 1640s onward that was characterized by the outbreak of new religious movements like the Quakers. For example, in 1656, John Naylor led his fellow Quakers on a pilgrimage in which they threw off their garments, crying "Holy, holy, holy" in imitation of Jesus' entry into Jerusalem, implying that all men were Christ. Naylor was jailed. Mathew Fox, who was already imprisoned, had founded the movement earlier in the mid-seventeenth century. Rent by controversy during the 1660s and the 1670s, the Quakers went on to eventually find a safe haven in the New World.

1722–1732 Conjunction (15°)

In alignment with the freedom principle represented by Uranus, this was the heart of a period of greater openness toward new information and for allowing diversifications of opinion greater scope. The religious wars were over and religious tolerance was gradually spreading. In science, after Newton, there was a fresh breeze blowing that aided the spread of new discoveries and concepts. The results of New World exploration in terms of the comparing of other cultures with the European, and the discovery of novel plant and animal species, was also an enlightening factor during this period. Jonathon Swift's novel *Gulliver's Travels* appeared in 1726, famously satirizing the notion of encountering other vastly different cultures, and how by describing these a traveler might make his reputation. Swift himself was born in 1667, during the preceding Uranus–Eris opposition.

This was also the early ascendancy of the freedom-loving Voltaire who established an international reputation by skewering the conventionality of traditional religious and political viewpoints of his day. His exile in England, from 1726-1728, greatly enhanced his international influence. After returning to France, he began his long relationship with Émilie du Châtelet, and together they studied Newton's work. Eventually, her translation of Newton's *Principia* was to promote the wider acceptance of Newton's scientific achievements and his philosophy.

1780–1790 Opposition (15°)
This was when the American revolutionary war was raging, and when the aftermath of the British departure allowed the colonists to establish the beginning of their own sovereign state. The symbolism is appropriate. The U.S. Constitution was ratified in 1788. The swearing in of Washington as the country's first president was in March of 1789.

The Bill of Rights, a refinement of the original constitutional document, came in 1791, during what Tarnas refers to as the "penumbral" period, that is, when the opposition was within 20 degrees of exact.

The long parade to bring the remains of the radical iconoclast Voltaire to be re-buried in Paris, in July of 1791, was attended by a million people, also during the penumbral period of this Uranus-Eris opposition.

1829–1838 Conjunction (15°)
The historic second voyage of HMS Beagle from December 27th, 1831 to October 2nd, 1836, which the young Charles Darwin was invited to join for purposes of scientific and geological exploration, fits neatly into this time period and makes a great deal of sense in reference to the Uranian symbolism of the liberation of men's minds from the dogma of the past. Perhaps no other theory to emerge out of the Victorian era would so greatly shake up and overturn the established truth of the day than would the *Theory of Evolution.*

1855–1863 Opening Square (10°)
Darwin's epic work announcing and explaining his discoveries, *On the Origin of Species*, was finally published on November 24th, 1859, when he was fully ready to back up his extravagant claims. Interestingly, on that date Uranus and Eris were in exact alignment, within 10 minutes of a degree, at 5¾ degrees of Gemini and Pisces. The publication of *Origin of Species* ushered in an era in Western culture that was more humanistic in its thinking and less based on religious ideals of self-abnegation.

One of the landmarks of the American Labor Movement also occurred during the peak of this square alignment, early in 1860, with 6,000 shoe workers marching in Lynn, Massachusetts, in a strike for better pay and conditions that soon spread throughout New England.[2] Eris was in close sextile to Pluto at the time as well, to the degree.

1877–1885 Opposition (15°)
The invention of the electric filament lamp in 1878 made possible the widespread use of electric lighting. This was a simultaneous discovery by Joseph Swann and Thomas Edison, separated by several months. The first street to be lit with electricity took place in America in 1882, when the conjunction peaked. The symbolism of the archetypal combination is consistent with a new pioneering commercial medium using electricity, Uranus symbolizing electricity.

This was also the heyday of a period of peace, prosperity and progressive thinking dubbed the Gilded Age in America and the Belle Époque in France. In England this period coincided with the beginning of the latter half of the Victorian era. Progressive social agendas included the rise of sociology as a science and the concept of "Social Darwinism" as promoted by the philosopher Herbert Spencer. This was a move in the direction of freedom of thought and away from the more straight-laced thinking of earlier and more strictly religious times.

1923–1932 Conjunction (15°)
The Roaring Twenties, the Stock Market Crash and the subsequent beginning of the Great Depression fall within this period. The connection between the Uranus archetype and the wild and licentious 1920s – especially in America – is easy to recognize. In America, with Prohibition in effect, an important component of the law of the land was being ignored on a grand scale by all classes of society, particularly the well-to-do. Due to bootlegging, gangsters established a huge foothold in American life. This was the essence of this entire period, leading up to the softening and then repeal of the ban on alcohol sales during the penumbral period of 1933.

It was also a period of extraordinary breakthrough in physics, the birth of what came to be known as the new field of quantum physics, with discoveries such as the Heisenberg Uncertainty Principle and the unification of the theory of quantum mechanics. The year of 1927 is considered the year of most rapid development in physics in the entire history of the science. The famous Solvay Conference of October 1927 in Brussels solidified these understandings and saw Albert Einstein and Niels Bohr in discussion over the ultimate meaning of the new developments in quantum theory with Einstein's famous statement that "God does not throw dice." It is interesting to note that Uranus and Eris both occupied the middle of the first degree of Aries in October 1927, with not more than 10 arc-minutes of separation between them.

1967–1975 Opposition (15°)

The year 1968 brought student revolution to the streets of Paris, and in America the anti-war movement against the Vietnam War. The 1968 Democratic convention Chicago was protested and bloody confrontations with the police ensued. Note that this period overlaps with the end of the Uranus-Pluto conjunction that signaled the 1960s. The period of the overlap proves enlightening in this regard, since Eris would thus amplify Uranus-Pluto. This was 1967–1972, which included Woodstock and the first Moon landing, both during the summer of 1969, arguably the height of the Sixties. The finale of the Woodstock concert by Jimi Hendrix – including his red-bandana rendering of "The Star-Spangled Banner" – was considered a "defining moment of the 1960s".[3]

2012–2020 Conjunction (15°)

This is our current decade as of publication, the decade of the "Turbulent Teens." It is interesting to note: within the same year that Uranus comes to conjunction with Eris, using the 15 degree orb, for the first time since the 1930s, the Uranus-Pluto opening square becomes exact to the minute, in June of 2012, with Pluto conjuncting Eris in the U.S. chart and with Uranus also in sextile to the U.S. Uranus. Transiting Saturn for this month is exactly opposite Eris in the sky. A similar crisis to the 1930s was then gripping the American nation, following the 2008 housing bubble and subsequent recession. This relates more to the Saturn-Eris opposition that was partile at the time, although in another very obvious sense, great change was coming to America over this key period. It remains yet to be seen how this interesting period of radical transformation is related to stages of freedom. The real question is what will emerge in a further symbolic chime with this World Transit as the remainder of the decade unwinds.

Neptune-Eris

The theme would be: media, images, fashion, religious conflicts and take-overs. There could be an iconoclastic dedication for bringing new channels and forms of belief into existence, perhaps with violence or an extreme pioneering outburst of entrepreneurial spirit.

1360–1375 Conjunction (15°)

In 1360 Wycliff began his writings to the effect that there need be no inter-mediary between a man (or woman) and his or her God, not the priest nor even the Church. His writings prefigured the Protestant Reformation 150 years later. See also the preceding section for Uranus-Eris that was also in effect subsequent to this time period.

In 1362 English was declared to be the language of law and the courts of England. This was the beginning of the recovery of the English language after the Norman invasion of 1066. This was a cultural change as the "ver-nacular" became more readily available for business and legal discourse.

1450–1467 Opposition (15°)

This timing includes the beginning of a new medium of art and commu-nication with the pioneering invention of movable type by Gutenberg that precipitated great cultural change. This period began, famously, with the mass publication of a religious work (Neptune), namely *The Gutenberg Bible* in the early 1450s. By 1463 printing had spread throughout Germany and was on its way to other European sites. In 1467 Gutenberg died.

This period also saw the bloody and horrifying capture of Constantino-ple by the Turks in 1453, finally completely destroying the old Byzantine Empire, pillaging and re-purposing the capital of the last remaining Chris-tian outpost of civilization in Asia. This event is fully symbolized by these two archetypes in combination since it represented a violent overthrow by means of implacable willpower, achieving a long-cherished goal (Eris) to remove the last remnants of an existing culture (Neptune) and all in the name of religion.

1500–1510 Closing Square (10°)

The exploration of the New World was beginning, with a corresponding shift in consciousness as to what this world had to offer. Humanism was on the rise in Germany, in the years preceding Luther. Also, Martin Luther entered his monastic sojourn in the Augustinian cloister of Erfurt, which shaped the remainder of his life. His famous conversion to religious studies took place in 1505 and in April 1507 he was ordained as a priest; he entered the cloister on July 17 of the same year.

Also in 1507, the first map showing America as a separate continent was produced as a result of the explorations of the early 1500s.
The reign of Henry VIII of England began – on April 21st, 1509 – which would eventually spell a religious shift freeing England from the subjugation to the Pope in Rome.

The reign of Julius II, descended from the Medici of Florence, also signaled a cultural shift, and lasted for most of this period, from 1503 to 1513, taking the papacy to new levels in support of the arts, and of war, as emblematic of a truly Renaissance prelate. He was the most well-known patron of the arts among Medieval pontiffs.

1543–1560 Conjunction (15°)
In the first year of this period, Copernicus published his *De revolutionibus orbium coelestium* (On the Revolutions of the Heavenly Spheres). This was an essentially religious moment – the beginning of the transfer of intellectual power from Church to Science, completed with Newton's publication of Principia Mathematica in 1687, during the subsequent opposition.

In 1549 the *Book of Common Prayer* was introduced in England, a victory for Protestantism, and in the rebellion that formed against it several thousand Catholics were slaughtered.

In England the coronation of Queen Elizabeth I – in 1558 – signaled an end to the religious uncertainty of the reign of 'Bloody' Mary who preceded her and was Catholic. Elizabeth made the country more firmly Protestant and would reign for 45 years. In 1555 the Peace of Augsburg effectively ended the Holy Roman Empire, asserting the right of states to choose their religion. In 1560, Protestantism became the state religion of Scotland.

1670–1725 Opposition (15°)
At perihelion, Eris is not much farther away from the Sun than Neptune, hence the long period when they remained within 15-degree orb of their opposition.
    The middle to late 1600s was the time of Newton and Descartes… *The Discourse on Method* was published in 1637. *Principia Mathematica* followed in 1687, arguably initiating the modern age of science. The Glorious Revolu-

tion in England of 1688-1689 was in essence a Protestant take-over that forever removed the potential for a Catholic ruler. A new cultural awareness was ushered in, hastening the societal shift that followed from explorations in the New World. A new era of Protestant religious tolerance (although not extending to Catholicism) was birthed in England. See also the Eris-Uranus conjunction of 1722-1732.

On the leading edge of this period, in 1658, within the 20-degrees that Tarnas uses as his "penumbral" period, the Maryland Toleration Act, the first attempt at religious freedom in the colonies to be guaranteed by law, was finally passed, after being initially rejected. It lasted thirty years.

1779–1794   Opening Square (10°)
These were the years of the French Revolution, including the Reign of Terror, the entire period signaling a massive shift of power from the Church to the State. The suppression of traditional Christian religion in France during this period was similar to the Soviet revolution of 1907. The storming of the Bastille on July 14th, 1789, was the quintessential moment of the French Revolution, and is still celebrated as Bastille Day in France. In 1789 this day was accompanied by a near-exact Eris-Neptune square, making a T-square to Neptune from Eris opposed to Sun-Mercury within 2 degrees.

In 1791 the First Amendment to the U. S. constitution, guaranteeing freedom of religious expression, and denying the "establishment" of a state-sponsored religion, was passed as part of the Bill of Rights, sponsored by Thomas Jefferson. His correspondence would later show that he was trying to create a "wall of separation between Church and State."

1839–1856   Conjunction (15°)
This time period coincided with the more widespread availability of the photographic technique and the coining of the word "photography," in 1839. It is interesting that the onset corresponds not to the invention of the photographic process but to its mass acceptance, and the accompanying cultural shift.

As with the Gutenberg moveable type press, when Eris and Neptune were also in axial alignment, a new medium was being pioneered by dedicated practitioners and early adopters. In this case the medium was also concerned with image (Neptune).

1892–1904 Opening Square (10°)

This period coincided with the invention and early development of moving pictures, another media shift that became more available for mass consumption, resulting in great cultural transformation. In the early 1890s movie making was rudimentary, and a novelty. This situation gradually improved, as documented in Wikipedia:

> The first eleven years of motion pictures [from 1890 onward] show the cinema moving from a novelty to an established large-scale entertainment industry. The films became several minutes long consisting of several shots. The first rotating camera for taking panning shots was built in 1897. The first film studios were built in 1897. Special effects were introduced and film continuity, involving action moving from one sequence into another, began to be used. In 1900, continuity of action across successive shots was achieved and the close-up shot was introduced.[1]

The year 1900 saw the first film with editing and plot; and perhaps the most famous early film, *The Great Train Robbery*, was made in 1903. The notable French film company, Pathé, one of the first to achieve commercial success, was formed in 1904.

1936–1954 Opposition (15°)

This period encompasses the tremendous cultural changes that led from the Great Depression of the 1930s, and the rise of Nazism in Germany, to the involvement of most developed nations in World War II and its aftermath. There was a widespread disillusion that followed the end of "the last just war" as it is sometimes labeled, leading to the hypocrisy of the 1950s, and the response of the Beat movement, in America at least, that was in many ways the precursor to the cultural rebellion of the 1960s.

For film, this was the advent of color in movie making, such as Technicolor, "the most widely used color process in Hollywood ... [up to] 1952," initially used most commonly for filming animated movies such as *Snow White and the Seven Dwarfs* (1937) and *Fantasia* (1940) as well as live-action spectacles like *The Wizard of Oz* (1939) and *The Adventures of Robin Hood* (1938), also musicals such as *Singin' in the Rain* (1952).[5]

This period also corresponds nicely with the period of Film Noir, another developmental period in filmmaking, and one in which the dark side of a feminine symbolism is readily discernible.

1986–1997 Closing Square (10°)

This is the almost exact timeline for the birth of the modern Internet. In March 1989, a computer programmer in Switzerland named Tim Burners-Lee took existing networking a step further by inventing HTML and the World Wide Web. Although sharing of files had been going on for many years with leaps forward in 1985 and 1986, when network speeds became acceptable and the number of users grew exponentially, this was the first time that commonly addressable URLs came into use. Over the next few years, with Uranus and Neptune also in conjunction, and in the period of the Uranus-Eris square of the early 1990s, there were further strides in the establishment of this truly international and people-oriented communication and media system that seems to have the power to change the global political situation. In any case a brave new era was instituted, similar to the timing of the onset of the great cultural shift caused by the invention of the printing press, in the early 1450s, when Neptune was opposite Eris with Uranus in square.

Perhaps the height of the rapid development that followed took place in 1993, when Mosaic (the ancestor of Netscape) was created and graphical searches became commonplace. In 1993 there was also an exact Uranus-Neptune conjunction in precise square with Eris, never more than a few degrees apart from January to November, while over the summer the separation from a perfect square with Neptune narrowed to a half of a degree. By 1997 the number of sites had grown to over one hundred thousand, and a competition between the surfing applications Netscape Navigator and Microsoft's Internet Explorer had begun the "browser wars." This development changed the world as we know it, with another new medium; this is a theme we have seen again and again in the timing of these Eris-Neptune alignments.

This time period also corresponds to the rebirth of 3D in movies. The technique of 3D in moviemaking had become familiar in the 1950s but in a cruder form. By the time of the beginning of this period, as the reference below indicates, the technology had become advanced enough that a resurgence in popularity was possible.

In 1986, The Walt Disney Company began more prominent use of 3D films in special venues to impress audiences, *Captain EO* (Francis Ford Coppola, 1986) starring Michael Jackson, being a very notable example. In the same year, the National Film Board of Canada production *Transitions* (Colin Low), created for Expo 86 in Vancouver, was the first IMAX presentation using polarized glasses. *Echoes of the Sun* (Roman Kroitor, 1990) was the first IMAX film to be presented using alternate-eye shutterglass technology, a development required because the dome screen precluded the use of polarized technology.[6]

Even more importantly, advances in CGI from this same period permitted new breakthroughs in a different direction, as the first realistic CGI animal, credited with *Labrynth* (1986) was followed by *Jurassic Park* (1993), with dinosaurs that seemed "real," and *Toy Story* (1995), the first feature-length CGI animation.

After the success of *Toy Story*, computer animation would grow to become the dominant technique for feature length animation, which would allow competing film companies such as DreamWorks Animation and 20th Century Fox to effectively compete with Disney with successful films of their own.[7]

The next Neptune-Eris conjunction will take place from 2030–2045.

Pluto-Eris

The theme of Pluto-Eris would encompass raw power in the political arena, potentially violent or at the very least extremely and forcefully dedicated. Some of the most difficult historical periods fall into the years of these axial and square alignments between Pluto and Eris.

1481–1494 Opposition (15°)

These were the years of the beginning of the Spanish Inquisition, known for the extremity of its torture methods. This most feared branch of Catholic inquisition for deviations from orthodoxy was founded by Ferdinand and Isabella beginning in 1478, during the early penumbral period of 20 degrees of separation, and rose to become a favored instrument of preserving power and the uniformity of Christian faith by 1483. The period of its most powerful sway lasted to 1500, although the Inquisition was not officially disbanded until the 19th century.

1482-1492 was also the time of the conquest of Granada, expelling the Moors from the European mainland, by these same Spanish monarchs, and in 1492 all Jews were expelled from Spain.

The initial discovery of the New World took place in 1492 setting off a wave of exploration and plunder. Columbus and the Spanish conquistadors that followed him were notoriously cruel to the Native Americans that they encountered.

1527–1543   Closing Square (10°)
The beginning of this period saw the brutal Sack of Rome, in 1527, that effectively ended the Italian Renaissance.

These were also the years of the second part of the dramatic reign of Henry VIII of England who married five more times after his divorce from Catherine of Aragon. His mistress and second queen, Anne Boleyn was the first to be beheaded, while others died in childbirth or had the marriages annulled. Elsewhere in Europe the Pope was deposed and captured by the Emperor Charles I.

(For 250 years from opposition to conjunction, Pluto chases Eris at a similar distance from the Sun)

1746–1772 Conjunction (15°)
The Seven Years War raged in Europe, beginning in 1754 with the main conflict in the seven-year period 1756–1763. It involved most of the great powers of the time and affected Europe, North America, Central America, the West African coast, India, and the Philippines.[8]

These were also the years of the bloody French and Indian War (1754-1763) on the American continent, followed by colonial unrest leading up to the Boston Tea Party of 1773 and, eventually, the Declaration of Independence of 1776, during what Tarnas refers to as the "penumbral" period of the combination, within 20 degrees.

In England, George III became King in 1760. Although militarily successful throughout much of his long reign, he has the dubious distinction of being the English monarch to "lose" the American colonies to the War of Independence that began during the last stages of this period of strife. The Boston Tea Party was a response to a series of disagreements between the colonies of the New World and the tyrannical government of the Old that claimed ownership. This took place on December 16th, 1773, with Pluto just beyond the 15-degree mark and in trine with Uranus. Eris and Uranus were in close sesquiquadrate aspect.

1892–1923   Opening Square (10°)
Labor unrest in America, often spilling over into violence, is detailed below. In Europe as well there was conflict and much violence and death. The Russian Revolution was preceded by increasing labor unrest and conflict

at many levels of society, from 1905 to the Bolshevist victory of 1917, eventually leading to the establishment of the U.S.S.R. in 1922. World War I (1914-1918) was one of the deadliest conflicts in history, followed by major political changes, including revolutions, in many of the nations involved.[9]

In America, this was the age of the Robber Barons who consolidated their power in the aftermath of the Civil War and who now ran the country. The election of Grover Cleveland in 1892 signaled a call for reform that was ignored by the new administration, which served the interests of the very rich.[10] The impoverished workers of the 1890s had little recourse but to strike.

> The year of 1892 saw strike struggles all over the country; besides the general strike in New Orleans, and the coal miner's strike in Tennessee, there was the railway switchman's strike in Buffalo, New York, and a copper miner's strike in Idaho ... marked by gun battles and many deaths.[11]

Eugene Debs was inspired to write

> If the year of 1892 taught the workingman any lesson worthy of heed, it was that the capitalist class, like a devilfish, had grasped them with its tentacles and was dragging them down to fathomless depths of degradation.[12]

In 1893, as President, Cleveland used the army to break up a march on Washington inspired by the depression that gripped the country in the wake of the economic policies of the past several administrations.[13]. Depressions were more regular occurrences, in 1893, 1907 and 1919, leading up to the big one of 1929. The peak of this World Transit was 1906–1912, when the square was less than 1 degree. Conditions of labor grew worse and worse with the accompanying union activity in resistance, much of it bloody. The formation of the I.W.W. in 1905 had a socialist agenda. Attempts at reform were instated during the presidencies of Roosevelt and Taft, from 1905 to 1912. The remainder of this period saw a great deal of union activity because working conditions did not improve.

1969–1982 Opposition (15°)
This was the closing phase of the Vietnam War, leading to the American withdrawal of troops in 1972 followed by the evacuation from Saigon in 1975. There is an overlap with the period of Uranus conjunct Pluto and

the opposition from Uranus to Eris from 1967 to 1975. The Vietnam War began in 1964 after "American Advisors" were already in the country, and then escalated in the following few years, reaching a peak of violence that was increasingly opposed at home from 1968 to 1972. This was the war – and the anti-war movement – that helped to define the Sixties.[14]

The Kent State anti-war demonstration in which four student protesters were killed, took place in 1970. The Attica prison uprising of September 1971 ended in violence when inmates and hostages were attacked by the National Guard with assault rifles blazing and 31 prisoners and 9 hostages killed.[15] In America also, during the 1970s there were American Indian Movement confrontations, most notably at the town of Wounded Knee, North Dakota, in 1973, with a similarly violent ending.[16]

In Europe there were student protests, most famously in Paris in 1968 on the very eve of this period. The extremely violent "Troubles" of Northern Ireland also reached a peak of violence in the early to mid-1970s.[17] In Turkey there was increasing violence between left-leaning and conservative movements, with the May 1, 1977, incident, called "Bloody Sunday," with Pluto opposite Eris within 2 degrees of exact, one of the most violent.[18]

September 11, 2001 – Pluto trine Eris
Although Pluto and Eris were not in dynamic aspect when the events of September 11, 2001, changed history forever in an act of extreme violence against the United States, they were within seven degrees of trine each other, an aspect that Tarnas does not cover. It is fascinating to note that as Pluto opposed Saturn across the Ascendant / Descendant axis of the U.S. chart, transiting Eris conjoined U.S. Chiron within one quarter of a degree.

At the timing of the subsequent invasion of Iraq, on March 19, 2003, Eris and Pluto were in trine within one-quarter degree as Pluto opposed U.S. Mars. See Chapter 7 for a more extended treatment of this latter event.

March 11, 2011 – Fukushimi-Daiichi Nuclear Plant Disaster
This environmental disaster and massive radiation leak occurred with Pluto square Eris within 15 degrees, considered as the "penumbral" period for the square described in the following section, according to the formula arrived at by Richard Tarnas in *Cosmos and Psyche*. In fact not yet settled as of publication, with 300 tons of radioactive groundwater per day leaking into the ocean, the initial problem was caused by an earthquake and subsequent tsunami on this date that damaged three nuclear reactors out of a total of

six plants at the Fukushima complex and made them unsafe to be entered and repaired. Over 300,000 people were eventually evacuated from the region. The disaster is considered "man-made" in that adequate safety provisions were not in place.

2013–2027   Closing Square (10°)

In the first year of this period, the environmental movement to combat global warming reached new levels of desperation, as 350 organizations and the Sierra Club launched the year with the biggest climate action rally yet. Meanwhile, California saw the onset of Carbon trading, and several Nuclear power plants closing around the U.S.: Crystal River in Florida; San Onofre, in California; Kewaunee and Zion in the Midwest. Electric utilities using coal went bankrupt, as the EPA finally moved to issue regulations on greenhouse gas emissions from existing power plants. Beijing struggled through months of toxic smog in the winter of 2012-2013. Tornadoes in the U.S. set a new record: 811. The Philippines were hit by a massive storm in Typhoon Haiyan.[19]

The Chart of ISIS

Also in 2013, an extremely violent development within the then-ongoing Middle-East conflict between militant Islam and Western democracies was recorded by the fresh outbreak of a jihadist rebel group calling itself the "Islamic State of Iraq" and later "Islamic State of Iraq and Syria," or ISIS. The chart for ISIS used by most mundane astrologers is for April 8th, 2013, which has an Aries stellium of Sun, Mars and Venus, with Mars and Venus at about 21 degrees. The position of Eris in this chart is in close conjunction to the stellium, at 22 Aries 14. In his article on the subject, published in the February 2015 edition of *The Mountain Astrologer*, Claude Weiss points out that the Mars-Venus position in the chart for ISIS aligns with Pluto in the chart for Islam itself, from 622 A.D. – and we could add to this salient point that the position of Eris (in conjunction with these two personal planets) in the chart for ISIS makes for an even closer match to the past event. Pluto in the chart for Islam is in the very same degree as Eris in the chart of ISIS, just 11 arc-minutes away, at 22 Aries 25. This is fitting for an organization intent on forcing their religion on the world against all odds and certainly with an excess of violence, going against the grain of higher-minded Islam.

Notes

1. Wikipedia http://en.wikipedia.org/wiki/Jamestown,_Virginia

2. Zinn, Howard. *A People's History of the United States: 1492 – Present*, HarperCollins, New York, USA, 1980, 1999, 2003, pp. 226-227.

3. Daley, Mark (2006) "Chapter 5: Land of the Free. Jimi Hendrix: Woodstock Festival, August 18, 1969". In Inglis, Ian. *Performance and Popular Music: History, Place and Time.* Aldershot: Ashgate Publishing, Ltd. p.57. ISBN 0-7546-4057-4 – quoted in Wikipedia article on Woodstock.

4. Wikipedia http://en.wikipedia.org/wiki/History_of_film.

5. Wikipedia http://en.wikipedia.org/wiki/Technicolor.

6. Wikipedia article: http://en.wikipedia.org/wiki/3D_film.

7. Wikipedia http://en.wikipedia.org/wiki/History_of_film#1990s.

8. Wikipedia http://en.wikipedia.org/wiki/Seven Years' War.

9. Wikipedia http://en.wikipedia.org/wiki/World_war_I.

10. Zinn pp.256-260.

11. ibid p.276.

12. ibid p.278.

13. ibid p.260.

14. Wikipedia http://en.wikipedia.org/wiki/Vietnam_War…
see also http://www.english.illinois.edu/maps/vietnam/timeline.htm))

15. Zinn pp.520-521.

16. ibid pp.534-535.

17. Wikipediahttp://en.wikipedia.org/wiki/Provisional_Irish_Republican_Army.

18. Wikipedia http://en.wikipedia.org/wiki/Taksim_Square_massacre

19. http://www.pbs.org/wnet/americanmasters/episodes/a-fierce-green-fire/timeline-of-environmental-movement-and-history/2988/)

Bibliography

Ackroyd, Peter. *Blake: A Biography*, Alfred A. Knopf, New York, 1996.

Adler, Gerhard and Jaffe, Aniela (ed). *C. G. Jung Letters, Vol. 1*, R.F.C. Hull (trans), Bolligen Series XCV, Princeton University Press, Princeton NJ, 1973.

Amburn, Ellis. *Subterranean Kerouac: The Hidden Life of Jack Kerouac*, St. Martin's Griffin, New York, 1998.

Bair, Deirdre. *Jung: A Biography*, Little Brown and Co. Boston, New York, 2003.

Dworkin, Andrea. *Heartbreak: the political memoir of a feminist militant*, New York: Basic Books, New York, 2002.

_____ *Letters from a war zone: writings, 1976-1989*. E.P. Dutton, New York, 1989.

_____ *Life and death: unapologetic writings on the continuing war against women*. Virago, London, 1997.

Eisler, Riane. *The Chalice and the Blade*, Harper and Row, 1987.

Erdman, David (ed). *The Poetry and Prose of William Blake* Ed. Doubleday, New York, 1970.

Estés, Clarissa Pinkola. *Women Who Run With the Wolves*, Ballantine Books, New York, 1992.

Fölsing, Albrecht. *Albert Einstein : a biography*, translated from the German by Ewald Osers, Viking, New York, 1997.

George, Demetra and Bloch, Douglas. *Asteroid Goddesses*, ACS Publications, San Diego CA. 1986.

Goddu, André. *Copernicus and the Aristotelian Tradition: Education, Reading and Philosophy in Copernicus's Path to Heliocentricism*, Brill, Leiden/Boston, 2010.

Hayford, Harrison (ed). *Moby-Dick: The Writings of Herman Melville Vol. Six*. Northwestern University Press, Evanston, Il, 1988.

Hunter, M. Kelley. *Living Lilith: Four Dimensions of the Cosmic Feminine*, The Wessex Astrologer, Bournemouth, England, 2009.

Jung, C. G. *Memories, Dreams, Reflections*, Vintage/Random House, New York, 1965.

_____ *Psyche and Symbol*, edited by V. S. de Laszlo, Doubleday, New York, 1958.

_____ *The Red Book*, edited by Sonu Shamdasani, W.W. Norton Co. New York/London, 2009.

Kerenyi, Karl. *Athene: Virgin and Mother in Greek Religion*, Spring Publications, Zurich, 1978.

Kerr, John. *A Most Dangerous Method*, Alfred A. Knopf, New York, 1993.

Kinsley, David. *Tantric Visions of the Divine Feminine*, University of California Press, Berkeley, 1997.

Lawrence, D. H. *Kangaroo*, Viking Press Compass Books, New York, 1923.

_____ *The Fox/The Captain's Doll/The Ladybird*, (Penguin Classics) Penguin Books, London, Penguin Group (USA), New York, 1923, 1994.

_____ *Lady Chatterley's Lover*, (Penguin Classics) Penguin Books, London, Penguin Group (USA), New York, 1928, 1994.

_____ *Sons and Lovers*, (Penguin Classics) Penguin Books, London, Penguin Group (USA), New York, 1913, 1994.

_____ *The Rainbow*, (Penguin Classics) Penguin Books, London, Penguin Group (USA), New York, 1915, 1995.

_____ *Women in Love*, (Penguin Classics) Penguin Books, London, Penguin Group (USA), New York, 1920, 1995.Lennon, J. Michael. *Norman Mailer: A Double Life*, Simon & Schuster, New York, 2013.

Lindorff, David. *Pauli and Jung: The Meeting of Two Great Minds*, Quest Books, Wheaton, Illinois, 2004.

Miles, Barry. *Jack Kerouac – King of the Beats*, 1998, Virgin, London, 1998. Press, New York, 1973.

Olson, Charles. 'Call Me Ishmael', 1944, reprinted in *Modern Critical Interpretations: Herman Melville's Moby-Dick*, ed. Harold Bloom, Chelsea House Publishers, New York, 1986.

Pierrakos, Eva and Donovan, Thesenga. *Fear No Evil*, Pathwork Press, Madison, VA, 1993.

_____ *The Pathwork for Self-Transformation*, Bantam, New York, 1990.

Sanders, Scott. *D. H. Lawrence: The World of the Five Major Novels*, Viking, New York, 1973.

Shamdasani, Sonu. *Jung and the Making of a Modern Psychology: The Dream of a Science*, Cambridge University Press, Cambridge, England, 2003.

Singer, June. *The Unholy Bible - Blake Jung and the Collective Unconscious*, Sigo Press, Boston, 1986.

Stachel, John (ed). *Einstein's Miraculous Year: Five Papers That Changed the Face of Physics*, with the assistance of Trevor Lipscombe, Alice Calaprice, and Sam Elworthy. Foreword by Roger Penrose; Princeton University Press, Princeton, NJ c1998.

Tarnas, Richard. *Cosmos and Psyche*, Viking, New York, 2006.

Taylor and Hall (ed). *Poetry in English*, Macmillan Co., New York, 1963.

White, Michael. *Isaac Newton, The Last Sorcerer*, Helix Books/Addison-Wesley, Reading Massachusetts, 1997.

Zinn, Howard. *A People's History of the United States: 1492 – Present*, Harper Collins, New York, USA, 1980, 1999, 2003.

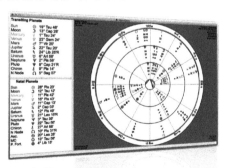 

Titles from The Wessex Astrologer
www.wessexastrologer.com

Martin Davis	Astrolocality Astrology From Here to There	Joseph Crane	Astrological Roots: The Hellenistic Legacy Between Fortune and Providence
Wanda Sellar	The Consultation Chart An Introduction to Medical Astrology Decumbiture	Komilla Sutton	The Essentials of Vedic Astrology The Lunar Nodes Personal Panchanga The Nakshatras
Geoffrey Cornelius	The Moment of Astrology		
Darrelyn Gunzburg	Life After Grief AstroGraphology: The Hidden Link between your Horoscope and your Handwriting	Anthony Louis	The Art of Forecasting using Solar Returns
		Lorna Green	Your Horoscope in Your Hands
Paul F. Newman	You're not a Person - Just a Birthchart Declination: The Steps of the Sun Luna: The Book of the Moon	Martin Gansten	Primary Directions
		Reina James	All the Sun Goes Round
		Oscar Hofman	Classical Medical Astrology
Jamie Macphail	Astrology and the Causes of War	Bernadette Brady	Astrology, A Place in Chaos Star and Planet Combinations
Deborah Houlding	The Houses: Temples of the Sky		
Dorian Geiseler Greenbaum	Temperament: Astrology's Forgotten Key	Richard Idemon	The Magic Thread Through the Looking Glass
Howard Sasportas	The Gods of Change	Nick Campion	The Book of World Horoscopes
Patricia L. Walsh	Understanding Karmic Complexes		
M. Kelly Hunter	Living Lilith	Judy Hall	Patterns of the Past Karmic Connections Good Vibrations The Soulmate Myth The Book of Why Book of Psychic Development
Barbara Dunn	Horary Astrology Re-Examined		
Deva Green	Evolutionary Astrology		
Jeff Green	Pluto 1 Pluto 2 Essays on Evolutionary Astrology (edited by Deva Green)	John Gadbury	The Nativity of the Late King Charles
		Neil D. Paris	Surfing your Solar Cycles
Dolores Ashcroft-Nowicki and Stephanie V. Norris	The Door Unlocked: An Astrological Insight into Initiation	Michele Finey	The Sacred Dance of Venus and Mars
		David Hamblin	The Spirit of Numbers
Martha Betz	The Betz Placidus Table of Houses	Dennis Elwell	Cosmic Loom
Greg Bogart	Astrology and Meditation	Gillian Helfgott	The Insightful Turtle
Kim Farnell	Flirting with the Zodiac	Christina Rose	The Tapestry of Planetary Phases

Lightning Source UK Ltd.
Milton Keynes UK
UKHW021541230922
409334UK00006B/1182